On this da

St Helens Rugby League Club

Alex Service and Adrian Lawrenson

London League Publications Ltd

To Brian —

Alex Serve   Adrian Law

On this day
St Helens Rugby League Club 1873 to 2018

© Alex Service and Adrian Lawrenson. Foreword © Eamonn McManus.

The moral right of Alex Service and Adrian Lawrenson to be identified as the authors has been asserted.

Cover design © Stephen McCarthy.

Cover photos: Front cover photo: Saturday 2 May 1953. A somewhat reserved skipper Duggie Greenall parades the Lancashire League Trophy to the Knowsley Road faithful before the Championship Semi-Final against Huddersfield. Saints lost to the same opponents the week before in the Challenge Cup Final at Wembley and were determined to make amends. No problems this time – Saints won 46–0 and went on to win the Championship Final. [Mirrorpix]
Back cover photos: left: Saints' fans know how to dress up for the big occasion and these ladies, at ringside in the 1966 Championship Final at Swinton, are no exception. [St Helens Local History & Archives/*St Helens Reporter*] Top right: Ben Barba leaves a trail of Castleford Tigers' defenders in his wake for a superb third try in the Challenge Cup tie at the Mend-a-Hose Jungle in 2018. [Bernard Platt] Bottom right: Two of the great wingers of the 1960s in combat. Tom van Vollenhoven (right) and Swinton's John Stopford were always extremely combative, with Stopford one of the few wingers capable of containing van Vollenhoven. [Alex Service]

Some of the photographs in this book are quite old and therefore have not reproduced perfectly. We thought that readers would prefer to have them like this rather than not at all! Unless otherwise credited, photographs and illustrations are from private collections. All photographs are as credited to the photographer or provider of the photo. No copyright has been intentionally breached; please contact London League Publications Ltd if you believe there has been a breach of copyright.

A CIP catalogue record for this book is available from the British Library.

First published in Great Britain in October 2018 by London League Publications Ltd, PO Box 65784, London NW2 9NS

ISBN: 978-1-909885-20-2

Cover design by Stephen McCarthy Graphic Design, 46, Clarence Road, London N15 5BB

Editing and layout by Peter Lush

Printed and bound in Great Britain by Ashford Colour Press Ltd, Gosport, Hants PO13 0FW

This publication is dedicated to six men who, in their own special way, made such significant contributions to St Helens Rugby League Club through the years and have left a vacuum at the club that remains quite unfillable: Geoff Cropper, Roy Haggerty, Ron Hoofe, Geoff Pimblett, Cliff Watson and Tom van Vollenhoven. We will never forget them and their legacy lives on in the hearts of every true Saints' supporter.

We are trailing in the footsteps,
Of those who've gone before,
And we'll all be reunited,
On a new and sunlit shore.

Come On You Saints

Foreword

One of the many pleasures and privileges which I have been bestowed as Chairman of St Helens RFC for the last 18 years is to deepen my knowledge and appreciation of its rich and colourful history since 1873. It is truly astounding in its depth and variety.

I would defy anyone to name either a rugby club or a town which have such fascinating and inspiring histories as those of the Saints and St Helens respectively. Neither has ever had a dull moment and both have produced performers and characters which have often gone on to international fame, and occasionally infamy.

No sport reflects the deep-seated characteristics of the towns and cities of its supporters as does rugby league, wherever in the world they may be. Honest, direct, uncomplicated and uncompromising but always tempered by a sense of humour and fair play. Our emotions and nerves are never, ever settled and we always expect disaster or triumph to be lurking around the next corner in equal measure.

It's great that Alex Service and Adrian Lawrenson have brought yet more of this to the fore in this latest magnum opus on the players and events surrounding our great club. Importantly, these are not in danger of diminishing in the future as the catalogue of characters and events continue to roll out. The "On this days" are simply in inexhaustible supply.

Eamonn McManus
Chairman St Helens RFC

On This Day: Eamonn is photographed at Saints' stadium at Langtree Park on 11 January 2012 – nine days before the first match at their wonderful new home against Widnes Vikings in the Karalius Cup. In just over a month would be the first Super League match against Salford City Reds. (Bernard Platt)

Acknowledgements and thanks

It is oft-quoted, but 100 per cent true nonetheless, that those who drink from the well must always be grateful of those who dug it! Needless to say, the authors would like to show their appreciation of a number of special people, without whom this publication would not have been possible.

There have been a number of different sources that have helped to compile this publication, but first and foremost we acknowledge the superb Saints' Heritage Society's website, www.saints.org.uk, for providing essential statistical, biographical and chronological information. Yet the people who first compiled the club's statistics, in pre-digital days, from a virtual blank canvas are indeed worthy of praise. Like Paul Cotham, the late Jack Leyland, Bill Bates, Curtis Johnstone – there must be more – have all made significant contributions. Talking of websites, Paul Cunliffe, Bill Bates and Dave Dooley have devoted many hours to the development of the Saints' Heritage website, which must not be overlooked.

Images have been provided from many sources and once again a vote of thanks to two doyens of the lens: Bernard Platt and Brian Peers, who have both contributed to the visual history of St Helens RFC in their own special way over the years; RLPhotos.com; Mirrorpix for the brilliant front cover image and others; Marie Roylance, Victoria Brokenshire and Bill Renshall, at the Heritage Library Service; Mike Appleton (St Helens RFC); Andy Fairclough; Merle Pimblett; Stan Ince; Robert Gate; Ron Lee; Curtis Johnstone; Dave Makin; Bill Bates; Nick Ellaby and Denis Whittle. Special thanks to St. Helens Townships Family History Society and Sutton Athletic club – Phil Thomas and Barry Graney – for their help; *Rugby Leaguer*, *St Helens Reporter* and *St Helens Star*. Particular thanks also to Paul McFegan at Sportsphoto Ltd. in Scarborough.

Other luminaries who have helped this project come into fruition include the following: Mike Appleton; Bill Appleton; Jimmy Flanagan; Ray French; Kevin McSweeney; Allan Rooney; Tony Brown; Brian Potter; John and Glynis Clegg; Duncan and Michelle at Triprint for several printouts of burgeoning ideas; Peter Harvey; Harry Edgar – *Rugby League Journal* remains a superb read for any diehard fan; Steve Leonard and the St Helens Players' Association. Author's royalties from this book will go solely to the Saints Community Development Foundation, who continue to inspire communities throughout sport. A worthy cause indeed.

Last, but by no means least, our thanks to Eamonn McManus for the superb Foreword. The authors would like to express their appreciation to Peter Lush and Dave Farrar of London League Publications, for providing the opportunity to publish this unique chronological and historical view of the mighty St Helens Rugby League Club.

Finally, any errors that sneaked in are our responsibility.

Alex Service and Adrian Lawrenson

London League Publications Ltd would like to thank Steve McCarthy for his design work on the cover and the staff of Ashford Colour Press Ltd for printing the book.

About the Authors

Alex Service (left) and Adrian Lawrenson presenting Louie McCarthy-Scarsbrook with a silver salver on behalf of Saints' Heritage Society to commemorate his 200 games for the club. [Mike Appleton]

Alex: St Helens-born, he is both proud and delighted that he spent some of his early years in the Wellington Hotel in South Naylor Street, which was a former Headquarters of the St. Helens Club – even though he was perhaps a little too young to appreciate it at the time. Then it was a move to another public House: The British Lion, back to the 'seat' of the family, in rugby league-mad Thatto Heath that shaped his early life. Alex has been involved with the documentation of Saints' history since the late 1970s and has produced a number of seminal publications relating to his major passion. A regular contributor to the Saints' matchday programme for many years, he has been at the forefront of numerous heritage initiatives involving the men in the red vee. Yet one aspect which gave him the greatest pleasure was re-uniting two former Saints' 'greats' – wing legend Alf Ellaby and his Welsh centre George Lewis after they had not contacted each other for many years. Favourite players? What about Tom van Vollenhoven and Jamie Lyon for starters?

Adrian: known as a Yicker, which, for the uninitiated, is someone born in the Haydock district, in his case the 'St. Helens end' of West End Road. It was his next-door neighbour who took him to his to his first game, when Saints beat Liverpool City at Knotty Ash, in March 1961. The sight of Tom van Vollenhoven scoring a seven-minute hat-trick remains a vivid memory! Later that year, the 1961 Challenge Cup Final proved to be the catalyst for what has become a life-long passion. A St Helens Council employee in the highways department for most of his working life, he once saw a photograph of the Saints' team that beat the Recs in 1926 which was instrumental in him embarking on a mission to find out more about the formative years of the club. Hours in the library followed and a complete season-by-season statistical account of Saints' progress ensued. His all-time favourite player is Tom van Vollenhoven, natch, but there is a penchant for unsung local heroes too: Jeff Heaton and Les Jones in particular. And did we mention Sonny Nickle?

Introduction

Doing this publication, it was important to produce not another assembly of mindless lists! What you get here is obviously date-driven - that is the nature of the beast – but we have tried to purvey the human aspects wherever possible. In fact we like to think that there is a good mix of entertainment, insight and odd facts. How can that go wrong? Well, not for a lack of effort. It has been written for Saints' fans by Saints' fans. No question about that.

The changing seasons in which our club has played in have made this project just that bit more interesting and viable, from the winter months of yore to the summer Super League, although 'cold' starts in February in the modern era does not necessarily seem to have changed things that much.

This is a reference book, certainly, but also something to dip into, as well as relate the contents to individual days. 'I wonder what was happening on my birthday?' or 'who did they play on our wedding day?' It is readable as an entity, too. Of course players and games dominate. Yet we have tried to produce as wide a cross-section of the club's history as we can, from its formation at the Fleece Hotel in 1873, to the club's 145th birthday in 2018.

Hopefully there is something for Saints' fans of all ages to relate to and, hopefully, to savour. You never know, even those who are not necessarily those of a red vee persuasion, might enjoy the read. If you are rugby league fans, like us, we won't mind a bit.

Alex Service and Adrian Lawrenson

Qualifying semi-final 24 September 2010: St. Helens 42 Huddersfield Giants 22. Bernard Platt's lens shows fans unfurling a banner to commemorate not only the last-ever game at Knowsley Road, but also those players who were leaving the club at the end of a momentous campaign: Keiron Cunningham, Matt Gidley, Maurie Fa'asavalu, Bryn Hargreaves, Jake Emmitt and Nick Fozzard.
[Bernard Platt]

Contents

St. Helens 4 Oldham 3 at Knowsley Road, Northern Rugby League 9 October 1937.
This superb image, provided by Curtis Johnstone, was taken at the corner of the Grandstand
side and Dunriding Lane End. St Luke's Church can be made out in the background.
Saints are wearing their blue change strip. A poor season ended with the club finishing 21st out of 29
teams in the league, one place above rivals St Helens Recs, who lost their professional status at the
end of the 1938–39 campaign.

Back row: Emlyn Hughes, Les Garner, Jim Cunliffe, Tom Mattinson, Ted Beesley, Peter McLoughlin;
middle: George Roberts, Jack Bradbury (Captain), Norman Hesketh, Jack Fearnley;
front: Harold Forsyth, Stan Powell, Glan Pryor.

January

A new beginning.

14 January 2010 at Knowsley Road. Ground staff, players and volunteers work feverishly to try and clear the pitch of snow. Despite a mammoth 24 hour effort, the proposed Testimonial match for Mike Bennett, against Barrow, had to be cancelled. [Alex Service]

This is the time that bad weather really starts to kick in, with obvious ramifications for sport generally. In days of yore it was part two of the holiday programme on New Year's Day, with the second match against St Helens Recreation to whet the appetite. In later years, it was Widnes, who were such a powerful team in the 1980s providing another eagerly-awaited clash. A time for large crowds and the biggest gate receipts. Interestingly enough, winters between the wars were amongst some of the coldest during the century and yet not one Christmas Day, Boxing Day or New Year's Day fixture was ever called off. It was a time to look forward to the Challenge Cup draw and possible pre-deadline signings that could well make all the difference to the rest of the campaign.

Things are somewhat different today. It is very much 'friendly' territory as the clubs prepare themselves for the big kick-off. Some matches could well be Testimonials, but mostly a chance for the players to have their first 'hit-ups' after copious time spent in the gym on their physical preparation. It may well be a chance for fans to see new signings, of course, but generally a time for final 'tweaks'. Given the potential for inclement weather and subsequent chaos with our transport infrastructure, perhaps this is all for the best. Indeed, given the seemingly constant constructional state of flux of the M62 and ever-increasing volumes of traffic, in particular, rugby league in the depths of winter is realistically no longer a viable option.

1 JANUARY

1896 Northern Union: St Helens 3 Manningham 8 at Knowsley Road. A try for winger Tom Sudlow was not enough as Saints struggled against the future first Champions of the professional rugby game. *1906* International friendly: England 3 Other Nationalities 3 at Central Park, Wigan. Frank Lee and Tom Barton are in the England team and thus become the club's first internationals in either code. *1924* Club founder William Douglas Herman, a former head chemist with the Pilkington Glass firm, died at his Rainhill home, Holm Lea, aged 72. He was cremated and his final resting place is a crypt niche at Anfield Cemetery, Liverpool.

2 JANUARY

1911 Northern Rugby League: St Helens 24 Hunslet 2 at Knowsley Road. Christopher Chavasse, the dashing curate at St Helens Parish Church, made a try-scoring debut on the left wing. His centre was Billy Belshaw. Meanwhile, on the other wing, local lad Jimmy Flanagan scored four sparkling tries. *1939* Northern Rugby League: St Helens Recreation 3 St Helens 5 at City Road. Requiem for the Recs, who resigned from the league at the end of the campaign. This was the last 'derby' clash after 20 years of turbulent, often rumbustious rugby, which lit up the lives of local supporters and created a fierce rivalry, even splitting families. The Recs were later resurrected as an amateur club in 1949 and remain a vibrant presence to this day.

3 JANUARY

1925 Northern Rugby League: St Helens 15 Wakefield Trinity 2 at Knowsley Road. Centre and later star stand-off Leslie Fairclough got married in the morning to Lilian Taylor, at St Helens Parish Church, played in the match and left for his honeymoon afterwards. Now that's dedication. *1959* Northern Rugby League: Leeds 12 St Helens 11 at Headingley. Van Vollenhoven, Greenall and Prinsloo were try-scorers, with Peter Fearis kicking a goal, but it was the end of a marvellous 21-match unbeaten run! Saints ended the season as worthy Champions, however.

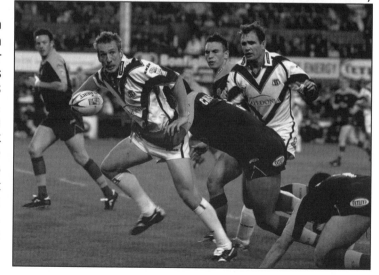

1979 Winger John Kirkpatrick was born in Preston. The former Preston Grasshoppers RUFC junior played 23 times for the Saints, scoring 11 tries, including a memorable hat-trick against Leeds Rhinos on 30 August 2002. Club photographer Bernard Platt captured him in action [right] during the game. He later joined London Broncos.

4 JANUARY

1976 winger Joey Hayes was born in Warrington and signed for the Saints from the Crosfields amateur club. Although relatively small in stature, he was an excellent finisher, scoring 29 tries in 44 matches. His first season form earned him a place in the 1996 Great Britain Australasian Tour squad. Joey later continued his Saints' connections as a much-valued physiotherapist on the backroom staff. *1996* Regal Trophy Semi-Final: St Helens 80 Warrington 0 at Knowsley Road. The Saints racked up their third-highest points 'for' in a home game in this one-sided affair, with young hooker Keiron Cunningham in what can only be described as virtually unstoppable mode. He was to become a thorn in the side of Warrington for the next decade and more. Warrington coach Brian Johnson resigned the following day.

Thirteen years after wreaking havoc in the 1996 Regal Trophy Semi-Final, Saints' skipper Keiron Cunningham receives the inaugural Vince Karalius trophy from Mrs Barbara Karalius after the 54–9 defeat of Widnes at Stobart Stadium in 2009 [Bernard Platt].

5 JANUARY

1921 Will 'o the wisp stand-off Eric Hesketh was born in Wigan. A former member of Wigan Old Boys RUFC, his father was the chairman of Wigan RLFC. He made 49 appearances, scoring 13 tries and endeared himself to the fans with his cavalier attacking style. Eric later joined Salford. *1968* Northern Rugby League: Barrow 17 St Helens 7 at Craven Park. Stand-off Austin Rhodes kicked two goals, with his scrum-half partner Tommy Bishop scoring the only try. It was also a losing start for new coach Cliff Evans, a disciple of open, attacking rugby, who formerly held the reins at Swinton.

6 JANUARY

1951 Jesse Skepper, who owned a laundry business in Spray Street and helped to found the St Helens Supporters' Club in 1924, died aged 76. One of his finest achievements was the fundraising to help build the original Popular Side enclosure at Knowsley Road in the mid–1920s. Jesse was also a member of the St Helens RFC Committee for a spell. *1993* Stones Bitter Championship Division One: St Helens 64 Leigh 9 at Knowsley Road. Saints were irresistible. Left winger Alan Hunte added to the on-field carnage with 4 brilliant tries. It avenged an 11–6 reversal at Hilton Park on 11 November 1992 which effectively cost Saints the First Division title.

7 JANUARY

1911 Northern Rugby League: St Helens 11 Swinton 10 at Knowsley Road. The St Helens Newspaper carried a full account of the pre-match drama: "The members and officials of the Swinton team had a rather lively experience on Saturday afternoon while on their way from the London and North Western Station to the Headquarters of the St Helens Rugby Football Club – the Talbot Hotel in Duke Street. They were being driven in a three-horse omnibus and at the corner of Lowe Street and Duke Street, where there is a curve, the bus came into a rather violent collision with a tramcar which was coming from Dentons Green." One of the Swinton players, winger Albert Morris, sustained cuts preventing him from playing in the match, but it could have been much worse. *1948* Half-back Matt Creevey was laid to rest in St Helens Cemetery aged 61. Known as the 'Human Panther' as a result of his extraordinary ability to achieve large distances from standing jumps, he was born in Pocket Nook and had two brothers, James and Charlie, who played in the same Saints team on several occasions. *1954* Half-back or centre Peter Glynn was born in Widnes. After an early spell as Saints' 'Supersub' in the Dad's Army team of 1976, he became a valued member of the squad,

playing 258 matches, scoring 118 tries and kicking 86 goals. Selected for the Great Britain tour in 1979, he joined Salford in 1983. A great player indeed. *1961* Northern Rugby League: Warrington 5 St Helens 8 at Wilderspool. A winning debut for Saints' local-born full-back Frank Barrow. His 'knock 'em down at all costs' style of play in both attack and defence endeared him to the Saints' fans. No frills, for sure.

Peter Glynn lines up a kick at Knowsley Road in the early 1980s. Notice the concrete dugouts in front of the Main Stand Paddock. [Brian Peers]

8 JANUARY

1966 Northern Rugby League: Oldham 13 St Helens 9 at Watersheddings. This was no place for the faint hearted in winter, for sure. Saints suffered their first league defeat for 26 matches. Winger Len Killeen scored all the points, with a try and 3 goals. He was really in his 'pomp' then. *1968* From the Boardroom: "It was decided to obtain regular reports on promising players in South Wales and it was left to the secretary to try and make suitable arrangements and to report back to the Board." Indeed, a vital ingredient in team-building at the time. Over the next few months names like Gerald Davies [Sale] and Phil Bennett [Llanelli] would be on the club's radar.

9 JANUARY

1894 The death occurred of Saints chairman, Alderman Thomas Charles Wilcock, at his home on Prescot Road. He owned the Phoenix Brewery in Peckers Hill Road, Sutton and succumbed to typhoid fever. As a result, his coffin was not allowed into Lowe House Church for the funeral service. He is buried at Windleshaw Chantry. Sad times indeed. *1988* John Player Special Trophy Final: St Helens 15 Leeds 14 at Central Park, Wigan. Our one and only win in the competition, but what a match in the cloying mud. Paul Loughlin scored two tries and kicked three goals, yet Neil Holding's drop-goal proved to be the difference in the end against a powerful Yorkshire team packed with Australian imports.

Centre Paul Loughlin scores against Leeds in the 1988 John Player trophy final. Dave Tanner [2] and Paul Forber are in support. Marty Gurr is the prostrate full-back for the Loiners. [Alex Service]

10 JANUARY

1956 Scrum-half Johnny Smith was born in St Helens. A clever footballer, with excellent hands, Johnny made 81 appearances, scoring eight tries, including the 1982 Lancashire Cup final against Warrington. His last matches for the club were on the 1985 New Zealand tour, against Waikato and Northland. *1970* Northern Rugby League: St Helens 22 Batley 9 at Knowsley Road. Scottish sprinter Alan Scott, a butcher from Hawick, played as a triallist in the first half and was replaced by regular winger Les Jones for the second stanza.

11 JANUARY

1941 War Emergency League: St Helens 3 Wigan 6 at Knowsley Road. Local-born Albert Johnson made an appearance for the Saints on the left wing and scored the only try for the homesters. He is best remembered as a Warrington legend, with over 112 tries in 198 matches. He also played 25 times for Wigan during the war years. A veritable double agent. *1943* Rumbustious full-back Frank Barrow was born in Thatto Heath. He was one of three brothers to play for the club, the others being Tony [centre] and Billy [hooker]. Unlike the Creeveys of pre-First World War fame, the brothers never all played together in the same Saints' first team. *2007* Former international sprinter and a Saints' signing from Bradford Northern, Berwyn Jones, passed away at Ross-on-Wye, Herefordshire. He was 67. Berwyn played four times scoring two tries before retiring from the game.

12 JANUARY

1934 Dynamic winger Mick Sullivan was born in Dewsbury. Described by many as one of the greatest wingers of all time, he was a world record signing from Wigan in 1961 for £11,000 [right] and made 82 appearances, scoring 31 tries before joining York in 1963. A brilliant defender and an established international – a really fine player. *1971* From the

Boardroom: "Sub-Committee business – the ground committee Chairman Charles Martin outlined a scheme of underground heating based on warm air. [The Cambridge Soil Warming System] He reported that test areas have proved to be successful and that Manchester City and Arsenal had accepted the scheme." The system was not adopted after a trial period on a piece of turf at the Pavilion End proved to be inconclusive.

Mick Sullivan signs on the dotted line to become a Saint, with Chairman Harry Cook next to him, positively beaming with delight. Secretary Basil Lowe oversees the process with his usual efficiency. [Alex Service]

13 JANUARY

1905 The *St Helens Reporter* carried this brilliant story: "The St Helens club are indeed lucky enough to have a President like Captain Michael Hughes, for apart from the interest which he takes in the doings of the team, his generosity is unlimited. This splendid sportsmanship was revealed in a striking manner when he announced that he was giving to the club the stakes which a horse of his had won that day at the Manchester Races, a 'small matter' of about £70 which is a vast sum to the St Helens club. The fact that Captain Hughes does not win out of his turn on the turf makes his gift all the more generous." Captain [later Colonel] Michael Hughes was the owner of the Sherdley Hall Estate and a real old Victorian country squire, with aristocratic connections. *1971* County Championship: Yorkshire 32 Lancashire 12 at Wheldon Road, Castleford. 2,000 spectators were admitted free because of the dense fog. Billy Benyon was at right centre, with Eric Chisnall and Eric Prescott making up the second row. Other former Saints for Lancashire included scrum-half Alex Murphy of Leigh and loose forward Doug Laughton [Wigan] who scored a try. *1996* Regal Trophy final: St Helens 16 Wigan 25 at the McAlpine Stadium, Huddersfield. A hard-fought contest, with Saints showing the promise that would see them become the inaugural Super League champions later in the year. Try-scorers were Joey Hayes, Paul Newlove and Keiron Cunningham. Skipper Bobbie Goulding kicked 2 goals.

Young guns! Doug Laughton (left) and Billy Benyon photographed in the mid–1960s, before Doug left for Wigan. Both played together for Lancashire in 1971. [Ged Morris];
Right: Welsh scrum-half Eddie Dowdall, who signed from Wigan in the late 1920s also played for Glamorgan and Monmouthshire in 1929.
[Alex Service]

14 JANUARY

1891 According to the *St Helens Reporter*: "The members of the Committee of the St Helens Football Club and a few friends met at the club's HQ, the Wellington Hotel, in response to the invitation of the President, Mr Councillor JP Mearns, to a sumptuous repast which was placed on the table in the host's usual excellent style." They certainly knew how to live in those days. *1942* Future Greatest 17 incumbent Kel Coslett was born in Tonypandy, South Wales. Like Chris Joynt years later, the team needed him on the field, such was his almost all-pervading influence on matches. His good friend Geoff Pimblett always referred to him as 'Skip' years later – a measure of the respect he engendered from his team-mates! *1969* Northern Rugby League: St Helens 13 Wigan 3 at Knowsley Road. This was a re-played league match after the Boxing Day abandonment at half-time. Saints' players were offered two shillings for every point scored above the Wigan total. So, an extra 20 shillings. For those unaccustomed to pre-decimalisation currency: a pound. *1990* Challenge Cup Preliminary Round: St Helens 39 Castleford 12 at Knowsley Road. Saints, under caretaker coach Shane Cooper, following Alex Murphy's dismissal, demolished Castleford. Teenage scrum-half Sean Devine, with nine goals and a try, picked up the Man-of-the-Match award. Former Hunslet second-rower Andy Bateman scored twice; Roy Haggerty and Stuart Evans also crossed the whitewash. Shane Cooper added a one-pointer.

15 JANUARY

1929 County Championship: Glamorgan and Monmouth 17 Yorkshire 22 at Sloper Road, Cardiff. Saints' signing from Wigan, Eddie Dowdall, was scrum-half for the Welshmen, who unfortunately lost all three matches in the tournament. *1945* From the Saints' Committee meeting: "Mr John Wilson wrote giving notice that a meeting of the rugby league clubs had been called for Wednesday, the 24 January 1945, at Manchester, to consider the application Workington Town RFC for admission to the Rugby Football League, and asking a representative to attend. It was agreed to support the application of the Workington Town RFC, and that a representative to attend the meeting would be appointed at the next meeting of the Management Committee." The Cumbrian outfit were allowed into the league for the start of the 1945–46 campaign and finished in 19th position in the league table – one place

above the Saints. *1949* Northern Rugby League: Belle Vue Rangers 5 St Helens 17 at Belle Vue showgrounds. Born in Widnes, signed from Halifax – Alan Prescott made a try-scoring debut for his new club from loose forward. Alan began as a winger and finished his career as one of the all-time great front-rowers. *1980* Towering front-rower Jason Cayless was born in Sydney, of Maori descent. The only UK based player to be selected for the 2006 ANZAC Test at Knowsley Road, Jason enjoyed considerable early success after signing from Sydney Roosters, although his later time in the red vee was hampered by injuries. Bernard Platt's image shows him in action against Bradford Bulls in 2006.

16 JANUARY

1907 Front rower and hooker Solomon Cotton was born in Wigan. The younger brother of Dave Cotton, who also hooked for the club, Sol was a reliable replacement in the engine room for several seasons before his transfer to Bradford Northern in 1933. *1909* Northern Union: Rochdale Hornets 3 St Helens 3 at the Recreation Grounds. The St Helens Newspaper seemed to like new signing Dai Harris, from Castleford Half-Acre: "On the other wing was Harris, whose square-jaw denotes determination – a most desirable qualification in a rugby footballer." Give us a team of square-jawed rugby players any day. *1929* The League Management Committee ruled that trainer Ted Forber must not speak to St Helens players during play either from the touchline or from the field. This was after an incident in the Warrington versus St Helens game when Alf Ellaby was spoken to at length by the referee for elbowing an opponent as he was scoring a try. The Saints' trainer came out onto the pitch and got himself involved in the incident. *1965* Northern Rugby League: Warrington 6 St Helens 4 at Wilderspool. Saints were beaten at last after a marvellous 22 match run in a closely-fought encounter that could have gone either way. The team went on to lift the League Leaders' bowl, with 56 points from 34 matches, yet lost to 8th placed Halifax in the Championship Final.

A pictorial pearl, this one! The great Alf Ellaby in action on his return to St Helens after his three-season sojourn at Wigan. Barrow are the opponents. Although Alf scored a try, the team lost 8–7, on 11 December 1937. Notice the sparse crowd at Knowsley Road. [Bill Bates]

17 JANUARY

1931 Northern Rugby League: St. Helens 8 Swinton 3 at Knowsley Road. A 'regulation' victory for the Saints, with tries from left-winger Tom Winnard and second-rower Ben Halfpenny. Full-back and captain George Lewis kicked a goal. The team finished in seventh position in the league table, somewhat different from their top spot at the end of the previous campaign. *1976* Northern Rugby League: Leeds 8 St Helens 17 at Headingley. Four goals from redoubtable full-back Geoff Pimblett, seemingly chipped over in his usual '9 iron' style, helped Saints to a welcome victory on Yorkshire turf. Crowd: 7,422.

18 JANUARY

1919 Competitive rugby restarted after the chaos and heartbreak of the war and Saints were defeated by St Helens Recreation 24–3 at Knowsley Road. This is the first 'official' fixture between the teams. Interest was high. Two hundred spectators also got in for free when the gates were rushed. *1924* Stand-off Ray Price was born in Blaina, South Wales. A former Abertillery rugby union player, he first signed for Belle Vue Rangers before joining Warrington. A tough customer, he played representative rugby league for Wales, Great Britain and Other Nationalities, before a final fling with the Saints. He is always remembered as the star of Tom van Vollenhoven's debut match against Leeds in 1957. *1947* Northern Rugby League: Featherstone Rovers 7 St Helens 11 at Post Office Road. Front row stalwart

George 'Porky' Davies played his 184th and last game for the Saints. Duggie Greenall was full-back that afternoon. George later joined Liverpool Stanley.

1949 Flying winger Stan McCormick, dubbed the 'Interception King' signed for St Helens from Belle Vue Rangers for a then record £4,000 fee. This was a real statement of intent that the Saints were determined to join the higher echelons of rugby league clubs.

1977 International front-rower Dave Chisnall was signed from Leigh. Although quite 'burly' Dave was extremely light on his feet with a deceptive turn of pace and a brilliant sidestep. He joined his brother Eric in the forward pack and played in the 1978 Challenge Cup Final classic against Leeds.

Stan McCormick on the way to the line against Salford at the Willows was the darling of the Knowsley Road fans and later became coach of the club in the 1960s [Alex Service]

10

19 JANUARY

1957 Northern Rugby League: Leeds 22 St Helens 11 at Headingley. A disappointing defeat for the Saints and a sad day for hooker Frank McCabe, who later announced his retirement after battling a persistent knee injury. *1962* Flying winger Barry Ledger was born in St Helens. This guy was brilliant and had so many natural attributes. It was always a pleasure to watch him in full flight as he streaked for the line. *1971* Front-rower Albert Halsall joined Swinton for a £1,750 fee. Saints' diehard fan Dave Dooley said that he "charged like a bull and side-stepped like a ballet dancer." We will always remember his scintillating hat-trick in the 1966 Championship Final against Halifax, when he did just that.

20 JANUARY

1973 First Division: Leeds 2 St Helens 5 at Headingley. A closely-fought affair between the two old rivals. Winger John Wills scored the Saints' try, converted by Kel Coslett. £8,000 second-rower George Nicholls from Widnes made a winning debut for his new club. What a signing. *2012* Karalius Cup: St Helens 42 Widnes Vikings 24 at Langtree Park. Dawn of a new era. Second-rower Sia Soliola (captured in full flow by Bernard Platt's camera, below) became the first Saints' player to score a four pointer in the club's magnificent new home at Peasley Cross. Appropriate – he was a huge fans' favourite.

21 JANUARY

1984 Popular forward from the 1940s Bill Fishwick died aged 64 in St. Helens. Bill was the brother of hooker Ike and the uncle of loose forward Harry Pinner. *1996* Stones Bitter Centenary Championship: Halifax 32 St. Helens 24 at Thrum Hall. Our last league match in 'winter' rugby, in typically freezing conditions, saw Halifax finish above us in third place in the table. Super League beckoned and much warmer climes, fortunately.

22 JANUARY

1910 Friendly match: Coventry 19 St. Helens 11 at Coventry. This was a visit to help with the eventual formation of a team to play in the Northern Union, which did take place, by the following season. The fledgling club lasted for three seasons before disbanding at the end of the 1912–13 campaign. *1921* Northern Union: St. Helens 8 Hunslet 7 at Knowsley Road. Saints' forwards certainly showed some improvement in this match. The *St Helens Newspaper* explained why: "Mr. Harold Molyneux, who is well-known as a physical culture expert and who has various diplomas to his name has been engaged by the Saints' Committee to give a special course of training to his players." *2009* Forceful back-rower Joe Robinson died aged 60 in St. Helens. He played 29 times for the seniors, scoring two tries. Joe was on the bench for the 1967 Championship Final and subsequent replay. A popular figure in local council circles, he later joined Barrow.

Saints' first team squad training at Knowsley Road for the 1967 Championship Final versus Wakefield Trinity. Back: Bob Dagnall, Bill Sayer, Cliff Watson, John Mantle, Ray French, Joe Robinson, Les Jones; front row: Wilf Smith, John Houghton, Tommy Bishop, Frank Barrow, Tony Barrow, Peter Gartland, Len Killeen. [Alex Service]

23 JANUARY

1943 Challenge match: Northern Command Rugby League XV 18 Northern Command Rugby Union XV 11 at Headingley, Leeds. The League XV included our own Private Jimmy Stott, at right centre and were mostly lower ranks. Receipts from the 8,000 crowd went to Service Charities and the game was played under union rules. Yet as Robert Gate succinctly puts it in his excellent *Illustrated History of Rugby League:* "there is no record of any Union player dying from contact with the League men". Ouch. *1965* Northern Rugby League: St Helens 16 Whitehaven 3 at Knowsley Road. Former Newport and Welsh international rugby union forward John Mantle made his debut in the second row. Strong, mobile and a real handful on the field, he went on to play 435 times for the club – a fantastic signing. *1971* Powerhouse right centre Scott Gibbs was born in Bridgend, South Wales. He played 48 matches for the Saints during his somewhat brief two-year dalliance with the XIII-a-side code, scoring 23 tries, but certainly gained the respect of his team-mates and anyone unfortunate enough to be marking him. Scott won the Super League and Challenge Cup 'double' in 1996 before returning to Wales and professional rugby union. *1988* Hooker Scott Moore was born in St Helens. A team mate of Paul Clough's at the Blackbrook amateur club, Scott was an excellent acting half-back, with good distribution skills, who made his debut at the age of 16 years, six months, against Wigan at the JJB stadium on 20 August 2004 at scrum-half, the youngest Super League debutant.

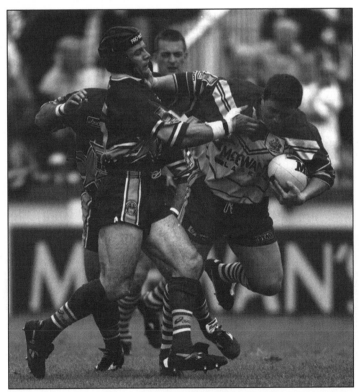

Tough as teak! Welsh centre Scott Gibbs takes on the Leeds Rhinos defence at Knowsley Road in 1996. He ended the season with a Super League and Challenge Cup winners' medals.
[Sportsphoto Ltd]

24 JANUARY

1889 Friendly match: St Helens 1 goal 2 minors Wigan 2 goals 1 try 3 minors. This was a match illuminated by 12 Wells Patent Electric lamps at the Saints' Dentons Green ground that drew a huge 7,000 crowd. Wigan, assisted by Jack Hurst, the crack centre from Leigh, won a most memorable match for all concerned. *1948* Northern Rugby League: St Helens 8 Rochdale Hornets 9 at Knowsley Road. A double debut for Welsh rugby union players winger Stuart [Steve] Llewellyn and second-rower George Parsons ended in disappointment. They did manage to make significant contributions to the Saints' cause over the next decade, however. *1982* Centre supreme Jamie Lyon was born in Narrabri, New South Wales, Australia and brought up in Wee Wah. In 63 matches for the Saints, he scored 46 tries and kicked 206 goals. Effortlessly. On returning home to play for Manly, Jamie also became only the fourth NRL player to score 100 tries and kick 500 goals in his career. The others: Ryan Girdler, Hasem el Masri and Luke Burt. *2000* World Club Challenge: St Helens 6 Melbourne Storm 44 at the JJB Stadium, Wigan. A real disappointment, on top of the match not being played at Knowsley Road in the first place. Saints were well and truly out-classed on the evening. Definitely one to forget.

25 JANUARY

1903 Lou Houghton, a rugged, hard-working forward, was born in Haydock. Lou has the distinction of scoring Saints' first-ever try in a Challenge Cup final at Wembley, in 1930, when the Chemics pulled off a shock victory against the odds. *1964* First Division: St Helens 28 Keighley 3 at Knowsley Road. Right winger Tom van Vollenhoven scored two tries. His centre, making his one and only appearance for the seniors was former Bradford Northern signing Lance Davies On the other flank, not to be outdone, Peter Harvey scored 4 tries. *1976* Tenacious centre Viliamu [Willie] Talau was born in Apia, Samoa. He began his career in New Zealand with the Taranaki Rockets, before joining the Saints from Canterbury Bulldogs in the NRL. He was terrifically strong for his size and scored 65 tries in his 149 matches for the

Saints. *2002* In a special service at the Parish Church of St Helen, conducted by Canon Leo Stoker, St Helens RFC was presented with the Honorary Freedom of the Metropolitan Borough of St Helens – a most prestigious honour indeed. The processional hymn: *Abide with me*; the recessional hymn: *When the Saints go marching in* – fitting on both counts! Bernard Platt's fine image shows the Casket containing the Freedom Scroll being presented to Chairman Howard Morris by the Mayor, Councillor Keith Roberts. The ceremony was followed by a celebration dinner at the World of Glass.

26 JANUARY

1931 Second-rower Roy Robinson was born in the 'Bruk' area of St Helens town centre. A fine, mobile forward, from the UGB club, he made his Challenge Cup debut at Wembley, in 1956. After 57 appearances and 15 tries he later signed for Barrow, outside the glassworks where he worked at Canal Street. *1957* Test Match #100: France 19 Great Britain 19 at Toulouse. Front-rower and Captain Alan Prescott became the first Saints' player to score against the French in an official test match and a real belter it was. He showed great strength and pace to smash his way through a mass of defenders 10 yards inside his own half and went on to score from 60 yards. Brilliant stuff. *2001* World Club Challenge: St Helens 20 Brisbane Broncos 18 at the Reebok Stadium, Bolton. Never mind the sleet and freezing rain: we are the Champions – of the world! Let's sing it again eh? What a mighty time for all connected with the Saints.

27 JANUARY

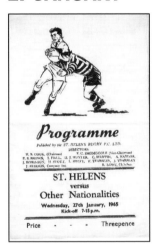

1965 Friendly match: St. Helens 19 Other Nationalities 2 at Knowsley Road. A special game to inaugurate the club's new floodlighting system and as such, a real milestone in the club's history. Club President Lord Pilkington performed the all-important ceremonial 'switch on'. Keith Northey scored 2 memorable tries on a crisp, frosty evening, showcasing his fantastic sidestep! The Other Nationalities team were guaranteed £20 to turn out, plus reasonable travelling expenses. The match programme is shown on the left [Alex Service] *2003* Cross-code challenge match: St. Helens 39 Sale Sharks 41 at Knowsley Road. Sale won the first half under union rules 41–0. The second half of rugby league saw Saints score 39 points without reply doing what they did best. It was arguably more interesting than the usual 'friendly' clash. Yet it emphasised the technically different aspects of the two codes. Never the twain? You bet!

28 JANUARY

1948 Quicksilver stand-off Jimmy Honey was signed from the famous junior club Vine Tavern in Thatto Heath. Mine Host of the famous public house on Elephant Lane for many years was former Recs and England star forward Frank Bowen. *1961* Test Match #124: Great Britain 27 France 8 at Knowsley Road. Despite the muddy conditions, this was a terrific display of open rugby from the Brits, who were 20–8 up at half-time to the delight of the near–15,000 crowd. There were four Saints' representatives on view: Mick Sullivan [at right centre, with Billy Boston outside him], Alex Murphy at 7; Abe Terry in the front row and Vince Karalius at loose forward. *1969* From the Boardroom: "A letter from Batley asking for support that touch judges have more authority in the control of matches was not supported". Obviously a contentious issue at the time. It probably still is. *1978* Players No.6 Trophy Final: Warrington 9 Widnes 4 at Knowsley Road. Legendary former Saints' centre Billy Benyon was Warrington's player-coach in a real arm-wrestle affair in the winter mud. He later re-joined his hometown club as coach in the mid–1980s.

Going for the gap! Stand-off Jimmy Honey scores against Liverpool Stanley in 1950, one of a hat-trick, when the new stadium at Knotty Ash was first used by the Liverpool club. [Alex Service]

29 JANUARY

1968 Front-rower Dave Cosgrove was born in Widnes. The former Farnworth junior was popular with the fans and was always a determined character on the field with his bustling runs and work rate. One of his most memorable matches was the one point victory, 27–26, over the visiting Kiwis at Knowsley Road on 1 October 1989. *1989* Challenge Cup Round 1: Swinton 5 St Helens 16 at Station Road, Swinton. The home team, with former Saint Frankie Barrow as coach, gave as much as they got at times, but Saints began their eventual Wembley odyssey with tries from Les Quirk, Neil Holding and Captain Shane Cooper. Centres Michael O'Connor and Paul Loughlin added a goal apiece.

30 JANUARY

1911 The *St Helens Newspaper* announced the signing of Cumberland County threequarter Plato Harrison, from Kendal RUFC. Further information included his membership of the Westmorland and Cumberland Territorial Yeomanry. He saw service as a bugler with the Border regiment during the Boer War and was under fire several times. Before he was 17 years of age, he could boast a medal and five clasps. A brave lad indeed. *1932* Hooker Bob Dagnall was born in Thatto Heath and attended Grange Park Secondary School. An old school hooker who knew every trick in the book to get the ball, he began his career with Rochdale Hornets and won every honour in club rugby when he signed for the Saints. He played for Great Britain too. *1963* Welsh centre Cenyyd Williams [Cardiff RUFC] signed for the Saints in Cardiff which, like most of Britain, was in the grip of the Big Freeze. A member of a famous Welsh rugby-playing family, he was a classy player and became one of Tom van Vollenhoven's centre partners in 1967–68.

31 JANUARY

1874 The *St Helens Standard* carried a report of Saints' very first match, against Liverpool Royal Infirmary, at Boundary Road. Details of the score and scorers are rather sketchy, to say the least, but, according to the paper: "On no side being called the Liverpool men had added another touchdown to their score, a very pleasant game thus terminating in a draw in their favour". Club Founder William Douglas Herman captained the team from full-back. Recent research has revealed that Herman played rugby when he was studying at the Royal College of Chemistry in London, in the early 1870s, before joining Pilkington's Crown Glass Works in St. Helens as Head Chemist. He turned out for the Crescent club as a forward, with his elder brother, Arthur. Playing home games at Battersea Park, their opponents included some of the teams who went on to form the Rugby Football Union, such as Belsize Park, Flamingoes, Mohicans and Queen's House. *1981* European Championship: France 35 Wales 5 at Stade de l'Egassiaral, Narbonne. Bustling front-rower Roger Owen made his Welsh debut and replaced fellow Saint Mel James from the bench. Clive Griffiths was the other replacement, with Roy Mathias at loose forward. Swinton's Danny Wilson, father of footballer Ryan Giggs, was at stand-off for the Welshmen. *1986* Front-rower Peter Souto was signed from Widnes. This talented former Fulham forward played only six matches, but impressed in virtually all of them. He won a John Player Trophy winner's medal in the 1988 Final against Leeds. What a pity we didn't see more of him in the red vee.

Welsh front-rower Roger Owen in action for the Saints against Hull KR in the early 1980s.
His Welsh international team-mate Clive Griffiths is behind him [Brian Peers]

February

Up and running and on top of the world.

A captain's part: Chris Joynt races away to score a vital try in Saints' first-ever World Club Championship success, against Brisbane Broncos at the Reebok Stadium in 2001. And yes; the white bits are sleet – not exactly welcomed by our friends from Down Under. [Bernard Platt]

Good old Mother Nature. The start of the Summer Super League has been pushed back quite a bit since the inaugural round of matches on 31 March 1996. For quite a while, early Challenge Cup rounds were the reason. Little wonder that people 'railed' at the 'pre-season competition' nature of the famous trophy and since then, rounds have been staggered throughout the season, with the Wembley date in August, which, in itself, is a real bone of contention! From 2003, every league campaign has begun in February. There has been another 'extra' fixture impact for the calendar in recent years, with NRL and Super League clubs vying for the World Club Challenge matches. It is unfortunate that Knowsley Road was not seen as adequate to stage the initial Saints matches in the Noughties. The first, against Melbourne Storm, in 2000, was played at Wigan. Then the games were at Bolton's Reebok Stadium, where the Saints became World Champions in 2001 and 2007. Memorable times indeed, but it was 2015 before we had the chance to watch our team on home soil, in the magnificent new stadium at Langtree Park – a fabulous setting, for sure. A great pity that the South Sydney Rabbitohs won so comprehensively. No wonder owner Russell Crowe preferred it to the Oscars. Wouldn't we all.

1 FEBRUARY

1864 Star fly-half Billy Cross was born in Barrow. The former Kendal Hornet remains Saints' most prominent early player in the last vestiges of the club's rugby union days. He had great skills and was a brilliant organiser. Really, he could be classed as 'Captain-coach' such was his overall influence. Billy was licensee of the Duke of Cambridge in Duke Street, which was also the Saints' headquarters for a spell. *1880* Meanwhile, over in London on this date, Hubert Sydney 'Jum' Turtill was born. The family migrated to New Zealand when he was young, when his rather portly appearance earned him the nickname 'Jumbo' later shortened to 'Jum'. A rock-solid full-back, he joined the Saints in 1909 and played 140 games for the club, kicking 200 goals. The licensee of the Nelson Hotel in Bridge Street, he lost his life in the First World War. *1972* From the Boardroom, with Mr FC Dromgoole in the Chair: "The Secretary [Basil Lowe] informed the Board that a Tommie Smith, the 1968 Mexico Olympic 200 metres winner [in a world record 19.83 seconds] was anxious to play a professional sport in Great Britain, he had some experience through playing American rugby for two years and had also completed a season in Canada. His statistics were 6 feet 5 inches 15 stone 6 pounds. 26 years. A school teacher and the current world record holder for the 100 and 200 metres. It was agreed that we were interested, and it was left to the secretary to find out further details." Unfortunately, it came to nought. Just to explain, Afro-American athlete Tommie Smith (gold) and fellow countryman John Carlos (bronze) provoked controversy during their medal ceremony on the podium as the *Star Spangled Banner* began. Each athlete raised a black-gloved fist and kept them raised until the anthem had finished. All three athletes, including Australian Peter Norman (silver) wore human rights badges on their jackets. Brave men who earned their own special niche in the promotion of human rights. Good on 'em.

Left: A Baines card featuring Billy Cross [Curtis Johnstone]; right: local newspaper cartoon extoling the popularity of 'Jum' Turtill, the former New Zealand full-back [Alex Service]

2 FEBRUARY

1868 The making of our town, but our team came five years later! Queen Victoria granted a Charter of Incorporation, defining St. Helens as a Municipal Borough. The first election of councillors took place later in May, followed by the first Town Council meeting on 18 May. *1929* Northern Rugby League: St. Helens 11 Salford 11 at Knowsley Road. This was the Benefit Match for stalwart local-born full-back Charlie Crooks. Unfortunately, the Saints had to play nine reserves as a result of illness and Crooks missed the game himself through injury. It poured down, too, keeping crowd numbers down.   *1971* It was announced at a meeting of the St. Helens directors that front-rower Cliff Watson wanted to play in Australia. He was eventually released to play for Cronulla Sutherland, in the Sydney competition for a £6,000 transfer fee, where he joined former team-mate Tommy Bishop. *2013* Super League Round 1: St. Helens 4 Huddersfield Giants 40 at Langtree Park. Saints, under new coach Nathan Brown – dismissed by the Giants the previous season - were expected to triumph. But Huddersfield ran riot, winning their first away fixture against Saints since 1978. Twelve months later, however, Brown had guided Saints to a Grand Final success against Wigan.

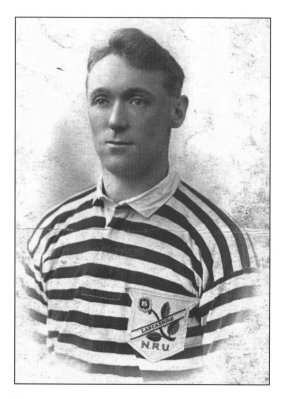 

Left: Charlie Crooks, in his Lancashire jersey, had a well-earned benefit in 1929. He spent his entire career with his home-town team and was a confirmed bachelor. [Alex Service]
Right: Great Britain front-row legend Cliff Watson, who announced his intentions to sign for Cronulla Sutherland in Sydney in 1971. [Robert Gate]

3 FEBRUARY

1962 Northern Rugby League: St Helens 36 Huddersfield 5 at Knowsley Road. Loose-forward Bill Major, signed from Widnes as part of the two-way Vince Karalius deal, made his debut, together with a five-try romp from winger Mick Sullivan. Bill was later appointed team captain. *1991* First Division: Oldham 16 St Helens 20 at Watersheddings. Two tries for powerful right wing star Alan Hunte in a hard-earned victory, in what was always such a difficult environment for visiting teams.

4 FEBRUARY

1950 Challenge Cup Round 1 (first leg): St Helens 10 Halifax 6 at Knowsley Road. Police used walkie-talkies for the first time to aid crowd control. Former Batley stand-off Eric Hesketh made his debut for the Saints. "My dad [a Wigan director] looks upon St Helens as the next best club to play for", he told the local press. *1967* Challenge Cup Round 1: Blackbrook 12 York 23 at Knowsley Road. Another occasion where local amateurs used the Saints' facilities. Blackbrook's utility back John Houghton later signed for St Helens on the strength of his performance in this match. *1996* Challenge Cup Round 4: Castleford Tigers 16 St Helens 58 at Wheldon Road. A hat-trick for centre Paul Newlove in his first Challenge Cup match for the club as Saints hit the Wembley trail at full pelt.

5 FEBRUARY

1945 From the Committee meeting at Knowsley Road: "The secretary was instructed to write to Sergeant J. Fearnley, Private H. Finney, and W/MA. Fearnley and ascertain their fitness and chance of obtaining leave to play in the forthcoming cup ties." Getting a team together in those dark days was always challenging, with greater priorities elsewhere. *1921* Northern Rugby League: St Helens 0 Rochdale Hornets 10 at Knowsley Road. A disappointing defeat, but Saints unearthed a future star at stand-off: Les Fairclough, the Little General.

6 FEBRUARY

1932 Don Vines was born in South Wales. He was a centre with Newbridge RUFC before turning professional with Oldham. He was a tough second-rower and Great Britain international when Saints signed him from Wakefield Trinity at the start of the 1960–61 campaign. He stayed for 12 months, winning a Lancashire Cup Final against Swinton and a Challenge Cup winner's medal, when Wigan were beaten 12–6 at Wembley, before returning to Trinity – a one-season wonder in the nicest sense. *1958* A terrible tragedy: 23 people were killed after BEA flight 609 crashed on take-off from Munich-Riem airport. Eight senior Manchester United players were killed. Full-back Bill Foulkes, grandson of former Saints captain Tommy Foulkes, survived the crash and was appointed club captain afterwards. He did play a bit of rugby in his youth and his favourite Saints player was legendary front-rower George 'Porky' Davies, a stalwart of the war years in particular. *2010* Super League Round 1: St Helens 12 Hull FC 32 at GPW Recruitment Stadium. The Humbersiders, including new signing Sean Long, pulled off a spectacular victory in the fog. The game nearly didn't take place at all as a result of the dense fog that shrouded the ground. The live television audience was equally nonplussed by the proceedings. Sean was in typically ebullient form and scored a try just after half-time that gave the visitors an unassailable 20–0 lead.

Left: In 2010 Sean Long returned to Knowsley Road for his new club Hull FC when dense fog made viewing a difficult option for many fans. Saints' Kyle Eastmond [left] comes in to tackle, with back-rower Willie Manu behind, who later joined St Helens
[Bernard Platt].

Below: a 1961 Challenge Cup Final programme signed by the team, including Don Vines
[Alex Service].

7 FEBRUARY

1948 Challenge Cup Round 1 (first leg): St Helens 48 Buslingthorpe Vale 0 at Knowsley Road. A predictably comprehensive victory against the amateurs from North Leeds. Right winger 'Sonny' Doyle led the scorers with four tries using his electric pace, while the back row of George Parsons, Len Aston and Jack Dixon all managed to get on the scoresheet with three-pointers themselves. The second leg, a week later was played at Headingley and the Vale gained much respect with a reduced 13–2 margin. *1967* Challenge Cup First Round Replay: St Helens 3 Salford 8 at Knowsley Road. After a 5–5 draw at The Willows, it seemed as though the Saints had done the hardest bit. Yet in front of a somewhat expectant crowd of over 14,000, the visitors pulled off a shock victory by defeating the Cup holders. Tom van Vollenhoven was the try scorer. A case of down to earth with a mighty crash.

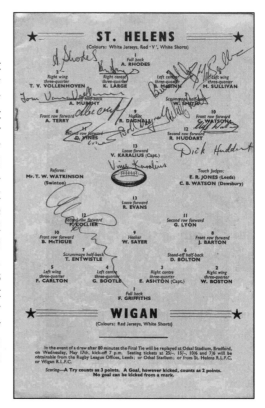

8 FEBRUARY

1930 Challenge Cup Round 1: St Helens 9 St Helens Recreation 7 at Knowsley Road. Flying winger Alf Ellaby scored and second-rower Jack Arkwright took over kicking duties from George Lewis and booted three goals from a pitch covered in slutch. Apparently, the aforementioned word is rarely used outside Lancashire and when BBC Commentator Ray French used it in one of his broadcasts it triggered a plethora of letters to Broadcasting House. "Confused of Kensington writes ..." *1964* Challenge Cup Round 1: St Helens 6 Castleford 13 at Knowsley Road. One local correspondent was totally fed up with the Saints' performance: "No passes out of the tackle, no forwards supporting the man with the ball, no constructive ideas". Castleford were, by contrast, "a snappy lot of ball-handlers" and worthy winners to boot. *2003* Challenge Cup Round 4: Union Treiziste Catalan 6 St Helens 70 at Stade Aime Giral, Perpignan. Sean Long scored four tries and kicked nine goals in this rather one-sided affair. The French club later entered Super League in 2006 as Catalans Dragons, who became much more formidable opponents, without doubt, over the ensuing years. The first Super League game against them in France was at the same venue.

Sean Long makes a break in Perpignan during the 2003 Challenge Cup tie against UTC in Perpignan. He scored four tries and kicked nine goals – a good day at the office, as the saying goes. [Bernard Platt]

9 FEBRUARY

1901 Second row forward and 'tackling machine' Albert Fildes was born in Runcorn. He originally signed for St Helens Recs. Then in October 1930, he was the subject of a potentially fraught transfer to rivals Saints, given the sheer volume of hatred between the two teams' spectators. Already a seasoned international, he made 129 appearances before retiring in 1934, scoring 19 tries.

1929 Challenge Cup Round 1: St Helens 32 Lindley Swifts 2 at Knowsley Road. This included a 'no pressure' debut for former Newport (rugby union) and Wigan scrum-half Eddie Dowdall against the amateur outfit from the Huddersfield area. *2017* Super League Round 1: St Helens 6 Leeds Rhinos 4 at the Totally Wicked Stadium. Former Halton Hornets stand-off Danny Richardson made his full debut. Comparisons with the great Sean Long sprung to mind. Theo Fages was his scrum-half partner and scored Saints' try. Mark Percival kicked the goal in a game of fine margins, unlike the often flowing rugby between the two old rivals.

10 FEBRUARY

1909 Tour match: St Helens 9 Australia 0 at Knowsley Road. Three tries without reply for the Saints to defeat the first Kangaroos. The scorers were winger Jimmy Flanagan, left-centre Jimmy Greenwood and feisty second-rower James 'Butcher' Prescott. *2001* Challenge Cup Round 4: St Helens 22 Wigan Warriors 8 at Knowsley Road. Full-back Paul Wellens returned just a fortnight after fracturing his cheekbone against Brisbane Broncos. After a disappointing effort from the visitors from over Billinge Lump, Mike Latham, in *League Express*, wrote: "The team that once dominated rugby league is now cast in the role of bridesmaid." How we loved that. *2012* Super League Round 2: St Helens 38 Salford City Reds 10 at Langtree Park. After a brilliant opening ceremony, featuring such playing luminaries as Keiron Cunningham, Alex Murphy, Kel Coslett (Club President) and Tom van Vollenhoven, the first Super League match took place in Saints' new stadium at Peasley Cross. 15,547 fans saw the Saints blow away the opposition in convincing fashion. *2018* Super League Round 2: Catalans Dragons 12 St Helens 21 at Stade Gilbert Brutus. Saints caught the French team cold – and it was cold too – with a stunning try from Jonny Lomax in the first minute, which brought up his 500th point for the club. Back-rower Morgan Knowles received his marching orders, yet Saints produced a marvellous backs-to-the-wall performance in adversity.

Tom van Vollenhoven – who else – brought the match ball into the Langtree Park arena before the opening match at Langtree Park and showed he still had the knack of putting the ball down.

[Alex Service and Bernard Platt]

11 FEBRUARY

1875 William 'Kitty' Briers was born in Thatto Heath. A superb athlete – he was a blacksmith's striker at Lea Green Colliery – perhaps the equivalent of any modern-day player's weight training. Billy was quick as well as durable and made 463 appearances for the club from 1895 to 1910, together with a sizeable chunk from the pre-Northern Union days. So why 'Kitty'? He was left-handed, also known as being 'kitty pawed' so there you are. *1969* From the Boardroom: "A letter from the Electricity Board gave the information that discussions are at present taking place with the Local Authorities for the dismantling of the overhead line which crosses some of the club property". The lines and their associated pylons were a prominent part of the skyline behind the Main Stand and railway line for many years.

1995 Challenge Cup Round 4: Wigan 16 St Helens 16 at Central Park. A try and crucial drop-goal by front-rower Ian Pickavance gave Saints another chance against the Old Enemy. He scored again in the replay at Knowsley Road, but Saints lost 40–24, a match covered extensively by the BBCs *Sportsnight* programme. A bitter blow. *2006* Super League Round 1: Harlequins 16 St Helens 40 at the Stoop. A try and six goals for Australian star Jamie Lyon, who then proceeded to kick at least one goal in the matches he played in until the end of the campaign: 34 games; 164 goals. He just seemed to love playing the game. *2016* Super League Round 2: Salford City Reds 44 St Helens 10 at the AJ Bell Stadium. Theo Fages, the first player of French origin to play for the club in rugby league, made his debut from the bench against his former team. Not the easiest of assignments.

Jamie Lyon in action against Harlequins (left) and booting over one of his 164 goals for the Saints during the 2006 'treble' campaign. [Bernard Platt]

12 FEBRUARY

1870 Winger Bob Doherty was born in Kendal. A slip of a lad, but quick for his size and elusive, he began with the Kendal Hornets, played for the Saints in their rugby union days and carried on to make 225 appearances in the Northern Union, scoring 38 tries, from 1895 to 1902. Although not necessarily a high strike rate, he was a Rottweiler in the tackle. Bob Doc was a real stalwart and the club made him a Life Member in later years. *1949* Challenge Cup Round 1 (first leg): Bradford Northern 3 St Helens 4. A real arm-wrestle of a game, with hooker Eric Battersby making his debut. As one correspondent wrote: "Wafted by a favouring gale from the junior field of Greenacres near Oldham to first class cup tie football in a few weeks." Eric played once more for the seniors, in the second leg at Knowsley Road, which the Yorkshiremen won 5–0 to go into the next round and win the Cup at Wembley.

1984 Challenge Cup Round 1: St Helens 16 Leigh 10 at Knowsley Road. Cumbrian Peter Gorley, a formidable back-rower, originally, added a new dimension to his career by playing in the front-row for the first time in the red vee. He was all knees and elbows and must have been a nightmare to tackle.

13 FEBRUARY

1897 John Patrick Mearns died aged 43. A solicitor, he had been President of St Helens RFC since the mid–1880s, taking over from Austin Cooper Carr and he helped the Saints' club over many potential difficulties. He suffered a compound fracture of the thigh and other injuries when he was hit by a cab during a business trip to London. He was a patient of Charing Cross hospital for many months and remained in poor health as a result. He is buried at Windleshaw Chantry, Hard Lane, in St Helens. Ted Forsyth (far right), Glyn Davies and John Bretherton are pictured during their restoration of the Mearns' grave in 2017. [Alex Service] *1939* Powerful forward John Warlow was born in Llanelli. A Welsh rugby union international, he joined Ray French and John Mantle to form a solid 'back three' at Wembley in the 1966 Challenge Cup Final against Wigan. He had two spells with the Saints, 1963 to 1969 and 1973 to 1975, making 235 appearances in the red vee. *1994* Challenge Cup Round 5: Whitehaven 4 St Helens 46 at the Recreation Ground. This was second-rower Chris Joynt's only hat-trick of tries for the club. He scored 121 in his long career, but never in threes until then. *2002* The club announced that Eamonn McManus was to take over as Chairman from Howard Morris. Apart from being at the helm during the club's marvellous 'three trophies' season in 2006, Eamonn's greatest achievement must surely be his role in the move from Knowsley Road to the marvellous new stadium at Peasley Cross. The main approach road is 'McManus Drive'. A fine tribute indeed. *2014* Super League Round 1: Warrington Wolves 8 St Helens 38 at the Halliwell Jones Stadium. A try on debut for new front-row signing Kyle Amor from Wakefield Trinity Wildcats. The big Cumbrian enjoyed a successful first campaign, ending with a Grand Final victory over Wigan Warriors at Old Trafford. He liked that – didn't we all.

14 FEBRUARY

1914 International match: England 16 Wales 12 at Knowsley Road. Over 10,000 witnessed this 'first' for the club at a ground that had seen several major improvements to the terrace banking and pitch. It was just a pity that there were no Saints representatives on view for the home supporters. *1959* Northern Rugby League: St Helens 71 Barrow 15 at Knowsley Road. Centre Peter Fearis kicked 13 goals in a points-scoring feast. Five of Saints' 13 tries were scored by Tom van Vollenhoven. What a pity Tom never secured the club match record of seven. It remained there for the taking in 2018. *1999* Challenge Cup Round 4: Hunslet Hawks 10 St Helens 40 at South Leeds Stadium. Barnstorming Sonny Nickle re-ignited his Saints' career after a spell with Bradford Bulls. He was joined in the second row with Chris Joynt and loose-forward Paul Sculthorpe. *2003* World Club Challenge: St Helens 0 Sydney City Roosters 38 at the Reebok Stadium, Bolton. They were too good for Saints on the night and included centre Chris Flannery and front-rower Jason Cayless, who would later wear the red vee with great success. But no consolation for us whatsoever in what has become an all-too-familiar story at club and international level.

15 FEBRUARY

1913 Northern Rugby League: St Helens 51 Coventry 9 at Knowsley Road. A fine hat-trick of tries from right wing powerhouse Tom Barton. He was really in form at the time and had scored three the previous week in the challenge match against Torquay in Devon. *1983* Challenge Cup Round 1: St Helens 52 Carlisle 0 at Knowsley Road. Full-back Clive Griffiths scored a try and kicked eight goals. His best performance with the boot during his time at Knowsley Road. *1998* Challenge Cup Round 4: Featherstone Rovers 24 St Helens 56 at Post Office Road. Record signing Paul Sculthorpe scored two tries on debut from the second row. Australian front-rower Brett Goldspink, a signing from Oldham Bears, also played his first match.

Left: Gotcha! Stand-off Tommy Martyn shows his one-on-one defensive skills by downing Sydney Roosters legend Anthony Minichiello in the World Club Challenge at the Reebok Stadium in 2003 [Bernard Platt]; Right: Welsh full-back Clive Griffiths lines up another pot at goal. [Brian Peers]

16 FEBRUARY

1924 Challenge Cup Round 1: Wardley 0 St Helens 73 at Swinton. Charlie Crooks, playing in the centre, scored a brace of tries against the non-leaguers. This was Saints' highest score against any opposition in competitive rugby before the Second World War. It remained the club's highest 'away' success until 2005, when Leigh Centurions were thrashed 78–4 on 4 September 2005. *1961* Challenge Cup Round 1: Widnes 10 St Helens 29 at Naughton Park. A ground record of 24,205 fans watched this match, as Saints continued on the Wembley trail, after a 5–5 draw in the first match at Knowsley Road. Tom van Vollenhoven and his centre Ken Large each scored a brace of touchdowns. *2018* During an open training day, held at Ruskin Drive, fans were able to watch the junior and senior squads put through their paces together. It was also a good opportunity for budding autograph hunters afterwards, with many youngsters enjoying their half-term holidays. A fine piece of PR by the club.

All smiles for Saints' players at the 'open' training morning at Ruskin Drive in 2018 [Alex Service].

17 FEBRUARY

1923 Challenge Cup Round 1: Norwood 3 St Helens 29 at the Boulevard, Hull. Welsh centre Gus Hayes scored a brace of tries against the plucky amateur outfit from Humberside. Where is Norwood? Think Beverley and you're quite near. *1951* Challenge Cup Round 3 (second leg): St Helens 4 Bradford Northern 0 at Knowsley Road. Despite two goals from Welsh centre Vivian Harrison, the Saints lost 11–10 on aggregate. The latest phase of post-war ground improvements saw the opening of the covered enclosure at the Eccleston End before the match, named after George Edington, the former Supporters' Club Chairman. Steelwork was by the local firm of Todd brothers in St Helens. *1974* First Division: St Helens 38 Rochdale Hornets 5 at Knowsley Road. Five tries from Welsh winger Roy Mathias. His fellow countryman Frank Wilson was his centre. When Roy had the line in his sights, he was tremendously difficult to stop with his direct no-nonsense 'route 1' approach.

18 FEBRUARY

1990 Stones Bitter First Division: Barrow 6 St Helens 46 at Craven Park. Job done, with a brace of tries from Phil Veivers and Roy Haggerty, plus seven goals from Paul Loughlin. In context, it proved to be a disastrous season for the homesters, with just one league win from 26 games during the campaign. *1991* First Division: St Helens 12 Hull FC 10 at Knowsley Road. Les Quirk's long-distance and last-ditch match-winner on the Popular Side had us all in raptures, not least jubilant video commentator Ron Hoofe, who described it as 'orgasmic'. And yes, it really was that good, trust me.

19 FEBRUARY

1966 Northern Rugby League: Wakefield Trinity 20 St Helens 12 at Belle Vue. Welsh second-rower Mervyn Hicks broke his arm in what proved to be his last game for the club before moving to Australia and North Sydney RLFC. Big Merv was certainly a handful and a fans' favourite at Knowsley Road. *2018* Another club favourite – former full-back Geoff Pimblett – passed away after a short illness. The first player to win both the Lance Todd and Harry Sunderland trophy, he was a brilliant all-round footballer and an integral part of the Saints' team of the 1970s. But for the phenomenal success of Paul Wellens in the Super League era, he would have been an automatic selection for the club's Greatest 17 selection in 2010.

Left: Skipper Geoff Pimblett with Saints' teddy bear mascot, Helen, at Wembley 1978;
Right: second-rower Eric Chisnall celebrates in traditional style after victory in the 1976 Premiership Final, against Salford. He played his 507th and last game for Saints in February 1982 [Alex Service]

20 FEBRUARY

1912 Northern Rugby League: Dewsbury 17 St Helens 8 at Crown Flatt, Dewsbury. Welshman Tom Browning, from Abertillery RUFC, made a solid debut at scrum-half. He was equally effective at centre or half-back and played 62 times for the club, scoring 14 tries. A member of the Royal Engineers during the First World War, he passed away back home in Blaina, South Wales, in March 1931. *2004* Super League Round 1: St Helens 30 Hull FC 16 at Knowsley Road. Two tries on debut for Nick Fozzard. The Wakefield-born front-rower became somewhat of a cult figure with both team-mates and supporters alike as a result of his occasionally 'eccentric' behaviour.

21 FEBRUARY

1919 Bill Fishwick was born in the Merton Bank district of St Helens. After making his debut in a Saints-Recs 'derby' match at Knowsley Road on Boxing Day 1938, Bill's rugby was interrupted by the war, when, as a member of the Parachute regiment, he was taken prisoner at Arnhem. Fortunately, he returned to the Saints afterwards and made 76 appearances before his transfer to Barrow in 1948. *1982* First Division: York 7 St Helens 19 at Clarence Street. Eric Chisnall played his last game for the Saints – his 507th – in the front row. He preferred the back-row, of course. A Saint through and through and remains so to this day.

22 FEBRUARY

1908 Tour Match: St Helens 10 New Zealand 21 at Knowsley Road. The first Kiwi tourists loved St Helens so much that they arranged a second match in the town during their inaugural tour. The chief 'mover and shaker' for the tour, Albert Baskerville, also turned out for the 'All Golds' that afternoon, in the second row – and scored a try. It must have been great to see. *1930* Challenge Cup Round 2: Leeds 5 St Helens 18 at Headingley. In his book, *The Headingley Story*, Ken Dalby writes as follows: "It was a game that had been awaited with great enthusiasm and which was a disgrace to the code. Pascoe, Moores [Leeds] and Halfpenny [Saints] were dismissed from the field, Stan Smith [Leeds] had to retire with a damaged hip and, as the final whistle sounded, Groves, the St Helens scrum-half was being carried off in a more or less unconscious state." For the record, Alf Ellaby, Trevor Hall and Bob Harrison scored Saints' tries; George Lewis kicked three goals. *2015* World Club

Challenge: St Helens 0 South Sydney Rabbitohs 39 at Langtree Park, St Helens. For several years it had been our dream to host Australian opponents in this competition and at last, we got our wish. Greg Inglis and his team were almost unbeatable on the night and it was so disappointing – yet a great spectacle nonetheless. Souths owner Russell Crowe said he would rather be in St Helens than the Oscars. Well, wouldn't we all.

All battered and blue. Centre Mark Percival troubles the South Sydney defence with his deceptive swerve and sidestep. [RLPhotos.com]

23 FEBRUARY

1997 Challenge Cup Round 5: St Helens 54 Hull 8 at Knowsley Road. Left centre Paul Newlove scored a fine hat-trick. He was so naturally strong and agile – a 'nailed on' member of Saints Greatest 17 team. In the summer of 1996, when scrum-half Bobbie Goulding directed play to his side there was always a terrific air of expectancy from the Popular Side at Knowsley Road. *2007* World Club Challenge: St Helens 18 Brisbane Broncos 14 at the Reebok Stadium, Bolton. Paul Sculthorpe shook off his injury hoodoo to help Saints win the World Club Challenge for the second time. They then held all four club trophies. Reasons to be cheerful? You bet. Follow that then?

Left: Kiwi second-rower Trevor Hall in relaxed mood before a match at Knowsley Road [Alex Service]; Right: skipper Paul Sculthorpe and Willie Talau celebrate Saints' second World Club Challenge success, against Brisbane Broncos, in 2007 [Bernard Platt]

24 FEBRUARY

1905 Second-rower Trevor Hall was born in Cambridge, a town in the Waikato Region of North Island, New Zealand He joined the Saints at the start of the 1929–30 campaign, with fellow Kiwis, winger Roy Hardgrave and front-rower Lou Hutt. Trevor made 130 appearances for the club, scoring 25 tries. A little-known fact is that his brother, Private Francis Hall of the 21st Battalion of the New Zealand Army was killed in action in Libya on 29 November 1941. Another casualty that day was Captain Alan Turtill of the same regiment, the son of former Saints' full-back 'Jum' Turtill, who died in the First World War. Both Francis and Alan are buried at Knightsbridge Military Cemetery. A truly poignant coincidence. *1970* Triangular Tournament: Wales 7 England 26 at Headingley. There were six Saints on show in Leeds, a good enough reason for fans to travel over the Pennines. For Wales: Frank Wilson (5), Bobby Wanbon (10) Graham Rees (11) and Kel Coslett (13). For England: Billy Benyon (4) and Cliff Watson (10). *1996* Challenge Cup Round 6: Salford Reds 26 St Helens 46 at the Willows. This included two bulldozing tries from the rampaging Vila Matautia. There was no stopping his Wembley odyssey. Salford had beaten Wigan in the previous round too, breaking their long grip on the coveted trophy. How could we ever forget that?

25 FEBRUARY

1916 This report from the day's *St Helens Newspaper* highlighted the horror of wartime for a Saints' forward: "Sergeant Archie Waddell of the New Zealand Expeditionary Force returned to St Helens having spent four and a half months in hospital in London as a result of his experiences with the Colonial forces at ANZAC Gallipoli. He was suffering the effects of concussion caused by a high-explosive shell and from the effects of an attack of dysentery." Say no more. ***1939*** European Championship: England 9 France 12 at Knowsley Road. A crowd of 10,000 watched Saints' new signing from St Helens Recreation, stand-off Frank Tracey, make his international debut. A film of the occasion still survives and what was the world's largest billboard, sponsored by Lewis's of Liverpool, which also had the function of a wind-break, quite prominent at the Eccleston End. ***1984*** Challenge Cup Round 2: St Helens 24 Hull FC 14 at Knowsley Road. A fine match to delight the live television audience on the BBC. Underdogs Saints triumphed against the all-star Humberside outfit, with Skipper Harry Pinner running the show and banging over a record four drop-goals. Brilliant! Hull FC fans seemed to be everywhere on the ground that afternoon, even taking over at half-way on the Popular Side. ***2011*** Super League Round 3: St Helens 18 Warrington Wolves 25 at the Stobart Stadium, Widnes. A perhaps understandable 'This wouldn't have happened at Knowsley Road' reaction from some Saints' fans after the first match in their temporary home. But at the season's end, the team was good enough to get into the Grand Final by beating Wigan Warriors for their sixth consecutive appearance at the Theatre of Dreams. All relative.

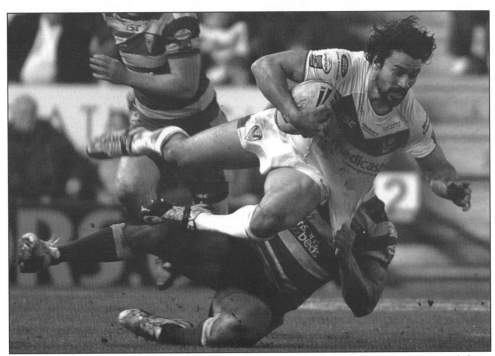

Powerhouse winger Ade Gardner tries to force his way through the Warrington Wolves defence during the club's first home match at Widnes in 2011. [Bernard Platt]

26 FEBRUARY

1920 Challenge Cup Round 1, second replay: St. Helens 3 Wakefield Trinity 12 at Headingley. The two previous matches were drawn 2–2, so a 'decider' was held on 'neutral' territory. The third game in five days for the clubs. *2000* Former Chairman Harry Cook died aged 95. In his tenure at the helm, the Saints were elevated into the upper echelons of rugby league clubs! The former local headteacher was chairman from 1950 to 1974. Astute and forward-thinking and in tandem with a capable Board of directors, he had a vision for the club which ultimately came into fruition.

Chairman Harry Cook presents 1962 Great Britain touring caps to Mick Sullivan, Dick Huddart and Alex Murphy (wearing his 1960 World Cup winning blazer). Great players, all and behind, the new grandstand marked another important phase in the upward development of the St Helens club. And how good do the red chest and arm bands look? [Alex Service]

27 FEBRUARY

1980 Full-back Paul Wellens was born in St Helens. A twin – sister, Claire, was born first – he became one of the most decorated players of any era. He has, as they say, got all the tee shirts, and more besides. *1994* Challenge Cup Round 6: St Helens 40 Doncaster 9 at Knowsley Road. Two tries for stand-off Tommy Martyn, in front of 8,695 fans. The Dons came to the same venue the following August after their promotion to the First Division and won 29–20. That really hurt.

28 FEBRUARY

1948 Challenge Cup Round 2: Oldham 5 St. Helens 0 at Watersheddings. Wigan-born full-back Jimmy Lowe made his debut. He was a stalwart who tends to go 'under the radar' somewhat and he made 173 appearances from 1948 to 1952, before the signing of Welshman Glyn Moses. *1967* From the Boardroom: There were discussions about the possibility of an exchange deal with Leigh: Ray French for goalkicking full-back Colin Tyrer. It didn't happen. But no smoke without fire. Ray later went to Widnes as part of the deal that brought stand-off Frank Myler to Knowsley Road. *2004* Challenge Cup Round 4: Bradford Bulls 10 St. Helens 30 at Odsal. A determined Saints performance was typified by a fantastic burst of speed by front-rower Mark Edmondson, who scored a brilliant try, more akin to a threequarter. There was Super League opposition all the way to eventual cup glory.

29 FEBRUARY

1924 Winger Steve Llewellyn was born in Abertillery, where he attended the same school as second-rower George Parsons, the player who joined the Saints at the same time, in 1948. In his 10 years at Knowsley Road, he scored 259 tries in 287 appearances, the majority ending with his trademark swallow dive. A popular deputy headteacher at Grange Park High School (Geoff Pimblett also taught there), he was a well-respected personality in the town. *1964* Northern Rugby League: Warrington 10 St Helens 17 at Wilderspool. New signing Stan Owen, a rugged campaigner from Leigh made his debut in the front-row. Signed for his leadership and ball-handling ability, the experienced Welshman lined up in the scrums with Cumbrian John Tembey and hooker Bob Burdell.

Welsh front-rower Stan Owen seemingly spills the ball under pressure from the Swinton defence and tackling full-back Ken Gowers in particular during the 1964 Western Division Championship Final at Central Park. [Alex Service]

March

High hopes or broken dreams?

Hands up. Karle Hammond (second from left) celebrates Saints' first-ever victory in Super League, against deadly rivals Wigan Warriors at Knowsley Road in 1996. Derek McVey, Danny Arnold and Keiron Cunningham share the moment. (Sportsphoto Ltd)

One of the most significant events in rugby league history occurred in late March 1996, when the Summer European Super League kicked off and knocked everyone's sporting body clocks into total disarray. Saints went up to Derwent Park, Workington and won 62–0 at a canter. Would they have done that in the depths of winter? It was a new beginning and, for players, officials and supporters, a time to re-jig their timetables. What about our summer holidays? What about cricket? How can we fit everything in? Given too, the habitual switching of match dates by the television-led orchestrators of the modern game, it is not easy to see why the modern watcher finds it increasingly difficult to attend matches at certain times during the season, which now begins earlier than ever. The 2018 campaign for the Saints began on 2 February.

A number of Challenge Cup semi-finals were also played in March and the Saints appeared in 13 of them all told – the rest were in April – winning seven, losing five, with one draw. Perhaps the most poignant were the 1989 and 1991 clashes against a powerful Widnes outfit, when hopes were raised after two brilliant performances, only to come back down to earth with a wallop against the old enemy, Wigan, at Wembley.

1 March

1930 The 'Third Man' Wilf Roach was born in St Helens. This was his own take on the fact that he was behind centres Duggie Greenall and Don Gullick in the pecking order. Wilf made 37 appearances for the seniors, scoring 13 tries, but he was the perfect utility man to have around and played in the 1952 defeat of the Australian tourists. He joined Rochdale Hornets in the mid–1950s where he gave everything on the field as he always did. *1958* Pre-World War One legend Tom Barton died aged 75. The former bricklayer made 225 appearances, mostly as a winger or full-back and scored 95 tries and 118 goals. The outbreak of the First World War eclipsed his hopes of becoming the first Saints player to score 100 tries and kick 100 goals. That distinction fell to South African winger Len Killeen some 50 years later. *1987* Challenge Cup Round 3: St Helens 41 Whitehaven 10 at Knowsley Road. Australian front-rower Pat Jarvis made his last appearance for the club before returning home to resume his career with Eastern Suburbs in Sydney.

2 March

1895 Friendly match: St Helens 13 Stockport 0 at Knowsley Road. Right winger – and occasional professional sprinter – Tom Sudlow was the dominant force in this somewhat languid encounter, with two tries and two goals. *1929* Oh no! The Saints' programme notes for the game against Leigh said that second-rower Ben Halfpenny might have to give up playing rugby because of work commitments at Widnes United Alkali Works. Fortunately, it never transpired. *2009* Flying winger Frank Carlton was laid to rest in St Helens Cemetery, aged 72. This was the man who scored the breakthrough try at Wembley in 1956 against Halifax that did so much to help his team lift the coveted Challenge Cup for the first time (see below), Frank made 156 appearances for the Saints, scoring 129 tries before his transfer to Wigan. Ray French, a spectator at Wembley in 1956, later gave a superb oration at his funeral at St. Mary's in Blackbrook.

Ken Dean and Halifax legend Johnny Freeman are left in Frank Carlton's wake as he scores in the 1956 Challenge Cup Final. Wonderful stuff. [Alex Service]

3 March

1956 Challenge Cup Round 2: St Helens 48 Castleford 5 at Knowsley Road. Right winger Steve Llewellyn equalled the individual try-scoring record, previously set by Alf Ellaby, with six brilliant tries. He was to repeat the feat on 20 August 1956, in the League against Liverpool City at Knotty Ash. *1962* Challenge Cup Round 2: St Helens 2 Huddersfield 13 at Knowsley Road. An expectant crowd hoped that the Saints would blow away their Yorkshire opponents just as they had done, 36–5, in the league match at the same venue on 3 February. Nothing is certain in sport. Huddersfield loose-forward Peter Ramsden unleashed a stiff arm on Tom van Vollenhoven on the Popular Side that left him poleaxed. Cue general mayhem, with Alex Murphy receiving his marching orders. Fans threw snowballs at the Huddersfield players and Saints' grip on the game was lost. *1974* First Division: St Helens 25 Castleford 5 at Knowsley Road. Young stand-off Tony Atherton made his one and only appearance for the seniors. The following week he suffered a serious head injury in the 'A' team game against Leigh which subsequently ended his career. *2000* Super League Round 1: St Helens 10 Bradford Bulls 32 at Knowsley Road. Before the game, a minute's silence was observed as a mark of respect after the death of former Chairman Harry Cook. This was an emotional time for everyone at the club.

Saints are all smiles before the Huddersfield cup tie at Knowsley Road in 1963. What followed was certainly not in the script. Players' positions on the day are indicated by their on-field numbers.
Back: Tom van Vollenhoven (2), Mike Knowles (8), Cliff Watson (10), Bob Dagnall (9), Ray French (11), Keith Ashcroft (12); front: Bill Major (13 Capt), Brian McGinn (3), Mick Sullivan (5), Alex Murphy (7), Wilf Smith (6), Austin Rhodes (1), Dick Huddart (4).
[Alex Service]

4 March

1962 A still dazed Tom van Vollenhoven recorded a radio segment at Knowsley Road as part of the *Down Your Way* programme on the BBC Home Service, with host Franklyn Engelmann *1968* From the Boardroom: "It was reported that Vollenhoven had booked his passage to South Africa to leave in July." After a few 'false starts' in previous years it was quite definite this time. Truly the end of an era at Knowsley Road. *1990* First Division: Castleford 34 St Helens 24 at Wheldon Road, Castleford. Saints' title hopes took a jolt in a high-scoring affair. The team eventually finished in fifth place in the league, behind Bradford Northern, Widnes, Leeds and Wigan.

5 March

1932 Northern Rugby League: St Helens 36 Barrow 15 at Knowsley Road. Alf Ellaby scored six tries for the rampant Saints. Local lad Jimmy Gerrard made his senior debut at loose-forward. *1960* Northern Rugby League: Warrington 16 St Helens 19 at Wilderspool. Bob Dagnall (St Helens-born) made a successful debut at hooker after his transfer from Rochdale Hornets. His front-row compatriots were Captain Alan Prescott and Yorkshireman Len Hammill. *1978* First Division: St Helens 71 Bramley 7. Saints scored 53 points in a storming second half display, with full-back Geoff Pimblett notching 13 goals in his usual imperious style. He finished top of the overall kicking charts with 178 at the end of the season.

6 March

1937 Northern Rugby League: St Helens 2 Swinton 6 at Knowsley Road. Scrum-half and former Parr Central pupil Harold Briscoe made his senior debut three weeks short of his 16th birthday. He was born on 27 March 1921 and remains the youngest-ever Saints debutant. Welshman Stan Powell, aged 20, was his stand-off in the match. *1965* Winger Les Quirk was born in Ulverston. Les scored 98 tries in 160 appearances and played in four major finals, winning just one – a great pity. He was a superb winger on his day, no question about that.

7 March

1875 Friendly match: Waterloo RFC [1 try 2 rouges] St Helens RFC [1 goal 3 tries 4 rouges.] A 'rouge' was a minor point awarded, for example, for an opponent trapped in his own 'in goal'. Jackson kicked the goal to win the game for Saints. The *St Helens Standard* later thought that certain basic equipment had been found wanting: "the ball itself was not properly 'blown' and, instead of being hard and almost incompressible, was as soft and flabby as a plum pudding". *1945* Centre Billy Benyon was born in St Helens. A skilful and durable footballer, he is a member of Saints 500 appearances club; played in a Lancashire Cup final as a 17-year-old in 1962; captained the team in 1976–77 and returned for a spell as coach in the early 1980s. A true legend of Saints rugby. *1953* Northern Rugby League: St Helens 69 Wakefield Trinity 17 at Knowsley Road. Right centre and Captain Duggie Greenall scored four tries and kicked four goals. Second-rower George Parsons kicked eight. *2008* Super League Round 5: St Helens 30 Hull FC 29 at Knowsley Road. Scrum-half Matty Smith kicked a last-minute penalty from the touchline to win the match for the Saints. Bernard Platt's image captures the moment of triumph. He has been involved in a few 'last ditch' victories, care of his trusty boot!

The lad's only gone and kicked it! Matty Smith's penalty about to go between the posts to seal a last-gasp win against Hull FC in 2008. Conditioner Apollo Perelini already has a broad smile of expectation and ultimate acclamation. [Bernard Platt]

8 March

1952 Challenge Cup Round 2: Workington Town 15 St Helens 4 at Derwent Park. There was a 20,403 ground record crowd for this one. Scrum-half George Langfield kicked two goals for the Saints. *1966* Northern Rugby League: St Helens 16 Liverpool City 2 at Knowsley Road. Scrum-half Tommy Bishop scored two tries. Peter Harvey was at stand-off. Saints were well on their way to a 'double' success in their league campaign, winning both the Lancashire League and League Leaders' Bowl.

9 March

1946 Northern Rugby League: St Helens 13 Halifax 0 at Knowsley Road. The BBC broadcast the second half of the match on the radio, for which the club received a fee of 5 guineas, a welcome source of additional income in those early post-war days. *2007* Super League Round 5: Warrington Wolves 12 St Helens 48 at the Halliwell Jones Stadium. New-season signing Matt Gidley, from Newcastle Knights, scored a memorable first hat-trick for the Saints, in a crushing victory for the visitors.

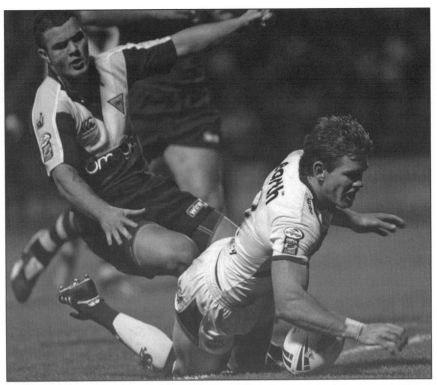

Hat-trick king. Centre Matt Gidley touches down against Warrington Wolves in 2007. He followed Jamie Lyon at Knowsley Road. What a golden era for centres it really was for the Saints.
[Bernard Platt]

10 March

1965 Towering second-rower John Harrison was born in Ashton. Basketball players seemed small compared to him. The former Parkside amateur made 120 appearances for the club and many judges reckon he was unlucky not to have played at representative level. Remember when he headed the ball in the match against Sheffield Eagles for Alan Hunte to score? They changed the rules because of that! *1967* From the Boardroom: "The Chairman reported that [Len] Killeen had received an offer of $10,000 for a season in America to play for Houston Oilers plus a $1,000 bonus to be paid on arrival." Yikes. Lenny could, potentially, have made a fortune as a kicker in the Lone Star State, but really wanted to join an Australian Rugby League club. Newtown originally showed interest, but he became a Balmain Tiger. *1990* Challenge Cup Semi-Final: St Helens 14 Wigan 20 at Old Trafford. Remember Les Quirk's magnificent effort on the South Stand side? He scored twice that afternoon. And what about the winning try from Denis Betts, which even Wigan fans thought was a bit dubious. Altogether now: FORRRWWAARRDDD! *2000* St Helens RFC announced that the contract of Coach Ellery Hanley had been terminated for 'fundamental breaches of contract', including comments at a sponsors' launch; failure to give an interview to the BBC prior to the Challenge Cup game against Leeds Rhinos and his non-attendance at the Super League launch. A great pity – we will remember him for guiding the team to Grand Final glory in 1999. The lads would run through a brick wall for him.

11 March

1953 Hooker Tony Waller was born in St Helens. He made 26 appearances for the seniors, from 1972 to 1973 before joining Warrington. *1989* Challenge Cup Semi-Final: St Helens 16 Widnes 14 at Central Park, Wigan. Widnes were down to 12 men and had seemingly weathered the storm, but Saints scored a try from Les Quirk late on, following great work from hooker Paul Groves and centre supreme Paul Loughlin on the riverside touchline. The final proved to be a match too far in many respects.

12 March

1949 Northern Rugby League: St Helens 18 Belle Vue Rangers 0. Left-centre Duggie Greenall scored a hat-trick of tries. He could score 'em as well as make 'em. The complete centre in many ways. *1972* Test Match #182: Great Britain 45 France 10 at Odsal. Left-centre Billy Benyon scored a try, John Walsh later came off the bench to replace him and scored a three-pointer on his international debut. Youngster Ken Kelly was at stand-off. *1978* Centre or second rower Lee Gilmour was born in Dewsbury. What a good player he was; 178 appearances and 52 tries from 2004 to 2009. Mobile and skilful, Lee was an integral member of the 2006 'treble' winners. How we missed him when he left Knowsley Road. *1995* First Division: Hull FC 32 St Helens 43 at the Boulevard. Keiron Cunningham scored his first try for the Saints at senior level. Jon Neill and Ian Pickavance started the match with him in the front row.

Sheer delight in Cardiff. Lee Gilmour scores Saints' first try after just three minutes in the 32–16 defeat of Wigan Warriors in the 2004 Challenge Cup Final. [Bernard Platt]

13 March

1942 Second-rower John Mantle was born in Cardiff. He became a veritable giant of rugby league. Supremely strong, mobile, with a great work rate and totally uncompromising, John was a regular for Wales and Great Britain. He made over 400 appearances for the Saints, winning four championships and three Challenge Cups. John eventually hung up his boots in March 1982 at the age of 40. He was at Blackpool Borough then and scored a try in his last match. *1944* A resident of Willow Road, parallel to the Popular Side, complained to the club that a ball had twice come over into his garden during the game with Huddersfield on 4 March, causing damage to his greenhouse and cold frame. Saints' Secretary Bert Murray inspected the damage and a financial agreement with the aggrieved resident was reached. *1962* Northern Rugby League: St Helens 31 Liverpool City 7 at Knowsley Road. Former Cowley Grammar School pupil Mike Beddow made his debut at stand-off. Alex Murphy was at scrum-half. Beddow later concentrated on his professional cricket career with Lancashire, 33 matches from 1962 to 1966. And there's more: second-rower Ray French scored his first try for the club – one of 10 for the Saints during his career. *2000* Leigh's Australian-born Head Coach Ian Millward was appointed as Ellery Hanley's successor at Knowsley Road. A new era of success for the club was about to begin.

Great days. Coach Ian Millward (right) and Paul Wellens with the coveted Challenge Cup after Saints' 2004 Challenge Cup success against Wigan Warriors at Cardiff. Jason Hooper is in charge of the base of the trophy and chairman Eamonn McManus is on the far right, savouring the moment – and why ever not. [Bernard Platt]

14 March

1889 Tour match: St Helens 0 New Zealand Maoris 3 tries, 1 drop-goal, at Denton's Green. The visitors were later entertained to dinner at the Fleece Hotel and enjoyed a performance at the Theatre Royal, a welcome respite for the squad, who had been on tour since the previous October. *1953* Challenge Cup Round 3: Leigh 3 St Helens 12 at Hilton Park. A fine win for the Saints, with tries by Welshmen Glyn Moses and Don Gullick, with 3 goals from Yorkshire-born scrum-half George Langfield. A record 31,326 fans packed into the ground. *1959* Test Match #113: Great Britain 50 France 15 at Headingley. 19-year-old scrum-half Alex Murphy bamboozled the visitors with four devastating tries. He was some player, with lightening acceleration. Alex scored 31 tries for his club that season and was truly devastating with the ball. *1987* Challenge Cup Semi-Final: St Helens 14 Leigh 8 at Wigan's Central Park. Tries for Kevin McCormack, Andy Platt and Chris Arkwright, plus a goal from Paul Loughlin did the trick. But what about Barry Ledger's 'where did *he* come from' tackle on Leigh's John Henderson, when all seemed lost? Marvellous, heart-stopping stuff.

Wembley bound. Young winger Kevin McCormack zooms in for a try against Leigh in the 1987 Challenge Cup Semi-Final. He was on good form during the season, with 20 tries from 40 appearances. [Alex Service]

15 March

1981 Challenge Cup Round 3: Oldham 5 St Helens 6 at Watersheddings. A great win in front of 8,712 fans, with no scoring in the second half. Graham Liptrot scored Saints' only try; Clive Griffiths converted and Peter Glynn popped over the winning drop-goal. *2013* Super League Round 7: St Helens 52 Wakefield Trinity Wildcats 18 at Langtree Park. Three tries and eight goals for full-back Jonny Lomax, the undoubted star of the show! But there was a downside: hooker supreme James Roby suffered ankle damage and did the same injury to his other ankle at Castleford Tigers on 7 July. Fortunately, after his two bouts of surgery, he was named in England's World Cup squad at the end of the campaign – one of the most durable players the Saints have ever had.

16 March

1904 Northern Union: Millom 0 St Helens 3 at Millom. Saints' try was scored by stand-off Dicky Rothwell, and future legend Tom Barton made his debut at full-back. Millom remain as 'the world's oldest amateur rugby league club' to this day, formed in the same year as the mighty Saints, 1873. *1989* Centre Steve Tyrer was born in St Helens. A strong, forceful player, he made his debut as a 17-year-old against Catalans Dragons at Knowsley Road in July 2006 and once kicked 11 goals in a Challenge Cup match against Batley Bulldogs.

17 March

1932 The England players, including Ellaby and Fildes, met to sign their agreement and passport form for the forthcoming Australasian tour. They were all given the following message from the RFL Chairman: "You are having a chance to see the world that falls to the lot of few men. You are going out as representatives of the Rugby League, and I ask you to uphold the dignity of that body both on and off the field. This I know you will do. While we hope you will retain the Ashes, we want you to do this by clean play. When far away remember you are representatives of Great Britain, and member of a league of which all connected with it are proud. You are going out under the management of two fine sportsmen. I ask you to be loyal to your managers, and to give them no cause for complaint. Good luck to all."

Boys of 1932. Four British Lions threequarters pose for the camera in their distinctive kit just after their arrival in Sydney: Barney Hudson (Salford), Stan Smith (Leeds), Alf Ellaby (St Helens) and 'Tank' Woods (Barrow). Saints' legend Alf Ellaby played 14 matches during the tour, scoring 21 tries. Little wonder he became a legend on two continents.
[Alex Service]

1971 Test Match #177: Great Britain 24 France 2 at Knowsley Road. It was 13–0 at half-time and ended in a convincing win for the Brits. Saints' representatives were centre Billy Benyon, who scored a try, with Cliff Watson and John Mantle in the pack. *1976* First Division: St Helens 7 Wakefield Trinity 10 at Knowsley Road. Loose forward Harry Pinner made his full debut. He would later become captain of club and country. A real good 'un. *1991* First Division: St Helens 54 Featherstone Rovers 38 at Knowsley Road. In an often brutal encounter, Saints played some marvellous flowing rugby to appease a home crowd often 'severely critical' of the visitors' efforts to stop them at all costs.

Left: Big John Harrison powers his way over for a try against Featherstone Rovers in this marvellous picture from the lens of Brian Peers. Right: He survived the mayhem too – and is photographed before a fans' forum at Langtree in 2014. Not changed, apart from the headband, has he?
[Alex Service]

18 March

1913 Stand-off Jack Garvey was born in St Helens. One of Alf Ellaby's favourite players, Jack made 119 appearances, scoring 52 tries, from 1931 to 1934 and played in the club's first-ever Championship Final victory in 1932. *1961* Northern Rugby League: Halifax 12 St Helens 19. South African left winger Johnny Gaydon scored a try on debut. He scored in his next game, at home to Barrow and followed with a brace against Salford at Knowsley Road. *2012* Sensation! Australian coach Royce Simmons and his assistant Kieron Purtill were relieved of their positions after a five-match losing streak. The following day, head of performance Mike Rush was appointed head coach, with legendary former number nine Keiron Cunningham as his assistant, an arrangement that lasted until the end of the season.

19 March

1933 Committee Meeting in the Pavilion at Knowsley Road: "Resolved that a bonus of £5 per man be paid in respect of a win in the [Challenge Cup] semi-final v Warrington at Swinton on Saturday 25 March, 1933." Despite the inducement, Warrington won 11–5, with an injured Alf Ellaby scoring Saints' only try. *2004* Super League Round 3: St Helens 38 Widnes 20 at Knowsley Road. James Roby, called up to train with the senior squad from his studies at Cowley Language College, made his debut off the bench. His next match was a 54–8 reversal against Bradford Bulls at Odsal.

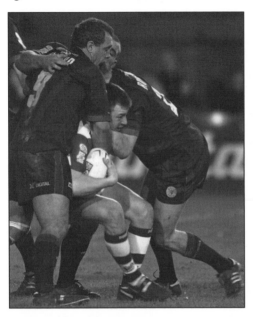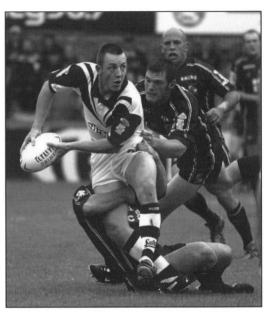

James Roby is all wrapped up by the Widnes Viking's defence (left) on his Knowsley Road debut in March 2004. The game against London Broncos, later in July (right) showed that James really had what it takes to be a future star. He scored his first try in the 30–10 victory. [Bernard Platt]

20 March

1897 Challenge Cup Round 1: St. Helens 58 Lees 0 at Knowsley Road. Saints' first-ever Challenge Cup tie and the team's first score of over 50 as a Northern Union outfit, against the amateurs from the Oldham district. *1924* Saints' Committeeman and Councillor Frank McCormack wrote to the Rugby League for funding to save the club from bankruptcy. Things were desperate in those days and McCormack himself instigated a successful S.O.S. fund (Save Our Saints). *1988* Stones Bitter Championship: Swinton 18 St. Helens 34 at Station Road. A comfortable victory for the Saints, who finished second in the table at the end of the campaign. They won 52–4 at Knowsley Road on 17 April to complete the double over the Lions. Swinton were subsequently relegated; Saints finished runners-up to Champions Wigan. *2008* Eric Ashton MBE died aged 73. A member of the Saints' Board and Chairman for a spell, Eric was a popular figure at Knowsley Road and his friendly demeanour and knowledge of the game was so important to the club. A true Piscean: selfless to a fault.

21 March

1896 Northern Union: Wigan 10 St. Helens 0 at Prescott Street. The first 'away' match against our rivals in the new professional rugby competition. James 'Pasha' Graham, the Cumbrian forward, made his debut for the Saints that afternoon. *1959* Challenge Cup Round 3: Featherstone Rovers 20 St Helens 6 at Post Office Road. Alex Murphy and Tom van Vollenhoven scored the tries. This was the only competitive match centre Peter Fearis played in where he failed to kick a goal during the season. It was the second year in succession that Post Office Road saw the end of Saints' Challenge Cup hopes.

22 March

1922 Half-back brothers George and Stan Lewis signed for the Saints for £400 from Pontypool RUFC. They wanted their fee in cash, not cheques – they insisted. Centre Gus Hayes also put pen to paper to go north. *1930* Second-rower Bill Bretherton was born in Pemberton. The former Triangle Valve junior escaped the clutches of his home town team and football – he was a centre half – to play 158 times for the Saints, scoring 10 tries. Tremendously strong, he later played for Wigan and Swinton. *1960* Centre cum second-rower Roy Haggerty was born in Thatto Heath. A genuine fans' favourite, or should that be folk hero, he made 363 appearances for the club, scoring 115 tries, from 1979 to 1991 and was a true Aries: athletic, adventurous and bold. *1997* Challenge Cup Semi-Final: St Helens 50 Salford 20 at Central Park, Wigan. A fantastic game for the spectators, especially if you came from St Helens. Alan Hunte and Anthony Sullivan roared in for hat-tricks and Keiron Cunningham scored a fantastic long-distance effort using tremendous strength and sheer belligerence. Young scrum-half Lee Briers kicked six goals, but didn't play in the final.

23 March

1940 Representative match: Lancashire League 10 Yorkshire League 13, at Craven Park, Barrow. Club colleagues Stan Powell [2] and Albert Butler [3] formed a partnership on the righthand side of the threequarter line for the Lancastrians. *1986* Slalom Lager Championship: Dewsbury 12 St Helens 18 at Crown Flatt. Attendance: 1,006. Relegation-battling Dewsbury certainly made it a difficult Sunday afternoon assignment for the Saints, who finished in third place in the table behind champions Halifax and Wigan. *2018* Super League Round 7: Hull KR 6 St Helens 30 at KCOM Stadium, Hull. A convincing victory on a chilly evening in Humberside. Full-back sensation Ben Barba scored two brilliant tries. Jonny Lomax, Luke Thompson and Dom Peyroux also crossed the whitewash. Five Danny Richardson goals ensured a happy trip back across the Pennines for us, despite several motorway closures.

24 March

1956 Challenge Cup Round 3: St Helens 53 Bradford Northern 6 at Knowsley Road. Saints' post-war cup hoodoo against the Yorkshiremen from the early post-war years was duly smashed. Winger Frank Carlton flew in for four tries in a brilliant individual performance. You just had to be there.

1967 Northern Rugby League: Wigan 7 St Helens 21 at Central Park. Right winger Les Jones scored a crucial interception try on debut. He went on to score 283 in 485 appearances, to become second in the all-time try-scoring list behind Tom van Vollenhoven.

25 March

1967 Northern Rugby League: Whitehaven 4 St Helens 3 at the Recreation Ground. Tony Karalius, who had originally played in the back row, made his first start as hooker and became a fixture in the number 9 jersey for well over a decade. He would win the ball and was superb in the loose too. *1974* Centre or winger Alf Frodsham died aged 71. A great servant to St Helens rugby as both player and coach – just after the Second World War – he was one of the town's 'Seven Stars' to be selected for the 1928 Australasian tour. *2012* Super League Round 8: St Helens 46 Leeds Rhinos 6 at Langtree Park. The majority of the visiting players came with their hair dyed as part of a charity initiative. Saints absolutely ran riot during the 80 minutes. New Zealand legend Lance Hohaia scored his first try for the club. It was the first game in charge for the newly-appointed Mike Rush and Keiron Cunningham management team. Who could ask for more?

The Walney Islander has landed. Ade Gardner scores a spectacular touchdown against Leeds Rhinos at Langtree Park in 2012 during their much-needed defeat of their Yorkshire rivals. His centre, Michael Shenton is about to lead the celebrations. Jordan Lilley of Leeds watches helplessly.
[Bernard Platt]

26 March

1960 Test Match #119: Great Britain 17 France 17 at Knowsley Road. Over 13,000 fans saw the home team do well to come away with a draw in the end after a disappointing performance. *1977* Challenge Cup Semi-Final: St Helens 2 Leeds 7 at Central Park. Hopes of a 'Dad's Army' return to the Twin Towers was thwarted by the Yorkshiremen, who eventually beat Widnes in the Final. *1994* Challenge Cup Semi-Final: St Helens 8 Leeds 20 at Central Park. Groundhog Day, 17 years later. Inspired by Ellery Hanley, Leeds won through. Stand-off Tommy Martyn scored all Saints' points, with a try and two goals. A real disappointment. Scoring chances were squandered. C'est la vie.

27 March

1915 Challenge Cup Round 3: Keighley 2 St Helens 3 at Lawkholme Lane, Keighley. Saints' scrum-half Fred Trenwith executed the famous 'burrowing' move from the scrum, to score the winning try, code named Beechams. The home crowd were upset, threw some stones and the ground was closed for a spell. *1926* Northern Rugby League: St Helens 34 Keighley 10 at Knowsley Road. 'We've got a real belter here'. Alf Ellaby, formerly a footballer with Rotherham County, made his debut in the XIII-a-side code. Subsequent fame on two continents beckoned. Who would have thought it? *1959* Northern Rugby League: Wigan 19 St Helens 14 at Central Park. Two Karalius brothers Dennis (11) and loose forward Vince were in Saints' back-row that day in front of a record crowd of 47,747. *1970* Centre Jarrod McCracken was born in New Zealand. The former Glenora Bear and son of Kiwi great Ken McCracken, on a short-term contract from Canterbury Bankstown was a huge favourite at Knowsley Road and certainly never took a backward step, especially against Wigan.

28 March

1931 Challenge Cup Semi-Final: St Helens 2 Halifax 11 at Recreation Grounds, Rochdale. The planned return to Wembley after the disastrous 1930 Final against Widnes never happened. Several Halifax players searched out Alf Ellaby afterwards, wanting his autograph. He was a big star, after all, but his Wembley dream never happened. *1953* Challenge Cup Semi-Final: St Helens 9 Warrington 3 at Station Road, Swinton. Saints were at Wembley for the first time since 1930, courtesy of a Don Gullick try and three goals from George Langfield in front of a huge crowd of 37,169. *1997* Super League Round 3: Wigan Warriors 10 St Helens 22 at Central Park. Pies duly devoured, you might say. Three goals and two drop-goals for young scrum-half Lee Briers, deputising for suspended skipper Bobbie Goulding. *2002* A rare defeat to London Broncos, 40–6, at Griffin Park. Miserable for Saints fans, but enjoyable for London's supporters, including the publishers of this book.

29 March

1909 Hooker Dave Cotton was born in Wigan. A tremendously durable character, he played 168 times for the Saints from 1930 to 1935 before joining Warrington. Dave was a member of the 1932 Championship-winning team and is the father of rugby union forward great Fran Cotton. *1930* Challenge Cup Semi-Final: St Helens 5 Wigan 5 at Swinton's Station Road. Over 37,000 witnessed 'honours even' with George Lewis (one goal) and try-scorer Les Fairclough just failing to break the deadlock. But Alf Ellaby did in the replay – and how – with a stunning hat-trick as Saints swept to Wembley. *1958* Northern Rugby League: St Helens 25 Blackpool Borough 11. South African forward Ted Brophy made his debut in the back row. His team-mates? Nat Silcock and Vince Karalius. A real character, Ted's first residence was above a chip shop in Liverpool Road. That was dinner and tea sorted. *1992* Stones Bitter Championship: St Helens 42 Hull 12 at Knowsley Road. Tea Ropati and Jon Griffiths scored doubles in a comprehensive victory for the Saints, who ended the season in second place in the table, behind Wigan. They were great entertainers, nonetheless.

30 March

1907 Northern Rugby Union: St Helens 68 Liverpool City 0 at Knowsley Road. A hat-trick of tries for Cumbrian centre William 'Gillie' Hillen in a proverbial 'walk in the park' for the homesters. *1929* Northern Rugby League: St Helens 47 Bradford Northern 5 at Knowsley Road. Right centre and local lad Bill Mercer was on top form with four blistering tries. *1933* International match: England 34 Other Nationalities 27 at Lonsdale Park, Workington. All the Saints' representatives scored a try: winger Roy Hardgrave for Other Nationalities; stand-off Jack Garvey and second-rower Jack Arkwright for England. 'Arkie' also kicked three goals.

Left: local born centre Bill Mercer, who scored four tries against Bradford Northern in 1929, registered a career total of 75 in 311 appearances, from 1925 to 1937 [Alex Service]; Right: Kiwi second-rower George Mann [right] takes on Widnes centre Andy Currier during the 1991 Challenge Cup Semi-Final at Central Park. [Brian Peers]

1991 Challenge Cup Semi-Final: St Helens 19 Widnes 2 at Central Park. A magnificent performance from the sizzling Saints, with two tries from Welsh half-back Jon Griffiths one of the many highlights. Such a pity that the Old Enemy lay in wait at Wembley. **1994** Front-rower Andy 'Gripper' Leathem was signed from Crosfields ARLFC in Warrington. A powerful forward, he enjoyed much success in Saints' inaugural season in the Super League in 1996, when the team won a fabulous league and Challenge Cup double.

31 March

1932 Toni Danieli (aka Rossi) was born in Italy. He used the 'Rossi' pseudonym in case he didn't make the grade in rugby league and had to return to rugby union. That's the way it was in those days. He first signed for Blackpool Borough before joining Saints, where he played two matches in the second row. He then joined Wigan, and returned home to set up a team in Padova and spent time with Venezia Mestre. Toni eventually returned to live in Cornwall for the rest of his life. Quite a story. **1973** The new bar and restaurant complex was opened at the Dunriding End at Knowsley Road. Based on the 'Salford model' at the Willows, this included provision for fans to watch the game and have a meal beforehand. Matches at the time were mostly on Friday nights, under the floodlights at Knowsley Road. **1996** Super League Round 1: Workington Town 0 St Helens 62 at Derwent Park. Saints' opening fixture in summer rugby saw the highest score registered without reply. Right winger Danny Arnold scored four tries. In his next five matches he went on to score nine more. **2001** Challenge Cup Semi-Final: St Helens 27 Leeds Rhinos 22 at the JJB Stadium, Wigan. A Tommy Martyn drop-goal, plus two tries from current Man of Steel Paul Sculthorpe helped to see off the challenge of the Rhinos in a cracking encounter. Cup glory in the Final ensued, against the Bradford Bulls at rain-lashed Twickenham.

Paul Sculthorpe was in irresistible all-round form in the 2001 Challenge Cup Semi-Final against Leeds Rhinos. Bernard Platt's images show him scoring a try and generally giving the Leeds defenders a torrid time. That's why he was double Man of Steel.

April

Warming up.

'Rhino-hunting' is bad for your health. Sean Long, with blood streaming from a head wound, takes a pass from Darren Britt (grounded, right) and makes a searing break against Leeds Rhinos in the epic 'extra time' Challenge Cup Semi-Final at Huddersfield on 12 April 2003. A truly classic encounter.
[Bernard Platt]

There was a time when some people couldn't wait for the rugby season to end. When the rules of the game were somewhat rudimentary [perhaps 'crude' would be more appropriate] it is little wonder that concerns were raised, as illustrated by this quote from the *St Helens Lantern*, at the beginning of May, 1887: "One of the advantages of the disappearance of spring is the disappearance with it of football. The growth of the game in popular terms during the last half dozen years has been marvellous. What is the explanation? I will venture on a reply to the question. Cock fighting, prize fighting, bull baiting are all prohibited by law. Englishmen cannot tire without some excitement of this kind; hence their fancy for football – fraught as it is, with danger to life and limb." Easter remains a busy time for rugby. In the old pre-Northern Union days, the Saints would often embark on short tours, or play matches against touring club teams. In rugby league terms, a time for more 'derby' thrills and spills, with Good Friday clashes against Wigan the highlight, backed up by Widnes on Easter Monday. It was a time too for Challenge Cup semi-finals and the prospect of a visit to the Twin Towers of Wembley. Fingers crossed, maybe it's our year, who knows?

1 APRIL

1984 First Division: St Helens 31 Oldham 20 at Knowsley Road. Local lad Paul Loughlin came off the bench and kicked his first goal for the seniors, one of the laudable total of 842 he kicked during his 12 years at Knowsley Road. *2011* Super League Round 8: St Helens 34 Hull KR 16 at Stobart Stadium, Widnes. Jon Wilkin missed the match after damaging his hand with a brush. This was no 'April Fool' joke either.

841 to go. Ever-alert photographer Brian Peers captures Paul Loughlin setting up and booting over his first Saints' goal.

2 APRIL

1930 Challenge Cup Semi-Final replay: St Helens 22 Wigan 10 at Mather Lane, Leigh. Arguably the club's finest moment to date against an 'all-star' Wigan outfit, in front of 24,000 baying fans. Centre Billy Mercer bagged a try, while Alf Ellaby ran in for a fabulous hat-trick, which he did with regularity, regardless of the quality of the opposition. *1952* Northern Rugby League: St Helens 13 Warrington 5 at Knowsley Road. This match saw the debut of Widnes-born fitness fanatic Vince Peter Patrick Karalius at loose-forward. For any scrum-half opposing him, life would be somewhat more difficult in future. The rest is the stuff of rugby league legend. *1978* First Division: St Helens 36 Wakefield Trinity 5 at Knowsley Road. Legendary second-rower George Nicholls scored twice in what was a comfortable victory for the red vee. George was in his 'pomp' then, winning the Lance Todd trophy, despite the narrow defeat against Leeds at Wembley on 13 May. *2004* Super League Round 4: Castleford Tigers 14 St Helens 22 at The Jungle, Wheldon Road. Former Samoan rugby union international Maurie Fa'asavalu made his debut off the bench. A powerful and belligerent impact player, Maurie really adapted well to his new code and was one of the stars of the 'three cups' season two years later.

3 APRIL

1965 Challenge Cup Semi-Final: Wigan 25 Swinton 10 at Knowsley Road. 26,658 fans saw this match, with the second half live on BBC1, with legendary commentator Eddie Waring at the helm. Wigan had beaten Saints 7–2 in the second round, in front of a huge crowd of 39,938 at Central Park, when we were all seemingly wedged in like sardines. *2012* Huddersfield Giants coach – and former St George hooker – Nathan Brown is appointed by St Helens on a three-year contract. His team won the League Leaders Shield and Grand Final in 2014, after an injury-hit rollercoaster campaign.

4 APRIL

1890 Friendly match: St Helens 1 goal 3 tries 3 minors Ulverston 0 at Dentons Green. The visitors from Cumberland included HL Stout, dubbed the 'Champion pole jumper of the World'. The match was on Good Friday and kicked off at 11am. *1980* First Division: St Helens 20 Wigan 17 at Knowsley Road. Young scrum-half Neil Holding ran in a brace of tries. The Saints' threequarter line was one of the youngest ever at senior level: Kevin Meadows aged 19, Steve Peters 20, Chris Arkwright 21 and Denis Litherland 21. *1994* Stones Bitter Championship: Widnes 20 St Helens 17 at Naughton Park. Ebullient stand-off Tommy Martyn was the star for the visitors, with two tries, two goals and a drop-goal for good measure. Despite a fine individual performance, he would have preferred a victory, though.

5 APRIL

1944 Winger Frank Wilson was born in Cardiff, under the fire sign of Aries. Hence, among other things, he was expected to be athletic, adventurous and bold. Frank certainly ticked those boxes. He was fast and elusive, like an eel in fact and gave us great entertainment on the terraces during his career as a Saint. [image courtesy Alex Service] *1958* Northern Rugby League: Hunslet 2 St Helens 33 at Parkside. A brilliant win for the visitors, with four stunning tries from Tom van Vollenhoven. It would be a recurring nightmare for the Hunslet lads, who could not prevent him running in a glorious hat-trick in the 1959 Championship Final. *1959* Test Match #114: France 24 Great Britain 15 at Stade Municipal Grenoble. The French beat Great Britain at the eighth attempt in test match football. Alex Murphy (7) and Albert Terry (8) were the Saints' representatives. *1996* Super League Round 2: St Helens 41 Wigan 26 at Knowsley Road. The first-ever home Super League fixture, with winger Danny Arnold scoring a fantastic hat-trick and blowing kisses to the camera. The 'Big Screen' also made its debut at the famous old ground. Saints were up and running and a famous League and Challenge Cup 'double' awaited.

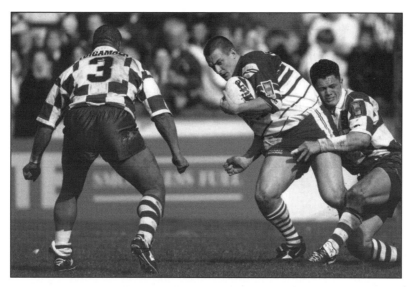

Saints are up and running in their first-ever Super League home game, against Wigan Warriors. Paul Newlove is halted by Wigan's stand-off Henry Paul. Centre Va'aiga Tuigamala, on the left, is about to complete the tackle. [Sportsphoto Ltd]

6 APRIL

1944 Tony Barrow was born in the Thatto Heath district of St Helens. Many supporters will always remember Tony as an excellent utility back, capable of filling in when injury struck the likes of Tom van Vollenhoven, like it did in the 1966 Championship Final. Despite his covering role, he was a capable and intelligent player in his own right: an aggressive runner and tackler, who could also take try-scoring chances with confidence. *2008* Super League Round 10: Castleford Tigers 30 St Helens 24 at The Jungle. The wheels came off, albeit temporarily in this snow-spattered affair in West Yorkshire. Maurie Fa'asavalu was sent off for punching to add to the woes. It was 'sending off sufficient' in the end at the Disciplinary Committee, but no consolation.

7 APRIL

1923 Northern Rugby League: Wigan 41 St Helens 10 at Central Park. A real towelling for the visitors, in front of over 9,000 fans. Saints' scorers were right-winger Jack Halsall and Alf Frodsham, on the other flank, who scored a try and kicked two goals. *1956* Challenge Cup Semi-Final: St Helens 5 Barrow 5 at Station Road. A true 'arm-wrestle' only settled the following Wednesday, at Wigan, when, in another dogged encounter, winger Steve Llewellyn's long-distance 'wonder try' broke the deadlock and got Saints to Wembley in front of 44,731 fans. The club went on to beat Halifax to claim the trophy for the first time. *1991* Stones Bitter Championship: Wakefield Trinity 8 St Helens 22 at Belle Vue. Second-rower Roy Haggerty played his last game for the club and 'signed off' with a drop-goal – the 20th of his career. A real crowd favourite, nay cult hero, Roy had a juddering, stuttering run and deceptive sidestep and would target the heart of the opposition's defence to open them up.

8 APRIL

1996 Super League Round 3: Leeds Rhinos 24 St Helens 46 at Headingley. The Saints were on their way to a fantastic cup and league double and were too mobile and clinical for the home team. A great game for the visiting fans, in particular, with two tries from Danny Arnold and nine goals from Bobbie Goulding's trusty boot. And Leeds? Work in progress. They finished in 10th place in the league. *2016* Super League Round 10: Warrington Wolves 22 St Helens 25 at Halliwell Jones Stadium. The Wolves were the current league leaders, but were beaten courtesy of a fine all-round team display, inspired by French half-back Theo Fages. The left side had an unfamiliar look about it, with try-scorer Jack Ashworth partnering young debutant winger Jake Spedding.

9 APRIL

1968 From the Boardroom: "A report on the Moss Bank v Walney match was read and a report on English amateur international full-back John Walsh was noted." Yes indeed – a rare talent. His team, coached by former Saint Josh Gaskell, later beat Wigan St Pats in the Lancashire Cup Final on 20 April at Knowsley Road and John was duly signed.

Langtree Park 21 July 2009. John Walsh is photographed with his commemorative award after his induction into the Saints' Players Association Hall of Fame. Austin Rhodes proposes a toast. Both are World Cup winners: John in 1972, Austin in 1960. [Alex Service]

1971 Northern Rugby League: Wigan 6 St Helens 9 at Central Park. Geoff Pimblett was selected at full-back for the first time. He resumed at stand-off after two more matches, however, before returning to the last line of defence shortly after. Geoff certainly made his mark as a Saints' all-time great in the number one jersey. *1999* Super League Round 5: London Broncos 18 St Helens 34 at Brentford FC's Griffin Park. Full-back Paul Atcheson notched a memorable hat-trick of tries in a convincing performance from the visitors. *2004* Super League Round 5: St Helens 21 Wigan Warriors 21 at Knowsley Road. This pulsating encounter – it was downright feisty, actually – included a brace of tries for new signing Lee Gilmour, formerly of Bradford Bulls and Wigan Warriors. Lee was a superbly mobile footballer who could play in the centres or back row with great effectiveness. How we missed him when he went.

A class act. Geoff Pimblett (left) scores against Hull FC [Alex Service]; Saints versus Wigan 2004: no holds barred. Paul Sculthorpe runs at Sean O'Loughlin [Bernard Platt]

10 APRIL

1890 Lancashire and Border Towns Union XV, featuring half-back Billy Cross, James Graham and Joseph Brownbill in the forwards, lost to Wigan at Central Park. This was an annual challenge match for the champion team to pit their wits against the cream of the rest of the league. Different times. *1936* Northern Rugby League: Wigan 14 St Helens 0 at Central Park. A disappointing result, especially for Saints' front-rower and workhorse Bob Atkin, who was playing his 400th match for the club. *1946* Northern Rugby League: Salford 6 St Helens 5 at the Willows. Future centre supreme Duggie Greenall made his senior debut at stand-off. He later switched to centre, with great success. *1957* Test Match #101: Great Britain 29 France 14 at Knowsley Road. Stand-off Lewis Jones of Leeds kicked seven goals and scored a try. Future Saint Mick Sullivan scored a brace, with Skipper Alan Prescott on view for the home fans. Austin Rhodes and Glyn Moses were reserves.

11 APRIL

1908 Northern Union: St Helens 11 Broughton Rangers 28 at Knowsley Road. Former 'All Golds' New Zealand tourist Joseph 'Tracker' Lavery played his only match in the seniors at right centre. He also played for Leigh, Salford and Barrow. *1914* Northern Rugby League: St Helens 47 Rochdale Hornets 5 at Knowsley Road. A four try and five goal performance from left-winger Tom Barton. *1942* Challenge Cup Round 1 (first leg): Featherstone Rovers 11 St Helens 21 at Post Office Road. Short-handed Saints are helped out by William Judge in the second row, a Featherstone player who happened to be a spectator. He was the only

Yorkshireman to draw winning pay that afternoon. *2008* Super League Round 11: St Helens 58 Harlequins 12 at Knowsley Road. Stand-off Leon Pryce scored 3 tries – one of his three hat-tricks for the club. Leon had been a superb addition to the Saints' attacking armoury since his signing from Bradford Bulls in 2006. *2014* Super League Round 8: Castleford Tigers 28 St Helens 30 at the Mend-a-Hose Jungle. The return of the comeback kings. Saints were 24–6 down and looking out of it at half-time. Yet three tries in the last 13 minutes clinched a memorable victory. When full-back Paul Wellens scored the penultimate try, in the 74th minute, it took him past 1,000 career points. Winger Adam Swift scored the winner with two minutes to go, the only time the visitors had been ahead. Fantastic stuff.

12 APRIL

1895 Fred Roffey, Saints' second-rower and captain in 1926–27, was born in South Godstone, Surrey. A Welsh rugby league international, he began his career with Wigan and was an 'experienced' addition to the 1926–27 team which he captained to Lancashire Cup glory. There have been several examples of forwards enjoying an Indian summer at Knowsley Road. Think: Kevin Ward and Paul Anderson, to name but two. *1909* Northern Rugby Union: Warrington 78 St Helens 6 at Wilderspool. Dark days indeed and a record defeat for the Saints. Forward George Thomas amassed 33 points for the Wire in the subsequent slaughter. It remains a record defeat to this day. *1968* Northern Rugby League: St Helens 24 Wigan 13 at Knowsley Road. Sheer ecstasy to beat our great rivals, of course, but with the added bonus of Tom van Vollenhoven scoring a glorious hat-trick in his last 'derby' clash. What could be better? *2003* Challenge Cup Semi-Final: St Helens 26 Leeds Rhinos 33 at McAlpine Stadium, Huddersfield. This was a truly gripping encounter that was only decided after 20 minutes extra time. The scores were level at 26–26 at full-time following a last-minute Leeds try, converted by Kevin Sinfield. Raymond Fletcher, in the *Rugby League and League Express*, described it as: "climax on top of climax. The first 80 minutes were exciting enough, and then they crammed in another 20 with an amazing finish. Unbelievable!"

13 APRIL

1934 International match: France 21 England 32 at the Buffalo Velodrome, Paris. The first time these old foes met in the XIII-a-side code. Alf Ellaby was on the right wing; Wigan and Welsh full-back Jim Sullivan played for England and kicked seven goals. It was not until 1954 that a match given 'test' status took place, during the World Cup in France in 1954. *1955* Representative match: British Services 15 French Services 7 at Headingley, Leeds. This was the days of National Service and Brian Howard played on the wing and was a try-scorer. The RFL organised the match; rugby league was banned in the Armed Forces at this time. *1961* Special training for the Challenge Cup Semi-Final versus Hull, at Odsal, was held at Ilkley and certainly paid dividends. Saints clearly meant business and produced a superb second half performance to win 26–9. Stand-off Wilf Smith scored two fine tries. *1965* From the Boardroom: "It was agreed to donate a sum of two guineas to the W. [hooker Bill] Sayer Testimonial Fund". Clubs always supported local rivals' players' testimonials. *1990* Division One: St Helens 35 Wigan 10 at Knowsley Road. Much-needed for morale. Mark Bailey, who came off the bench, scored his third try in as many games as the Saints gained some revenge for their defeat against their longstanding rivals in the Challenge Cup Semi-Final on 10 March at Old Trafford.

St Helens versus Hull in the 1961 Challenge Cup Semi-Final at a packed Odsal.
Stand-off Wilf Smith scores a glorious try, much to the delight of those fans on ringside.
Tom van Vollenhoven is in support. Note the length of the grass, too. [Alex Service]

14 APRIL

1904 Committee meeting, Talbot Hotel: "Application read from Hurling Club to rent football ground during summer months – not entertained". The Irish influence in St Helens led to the formation of this 'other' club maybe? *1939* Running second-rower Jim Measures was born in Thatto Heath. A player who would have benefitted from 15 or 17-man squads on match day. He would surely have made the bench for the 1961 Challenge Cup Final in such circumstances. He later joined Widnes where he won a Challenge Cup winner's medal and played for Great Britain. A lovely man. *1985* First Division: St Helens 30 Hull KR 14 at Knowsley Road. Saints put a temporary dent in Rovers' title hopes with Australian Superstar Mal Meninga notching a superb hat-trick, but it wasn't to be. Rovers ended up as Champions a few weeks later. *1991* First Division: St Helens 62 Warrington 16 at Knowsley Road. Centre Alan Hunte, in unstoppable form, scored four tries. File this one under 'end-of-season slaughter'. *2017* Super League Round 9: Wigan Warriors 29 St Helens 18. At the DW Stadium. Left winger Regan Grace, already a Welsh international, capped a fine debut with a superb try in the North-West corner, to the delight of the Saints' support. Unfortunately, such a fine try could not prevent a home win.

Left: Wooosshh! Welsh flyer Regan Grace endears himself to the Saints' faithful with this marvellous finish against Wigan Warriors in 2017. They don't come much better than this. [Bernard Platt]

59

15 APRIL

1905 Back-rower Arthur Lemon (left) was born in Tonna, South Wales. The former Neath RFC player joined the Saints after his omission from the Welsh rugby union squad in the early 1930s. According to his coach, fellow-Welshman George Lewis, Arthur wrote home to his dad expressing great glee at his new job as a carpenter at the Greenall Whitley brewery in St Helens. Arthur liked the odd pint or two. He later transferred to the Streatham & Mitcham club in London, before returning to Wales. [pic: Dave Makin] *1944* War Emergency League: Halifax 46 St Helens 4 at Thrum Hall, Halifax. This last game of the season meant that Saints had played 20 league games, losing 19 and were rooted to the bottom of the final table. *1968* Northern Rugby League: Swinton 16 St Helens 19 at Station Road. Tom van Vollenhoven scored his 392nd and last try in a Saints' jersey. The end of an unmissable era for St Helens RFC.

2018 Women's' Super League Round 1: St Helens 40 York 0 at Ruskin Sports village. A real ground breaker – the first game of the newly-instigated competition was a welcome breath of fresh air and long overdue. The Saints team on this historic day was as follows: Becca Rotherham; Rachel Yeates, Naomi Williams (two tries), Katie-May Williams, Leah Burke (three tries); Carys Marsh, Faye Gaskin (Capt, three tries, four goals); Sarah Lovejoy, Tara Jones, Dawn Taylor, Isabelle Rudge, Roxy Mura, Channy Crowl. Interchange: Zoe Harris, Charlotte Hill, Lizzie Gladman, Pip Birchall. Scrum-half Faye Gaskin scored the first-ever try after just five minutes.

Right: Loose forward Channy Crowl gets stuck in as Saints' Ladies get off to a winning start against York at Ruskin Sports Village. [Liam Platt]

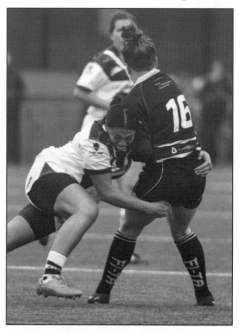

16 APRIL

1956 Northern Rugby League: St Helens 22 Whitehaven 7 at Knowsley Road. Former St Austin's schoolboy Alexander James Murphy made his first appearance for his home town team. And the rest, as they say, is history. *1966* Challenge Cup Semi-Final: St Helens 12 Dewsbury 5 at Station Road, Swinton. The Yorkshiremen, with former Saint Mick Sullivan as player-coach, threatened to derail Saints' hopes of a Challenge Cup Final, with a 'spirited'

performance. One St Helens fan, Minnie Cotton, took umbrage at the treatment metered out to her lodger, Saints' second-rower John Warlow and ran onto the pitch with a borrowed umbrella. Thankfully, the only damage done was to the umbrella. Len Killeen produced a match-winning two try and three goal performance to pull his team out of the mire. He is seen being congratulated by Tony Barrow and young fans after his vital three pointer.
[Photo: St Helens Local History & Archives/*St Helens Reporter*]

2004 A bombshell! The *Daily Mail*, in a two-page 'exclusive' revealed that Sean Long and Martin Gleeson had placed £1,000 bets on Bradford Bulls to win the game at Odsal on Easter Monday. Gleeson played that day and scored one of the tries in a 54–8 loss. The RFL Disciplinary Commission dealt with the matter, as bye-laws had been breached! Both players were suspended as a result.

Resplendent in the red vee and ready for the fray! Saints are photographed behind the Main Stand at Swinton before the 1966 Challenge Cup Semi-Final against Dewsbury.
Back: Ray French, John Warlow, Bill Sayer, Cliff Watson, Albert Halsall, John Mantle, Len Killeen;
Front: Billy Benyon, Frank Barrow, Alex Murphy [Capt], Tommy Bishop, Tony Barrow, Peter Harvey.
[St Helens Local History & Archives/*St Helens Reporter*]

17 APRIL

1933 Northern Rugby League St Helens 26 Broughton Rangers 0 at Knowsley Road. Irish loose-forward Tom Griffin scored a try, as did Harry Frodsham (7), Jack Garvey (6), Teddy Butler (5) Tom Winnard (4) and Kiwi flyer Roy Hardgrave (2). George Lewis kicked four goals. *2010* Challenge Cup Round 4: St Helens 56 Toulouse Olympique 16 at Knowsley Road. An eight goal debut for winger Jamie Foster. A red haze sunset was a result of the eruption of the Icelandic volcano, called Eyjafallajokull. Its billowing plume of dust caused havoc with air travel for over a week. The French team had to travel overland for the bulk of their journey and made it to Knowsley Road with just enough time to spare.

18 APRIL

1927 Hard-running second-rower Ben Halfpenny signed from Widnes. A good piece of business, for sure. Ben had quite a bit of pace for a back-rower and scored 59 tries in his 196 appearances for the club. He was selected for the Australasian Tour after his first season at Knowsley Road, one of four Saints to make the trip. The others were: Alf Frodsham, Alf Ellaby and Leslie Fairclough. *1951* Northern Rugby League: St Helens 9 Huddersfield 14 at Knowsley Road. Former Parr Central schoolboy prodigy John 'Todder' Dickinson made his debut at stand-off. His partner at scrum-half was another local lad, Jimmy Honey.

19 APRIL

1942 Front-rower Albert Halsall was born in Wigan. Big Albert? He holds a special place in our hearts after his marvellous hat-trick of tries in the 1966 Championship Final against Halifax and subsequent award of the coveted Harry Sunderland trophy. An inspired signing from Salford, he was a burly lad, but he could certainly shift. He was unlucky not to be selected for the Great Britain Australian tour Squad in 1966. *1972* Challenge Cup Semi-Final: St Helens 10 Warrington 6 at Central Park. A fantastic midweek crowd of 32,180 saw the two local rivals renew their acquaintance following the 10–10 score line four days before. Skipper Kel Coslett scored a brilliant diving try and kicked two goals; front-rower John Stephens added another in a dominant first half performance that was good enough to get the lads to Wembley.

20 APRIL

1927 Northern Rugby League: Leeds 10 St Helens 21 at Headingley. What a win, with Welsh centre George Lewis providing two tries for his winger, Alf Ellaby, plus three goals. George went on to make 428 appearances for the club, kicking 850 goals. George later trained the UGB team, where he worked, before returning to the family home at Pentrepiod, the house with the monkey tree, in Pontypool. *1964* From the Boardroom: "Mr Naylor [Director] reported on the formula of a new Committee which hoped to start a new club in the name of Bradford next season. It was agreed to buy 50 £1 shares to assist the club to obtain their target figure." Phoenix from the ashes – the re-formation of the Bradford Northern club was much-needed for rugby league in West Yorkshire.

George Lewis places a wreath at the Cenotaph in London and takes part in a goalkicking contest at Widnes. [Alex Service]

1967 Second-rower or hooker Bernard Dwyer was born in Thatto Heath. A 100 percent player right out of the top drawer. He had to run and tackle above his weight but it didn't matter to him. Bernard made the hooking role his own and will always be remembered for his 'Fred Flintstone' (Kevin Ward) and 'Barney Rubble' (Bernard) partnership in the front-row. *1977* First Division: St Helens 49 Leigh 2 at Knowsley Road. Left centre Eddie Cunningham roared in for three tries and repeated the performance on 10 May, with a dazzling hat-trick against Castleford at Wheldon Road. Eddie had bull-like strength to break through a raft of tacklers when his progress seemed surely to be halted.

21 APRIL

1908 Northern Union: St Helens 13 Bramley 16 at Knowsley Road. Despite the unexpected defeat, right winger and sprinter Jack Manchester scored a fine hat-trick. Although he later joined Hunslet for a spell, he was Saints through and through and became an avid spectator at Knowsley Road for the rest of his life. *1926* Second-rower George Parsons was born in Newbridge, South Wales, on the same day as HM Queen Elizabeth II. In fact, George later attended garden parties at the Palace in connection with his special date of birth. *1981* First Division: St Helens 24 Widnes 9 at Knowsley Road. Second-rower George Nicholls played his last game for Saints at the end of a stellar career. Apart from his many accomplishments at club level, with over 270 appearances for the club, he was also one of the most enigmatic players at test match level in the 1970s too.

22 APRIL

1939 Schoolboy prodigy Alex Murphy was born in Thatto Heath. Just prior to the 'witching hour' on the eve of his 16th birthday the outstanding young rugby player was salted away to director Joe Harrison's house in Eccleston, where he played games of snooker before becoming a Saint. An absolute 'nail-on' for the Greatest 17, he remains, to those who had the privilege to see him, many peoples' favourite Saint.

Two of the Thatto Heath district's finest players: Eddie Cunningham (left) and the perpetual motion man himself, Bernard Dwyer. [Alex Service]

1950 Challenge match: St Helens 48 Neath 10 at Knowsley Road. Saints' Welsh centre Viv Harrison bowled the referee over while side-stepping. The referee's whistle broke as a result. A goal kick also broke one of the Pavilion windows. Just one of those days! **1957** Northern Rugby League: St Helens 48 Blackpool Borough 10 at Knowsley Road. A real family affair. Denis Karalius made his debut in the back-row. His brother, Vince, was at loose-forward. Denis played 24 games for the Saints, scoring one try, before moving to Warrington.
Below: The Karalius brothers relax at the family home in Widnes. Denis is far left and Vince next to him. [Pic: Alex Service]

64

1969 From the Boardroom: "The Chairman reported on an Australian S.O.H. [stand-off half] named Pickup who was playing in the London Amateur League for Hackney. It was agreed to ask him to play trials." To cut a long story short, the former Manly RUFC player was on an extended 'working holiday' to Europe when he was spotted. However, things didn't work out at Saints and he joined Blackpool Borough, where he flourished. Australian clubs showed interest in the classy stand-off and he returned to play with great success for North Sydney and Canterbury Bankstown. Tim also played 11 times for Australia. Unusual fact: he attended the Woodstock music festival during his 'travelling years'!

2008 Saints appointed Catalans Dragons coach Mick Potter to succeed Daniel Anderson on a two-year contract, from the 2009 campaign. Mick had coached the French outfit in their run up to the 2007 Wembley Final, against the Saints.

2018 The death was announced of former second-rower Roy Haggerty, at the age of 58. Although not the biggest, he cut a formidable figure, with socks rolled down and a perennial bandage on his left knee as he plunged into the heart of the opposition, often beating opponents with his own unique sidestep. Two of his sons Gareth (Widnes Vikings, Salford City Reds and Harlequins) and Kurt (Widnes and Leigh Centurions) played professionally and represented Ireland in the Rugby League World Cup.

Above: 'Bet you've not been to Woodstock!' Future Australian star Tim Pickup (in dark jersey, right) shakes hands with John Nicholson of Workington Town before an 'A' team fixture at Knowsley Road.

Right: centre-turned second-rower Roy Haggerty was a huge favourite with Saints' supporters.
[Alex Service]

23 APRIL

1893 Forceful forward George Farrimond was born in the Thatto Heath district. A miner at Lea Green Colliery, he played 122 games for the Saints, including the 1915 Challenge Cup Final against Huddersfield. As the conflict in Europe escalated, he joined the Royal Army Medical Corps and went on to be awarded the Military Medal for his gallantry. A brave man indeed. *1904* Division Two: St Helens 35 Lancaster 2 at Knowsley Road. Saints' promotion hopes remained on track, although it took a special 'Test match' against Holbeck to ensure the return to the top flight. This game was also designated as the William Foulkes benefit match. A powerful full-back, from Thatto Heath, he had played for the club before the formation of the Northern Union in 1895 and skippered the team in the first-ever Challenge Cup Final, against Batley. *1910* Northern Rugby Union St Helens 20 Rochdale Hornets 11 at Knowsley Road. Saints' left winger Jimmy Flanagan raced in for a stunning hat-trick of tries, making his total for the season 33. As such, he became the first Saints' player to attain a top three place in the league's try-scoring charts. *1927* Championship Semi-Final: St Helens Recs 33 St Helens 0 at City Road. The homesters duly progressed into their first Championship Final, against Swinton, in a game chock full of controversy and downright bitterness between the local rivals. It was Saints' full-back Charlie Crooks's 35th match of a long season. Recs lost to Swinton in the Final. *1989* Premiership Trophy Round 1: Wigan 2 St Helens 4 at Central Park. Two goals from second-rower Paul Forber saw Saints come away with the spoils in a real arm-wrestle in the mud. Six days later, we were deflated after a Wembley defeat against the same opposition.

24 APRIL

1897 Challenge Cup Final: St Helens 3 Batley 10 at Headingley. The first of its kind and Saints were always disadvantaged after having to play their re-arranged Semi-Final, against Swinton at Broughton, the Monday before the Final, following its bad weather postponement. Opponents Batley, who had played on the Saturday, proved to be much the more dynamic of the teams as a result. *1968* Championship Play-off Round One: St Helens 20 Warrington 0 at Knowsley Road. The crowd payed homage to Tom van Vollenhoven in his last match on home turf. Unfortunately, the Great Man couldn't cross the whitewash. His centre, Cenyyd Williams did score, however. *1995* Centre Ken Large died aged 55. A fine threequarter, with pace to burn, he made 136 appearances for his home town club, scored 83 tries and kicked 27 goals. He later joined Leigh after leaving the Saints. *2000* Super League Round 7: Warrington Wolves 34 St Helens 47 at the Halliwell Jones. Legendary New Zealand threequarter Sean Hoppe scored his first Super League try for the Saints. Although approaching the veteran stage, he proved to be a superb signing for the club, making 98 appearances with 36 tries and featuring in three successful Grand Finals: 1999, 2000 and 2002. A real good 'un. *2005* Huddersfield Giants 22 St Helens 36 at Galpharm Stadium. An exciting clash in the West Yorkshire sunshine, with Saints' powerful attack the more clinical on the day. The race for the League Leaders Shield was in full swing.

Left: Ken Large shrugs off a challenge from Australian star Wally Macarthur of Rochdale Hornets to score a brilliant try at the Athletic Ground, in the late 1950s;

Below: end of an era! Tom van Vollenhoven is carried on his team mates' shoulders after his last game at Knowsley Road in 1968. [Alex Service]

67

All poise and balanced running, like a well-tuned Rolls Royce. Darren Albert scores one of his two tries against Huddersfield Giants in 2005, with Stanley Gene trying in vain to prevent the inevitable. Micky Higham also scored twice, with Jamie Lyon chiming in with six goals. Saints fully justified their 'great entertainers' tag during the campaign. [Bernard Platt]

25 APRIL

1953 Challenge Cup Final: Huddersfield 15 St Helens 10 at Wembley Stadium, London. A real shock for Saints' fans, who must have wondered when their Challenge Cup drought was going to end. The two teams met again in the Championship Semi-Final at Knowsley Road, with Saints gaining ample revenge to the tune of 46–0 on their way to their second Championship Final success. *2008* Super League round 12: Warrington Wolves 22 St Helens 30 at Halliwell Jones Stadium. Interchange forward Paul Clough scored a memorable, albeit rare, hat-trick of tries. As the saying goes, he was well-chuffed during the post-match interview on Sky Sports.

26 APRIL

1890 Friendly match: West Leigh versus St Helens 'A'. Tragedy struck when 19-year-old Saints' player Edward Smith, of Waterloo Street, St Helens, was seriously injured during the match. He was a new player and fell on his head during a scrimmage. He lost his footing because he had no bars on his shoes. A report of the incident even reached the Yorkshire Post [1 May 1890], where it said that: "paralysis speedily set in, and Doctor Jones, who was called in, ordered his removal to the Workhouse hospital, where he lies in a critical condition. He was the only support of his widowed mother." A truly sad tale from the early days.

1930 Championship Semi-Final: St Helens 6 Leeds 10 at Knowsley Road. Leeds put Jenkins, a forward, on the wing to keep Alf Ellaby quiet and succeeded by fair means or foul. "*He took Ellaby with or without the ball and downed him with almost monotonous regularity,*" wrote 'Zealot' in the *Daily Herald*. ***1940*** Iron man front-rower Cliff Watson was born in Stepney in east London. Probably not within the sound of Bow Bells, but definitely air raid sirens in what was a desperate time for our proud capital city. The family was actually bombed out by the Luftwaffe and moved to Cliff's father's birthplace, Dudley, in the West Midlands. He went on to make 30 full appearances for Great Britain – the most capped Saints' player in red, white and blue.

Above: despite the mere inconvenience of a broken arm, Cliff Watson seems to be in a happy mood before Saints' European Championship match in Toulouse in November 1970. The front-row that day read: Graham Rees, Tony Karalius and Eric Woodyer.

Right: Cliff back at Knowsley Road for the Saints versus Cronulla Sharks World Club Championship match in 1997. [Alex Service]

27 APRIL

1886 Friendly match [Good Friday]: St Helens 1 try 6 minors Warrington 1 goal 3 minors at Dentons Green. Warrington were the first holders of the West Lancashire and Border Towns Cup. *1959* Northern Rugby League: Oldham 15 St Helens 14 at Watersheddings. Saints scored tries from van Vollenhoven with two, Smith and Murphy, with a goal from Brian Briggs and this was enough for the team to become the first to score over 1,000 league points in a season, 1005 in fact. The following week in the Championship Semi-Final, they redressed the balance and how: St Helens 42 Oldham 4.

Alex Murphy scoring a try against Wakefield Trinity at Knowsley Road in his usual inimitable style. Ken Large is in the background. Alex raced over for 31 tries in 36 appearances during the 1958–59 campaign. Not bad for a scrum-half and a record for a number seven at the time.
[Alex Service]

1968 Championship Semi-Final: Hull KR 23 St Helens 10 at Craven Park, Hull. The curtain came down on Tom van Vollenhoven's magnificent career as a Saint after 409 matches. Will we ever see his like again? *1986* Premiership Trophy Round 1: St Helens 22 Leeds 38 at Knowsley Road. Since signing from Widnes 12 games previously, veteran stand-off Eric Hughes had won every one until this one – his 13th.

1996 Challenge Cup Final: St Helens 40 Bradford Bulls 32 at Wembley Stadium. It was Saints' first Challenge Cup Final success for 20 years and is regarded by many as being the best-ever final. Certainly the greatest come-back, for sure. To overcome a 14-point deficit in such a short time was surely in the realms of dreams, but became reality when Squadron Leader Bobbie Goulding started his aerial bombardment of the Bradford line, causing absolute mayhem, resulting in three key touchdowns. In this superb image, Alan Hunte and Bradford's Nathan Graham (left) tussle for the high ball.
[RLPhotos.com].

Wembley 1996: Saints' players acknowledge the fans after a real rollercoaster match. [RLPhotos.com]

28 APRIL

1894 Friendly match: St Helens 11 Tyldesley 0 at Knowsley Road. This season saw the club's first major honour in rugby. Before this friendly encounter with local rivals Tyldesley, known as the Bongers, the Second Division County Championship trophy was presented to Saints' captain Billy Cross by St Helens MP Henry Seton-Karr, Laird of Kippilaw in front of over 5,000 cheering supporters. Onwards and upwards, as they say. *1940* Centre Brian McGinn was born in St Helens. A fine all-round threequarter, he played in the 1959 Championship Final against Hunslet and the 1961 Challenge Cup Final, when Wigan were put to the sword. *1956* Challenge Cup Final: Tries by Frank Carlton, Steve Llewellyn and skipper Alan Prescott, together with two Austin Rhodes conversions enabled Saints to defeat Halifax by 13–2 to secure the club's first-ever Challenge Cup Final success. *2001* Challenge Cup Final: St Helens 13 Bradford Bulls 6 at Twickenham. In what was the actual 100th final, Saints had the game well and truly wrapped up with tries from Tommy Martyn and Keiron Cunningham. This was a clinical victory for the Saints, in both preparation and application, despite the horrendous weather on the day and the patched-up pitch. Did we care? Not at all. Players and staff, like us, were singing in the rain. [below, Bernard Platt]

29 APRIL

1933 Northern Rugby League: St Helens 39 Castleford 5 at Knowsley Road. A stunning five try performance from 26-year-old New Zealand winger Roy Hardgrave put the Yorkshiremen to the sword. On his day, this guy certainly wanted some stopping and was so elusive. *1935* 'The Idol of them All' Tom van Vollenhoven was born in Bethlehem, South Africa. The club's all-time leading scorer in an era when the opposition included such luminaries as Billy Boston [Wigan] and Warrington's Brian Bevan. A golden era indeed. *1989* Challenge Cup Final: Wigan 27 St Helens 0 at Wembley Stadium. A bridge too far for coach Alex Murphy's men, who had defied expectations somewhat by disposing of Widnes in a tremendous semi-final at Central Park. Just like the lads on the field, we were beyond sorrow.

30 APRIL

1927 Scrum-half Joe Ball was born in St Helens. A 'pocket battleship' figure, he was a popular member of the squad and attended Rivington Road School, where he came under the tutelage of Saints' Chairman Harry Cook. Joe went on to play for Barrow, as did his son, Ian. [Image: Alex Service] *1961* Demolition of the first section of the old Popular Side stand began, prior to its replacement with a more modern structure. Like the Main Stand, it was designed by local architect Clive Robinson, with steelwork by the local firm Todd Brothers. *1971* Top 16 Play-Off Round 2: St Helens 30 Hull FC 5 at Knowsley Road. Cumbrian left winger Bob Blackwood scored a try – something he would do in his next three matches, including a crucial three-pointer in the Championship Final against Wigan.

Lest we forget! Saints' players and officials visit injured hooker Frank McCabe in hospital with the Challenge Cup after their 1956 victory against Halifax. Frank got hurt after scoring his second try in the quarter final tie against Bradford Northern at Knowsley Road. [Alex Service]

May

Gathering Cups

That winning feeling at Wembley. Apollo Perelini scores Saints' last try after the incredible 'comeback' Final against Bradford Bulls in 1996. The best-ever? Lots of people think so. [Sportsphoto Ltd]

The traditional 'business end' time for the conclusion of the Challenge Cup, League Championship and Premiership Final, the month of May remained until the advent of the Summer Super League in 1996 as one of the most anticipated times of the year for the fans. If you supported the Saints, especially since Jim Sullivan's appointment as coach in 1952, you were truly blessed by the probability that the Red and Whites would, more often than not, be in contention for one of the game's top honours. The team appeared at Wembley on nine occasions in May during the winter season, winning five and losing four. There were also 10 Championship Final appearances; six were won, with three defeats and a draw in 1967. Of the seven Premiership Finals before Super League, the Saints won four.

1 MAY

1905 International centre Billy Mercer was born in St Helens. Billy was a superb player who made 311 appearances and scored 75 tires during his career, from 1925 to 1937. He also had two fliers outside him at various times: Alf Ellaby and Roy Hardgrave. He must have thought it was Christmas every match. ***1915*** Challenge Cup Final: Huddersfield 37 St Helens 3 at Watersheddings. It was a game too far for the Saints, who had massively over-achieved to get there. The attendance of 8,000, with receipts of £72, was the lowest-ever for a final. ***2000*** Super League Round 8: St Helens 50 Huddersfield-Sheffield Giants 30 at Knowsley Road. Powerhouse New Zealand centre Kevin Iro thundered over for five touchdowns, equalling the Super League record for tries in a match.

New Zealand winger Roy Hardgrave makes a break during the 1930 Challenge Cup Final against Widnes – the first time the team had played at the iconic venue. Widnes left-winger Harry Owen is left in his wake, with his team mate George van Rooyen covering in the background.
[Alex Service]

2 MAY

1904 Committee Meeting, Talbot Hotel. "Resolved: to nominate JH Houghton as secretary to the Northern Rugby League." A great administrator, Joe was also manager of the famous 1914 Rorke's Drift tourists Down Under. ***1953*** Championship Semi-Final: St Helens 46 Huddersfield 0 at Knowsley Road. Sweet revenge for the Wembley defeat seven days before, with second-rower George Parsons notching a superb hat-trick of tries. Meanwhile over at Wembley, the famous 'Stan Matthews Final', Blackpool versus Bolton Wanderers, was taking place. ***1959*** Championship Semi-Final: St Helens 42 Oldham 4 at Knowsley Road. Saints ran riot, with three tries from right winger Ken Large, who was deputising for Tom van Vollenhoven. ***1987*** Challenge Cup Final: Halifax 19 St Helens 18 at Wembley Stadium. The major talking point – Kiwi centre Mark Elia had the ball sensationally knocked from his grasp by Halifax loose forward John Pendlebury as he was diving to score a vital try. A Saints' equalising one-pointer would have been certainly followed by a replay victory, but they stuck to the belief that another try would come.

3 MAY

1886 Half-back Matt Creevey was born in Pocket Nook, St Helens. Matt had devastating speed off the mark and won a number of professional sprints when he wasn't playing rugby.
1919 Northern Rugby League: St Helens Recs 2 St Helens 8 at City Road, St Helens. Right centre Tommy Gormley, formerly with Warrington, made his Saints' debut. 65 matches later he joined the Recs and won the Lancashire Cup in 1923. *1930* Challenge Cup Final: St Helens 3 Widnes 10 at Wembley Stadium, London. Only the second rugby league cup final played at the iconic venue, it was Saints' first time and they were somewhat unprepared for the 80 minutes, with amongst other things, a visit to the House of Commons the night before.
1997 Challenge Cup Final: St Helens 32 Bradford Bulls 22 at Wembley Stadium, London. Clad in their black, red and white jerseys, the Saints retained the Challenge Cup for the first time after defeating the Bulls on the ground, with grubber kicks, as opposed to the aerial bombardment at the same venue 12 months before. *2017* Justin Holbrook, former assistant coach with Sydney Roosters was appointed as the new coach of St Helens RFC on a two-and-a-half-year contract.

Making history: Chris Joynt, Paul Newlove, Anthony Sullivan and (kneeling) Karle Hammond
show the Challenge Cup to the fans after Saints' first-ever successive Wembley
'double' victory, ironically against the same opponents – Bradford Bulls [Sportsphoto Ltd]

4 MAY

1970 Championship Semi-Final replay: St Helens 21 Castleford 12 at Knowsley Road. Over 12,000 saw the team struggle against a weakened Castleford outfit – they were at Wembley five days later, where they beat Wigan – with the result in doubt until relatively late on. Welsh winger Frank Wilson scored a blistering hat-trick, although he missed the Championship final, with his place on the wing taken by young back-rower Eric Prescott. *1975* Premiership Semi-Final: Wigan 16 St Helens 26 at Central Park. Comeback kings. Saints overturn an 11–2 deficit at half-time to triumph 22–16 in an amazing 'derby' clash. The team had to do something similar in the Final on the same ground against Leeds, but it was a bridge too far. *2012* Super League Round 13: St Helens 38 Wakefield Trinity Wildcats 12 at Langtree Park. Former Sydney Rooster Chris Flannery scored a hat-trick from the second row, with the great James Roby capping a comprehensive victory with a marvellous long-distance solo effort. What a player.

Trying to stop the unstoppable. The marvellous James Roby scores against Wakefield Trinity Wildcats at Langtree Park in 2012. [Bernard Platt]

5 MAY

1941 Yorkshire Cup Final: Bradford Northern 15 Dewsbury 5 at Odsal Stadium Bradford. Wartime shenanigans! Jackie Waring (3), Frank Tracey (6), Les Garner (11) and Jackie Bradbury (13) guest for the unsuccessful Dewsbury team, who also had Jim Sullivan at full-back. Guest players had to have their own club's permission in writing in order to guest with another club, so the Saints' secretary was obviously a busy man. *2007* Super League Magic Weekend: St Helens 34 Wigan Warriors 18 at Millennium Stadium, Cardiff. Magic was the word. Paul Wellens ran in four brilliant tries and continued with a brace of touchdowns in his next two matches, against Rochdale Hornets in the Challenge Cup and Wakefield Trinity Wildcats at Knowsley Road. As the Popular Side used to sing: "the best full-back in the world!" He was too, at the time.

6 MAY

1922 Challenge Cup Final: Rochdale Hornets 10 Hull 9 at Fartown. What's this got to do with the Saints? Well, former Saints' centre Teddy McLoughlin became the first St. Helens-born player to get a Challenge Cup winner's medal after his transfer to the Hornets. He came back to Knowsley Road later on in his career too. *1967* Championship Final: Wakefield Trinity 7 St. Helens 7 Headingley. The lightening flashed and the thunder crashed around the 20,161 fans, but it was honours even. Saints were well beaten in the replay at Swinton, however. *2008* The famous Knowsley Road ground was rebranded the GPW Recruitment Stadium, until the end of the 2010 season, when demolition began. As the song goes "...Money talks..." Who could blame them?

7 MAY

1932 Championship Final: St. Helens 9 Huddersfield 5 at Belle Vue, Wakefield. Ode to joy – the first time the club aspired to such lofty heights and that was without star winger Alf Ellaby and second-rower Albert Fildes who were on the boat with the England squad bound for another Ashes success Down under. *1960* Championship Semi-Final: St. Helens 9 Wigan 19 at Knowsley Road. Saints attempted a repeat Championship final appearance but failed somewhat disappointingly at the last hurdle. Full-back Austin Rhodes kicked three goals, giving him a total of 397 points for the campaign (19 tries 170 goals), although centre Neil Fox of Wakefield Trinity led the overall charts with 453 points. *1962* Challenge Match: St Helens 43 SHAPE Indians 8 at Knowsley Road. The visiting American servicemen, from NATO HQ in Paris, had to cope with a rampant Tom van Vollenhoven, who broke the individual try-scoring record. Pity it was an 'unofficial' match. He kicked a goal too, as did front-rower Cliff Watson. *2004* Super League Round 10: St. Helens 26 Wakefield Trinity Wildcats 20 at Knowsley Road. Young Gun front-rower James Graham made his senior debut and went on to become a legend in the red vee before moving to Australia in 2012. The complete forward.

Tom van Vollenhoven in irresistible form against SHAPE Indians, scoring seven tries! [Alex Service]

8 MAY

1909 Scrum-half or loose forward Jack Bradbury was born in St. Helens. He began with Wigan Highfield and signed for Saints from Bradford Northern, playing in 231 matches from 1934 to 1946, scoring 65 tries. Jack was a tough customer, a deadly tackler and a great leader, who could "marshal his troops like Montgomery," as one journalist wrote. *1972* A Gala Night took place at Knowsley Road, when supporters bade farewell to the team before their sojourn at Norbreck Hydro in Blackpool in preparation for Saturday's Challenge Cup Final against Leeds. The team trained at Blackpool Borough's ground. The team then left the Hydro on Thursday at lunchtime for their training base at Selsdon Park Hotel in South Croydon. *1976* Challenge Cup Final: St. Helens 20 Widnes 5 at Wembley Stadium, London. A new moniker for the team: Dad's Army. A lot of them were, after all, in the veteran stage, with the front-row of Kel Coslett, Tony Karalius and John Mantle sharing 99 years between them. Saints beat a younger Widnes outfit with two key tries from 'Supersub' Peter Glynn – a Widnes lad himself.

9 MAY

1953 Championship Final: St. Helens 24 Halifax 14 at Maine Road. The second league title victory in the club's history and what a cracking match it was, with over 51,083 cramming into the home of Manchester City FC. Saints' tries were scored by Glyn Moses, Duggie Greenall, Ray Cale, Peter Metcalfe and a brace from livewire hooker Reg Blakemore. Metcalfe also kicked three goals.

1953 Championship Final: Left: hooker Reg Blakemore scores one of his tries and, below, skipper Duggie Greenall accepts the cup from Lord Derby. Chairman Harry Cook is in the background. [Alex Service]

1976 Saints' victorious Challenge Cup squad return home to a rapturous welcome in Victoria Square before showing the cup to the fans on the Town Hall steps. **2015** Super League Round 14: Catalans Dragons 33 St. Helens 26 at Stade Gilbert Brutus. Left winger Adam Swift bagged four tries in this close-run reversal on French soil. Bien joué, Adam. Full-back Shannon McDonnell scored the other four-pointer; Luke Walsh, who later joined the Dragons, kicked three goals. The French team continued to dominate at rain-lashed Perpignan on 8 August, when they won 26–16 in what was the first Super 8 fixture for both clubs. Given the short notice of the inaugural second phase, Saints' travelling support was down in numbers as a result.

Health and safety? Forget it! Fans went to any lengths to catch a glimpse of their heroes with the Challenge Cup in Town Hall Square in 1976. [Alex Service]

10 MAY

1967 Championship Final Replay: Wakefield Trinity 21 St Helens 9 at Station Road. Saints were well-beaten, with a fine performance from Wakefield's scrum-half Ray Owen that sticks in the memory. *1987* Premiership Semi-Final: St Helens 8 Warrington 18 at Knowsley Road. Despite the defeat, centre Paul Loughlin kicked a goal – his 190th of the season to keep him top of the league's goalkicking charts. *2005* Saints' coach Ian Millward was relieved of his duties for 'gross misconduct' on three charges of swearing and abuse. He was the longest-serving in Super League at the time. On 23 May, he crossed the Rubicon and was appointed in a similar role at Wigan. *2009* Challenge Cup Round 5: St Helens 42 Catalans Dragons 8 at The GPW Recruitment Stadium. A complete victory for the Red Vee. Next match? Away against the same opponents in Round 13 of Super League and a 32–28 victory for the Saints.

11 MAY

1944 Full-back supreme Geoff Pimblett was born in the Laffak district of St Helens. A brilliant addition to the team in the early 1970s from St Helens RUFC, he was the first man to win both the Lance Todd and Harry Sunderland trophies. He was one of two Lance Todd trophy winners from Laffak and both full-backs. The other was Ray Ashby, of Wigan and Liverpool City. *1985* Premiership Final: St Helens 36 Hull KR 16 at Elland Road. A magnificent victory, full of open rugby, with Saints' loose forward and captain Harry Pinner untouchable in his 300 game for the club. The only downside: Big Mal Meninga played his last game. The referee was Saints' future kitman, Stan Wall. Brian Peers captured young Saints' star Paul Forber (left) in ebullient mood afterwards.

12 MAY

1874 Cuthbert 'Cuddy' Pennington was born in St Helens. A great all-round sportsman, who was adept at water polo, rugby and bowls – in later life – Cuddy was a nuggetty half-back who would frequently knock the stuffing out of opponents three stones heavier. He played 63 times for Saints and remained on the scene for many years afterwards as trainer for the senior squad at Knowsley Road. A wise old owl who had seen it all. *2002* Super League Round 10: Warrington Wolves 36 St Helens 44 at Wilderspool. Hooker Keiron Cunningham scored his 100th try for the Saints in a memorable 'derby' clash. *2018* Challenge Cup Round 6 Castleford Tigers 18 St Helens 36 at Mend-a-Hose Jungle. A rip-roaring victory for the visitors, including an attacking masterclass from full-back Barba, who scored a brilliant hat-trick. His third try was really one to savour, beating six would-be tacklers with the acceleration of Alex Murphy and the pace of van Vollenhoven. He also put winger Regan Grace away with a brilliant pass from his own line for a length of the field effort. We were truly glad all over and could watch it again and again and again. Sheer class.

Glad all over! Ben Barba seemingly strolls his way through the Castleford defence for a wonder try and the completion of his hat-trick. Simply magical. You just had to be there. [Bernard Platt]

13 MAY

1882 Half-back Teddy Toole was born in Pocket Nook. He played 97 times for the Saints, including the famous match against the first New Zealanders in 1907, when he was stand-off and fellow Pocket-Nooker Matt Creevey was scrum-half. After a severe engagement in the First World War with the Royal Field Artillery, he was missing presumed dead, but fortunately got back to his own lines intact. Teddy later joined Runcorn from Saints. *1961* Challenge Cup Final: St Helens 12 Wigan 6 at Wembley Stadium. A scorcher temperature-wise it was too, with centre Ken Large and his winger Tom van Vollenhoven showing perfect combination for the latter to score one of Wembley's greatest tries. *1972* Challenge Cup Final: St Helens 16 Leeds 13 at Wembley Stadium. Welsh front-rower Graham Rees scored a crucial first-minute try to 'kick start' Saints' success. Another Welshman, loose-forward and captain Kel Coslett won the Lance Todd Trophy for his brilliant performance, especially with the boot! Remember his post-match interview with BBCs Frank Bough: "We've got the Championship Final next Saturday, but we'll let ourselves go a bit tonight and have a few drinks, and some chips for Chissey." Brilliant stuff. *1978* Challenge Cup Final: St Helens 12 Leeds 14 at Wembley Stadium, London. A classic match, with Leeds overturning the Saints' 12–5 first-half advantage with sheer forward power. George Nicholls won the Lance Todd Trophy with a brilliant performance in adversity.

14 MAY

1904 Test Match: St Helens 7 Holbeck 0 at Fartown, Huddersfield. The two opponents were locked together with equal points in second place in the league and so a special match was organised. A forerunner of the 'Million Pound Game' in some ways. This was the latest finish to a Saints season since they joined the Northern Union. Defeated Holbeck duly resigned and, to cut a long story short, became Leeds United AFC. *1918* Former Saints' and Lancashire winger Sergeant James Flanagan was killed by shrapnel on the Western Front. A real tragedy for his family and the St Helens club. *1945* At the Committee meeting at Knowsley Road: "The Secretary [Bert Murray] was instructed to write to Mr R. Huyton and offer him the grazing rights till the end of July for the sum of ten pounds." The lawn mower did not need much petrol in the closed season, fuel was rationed, after all and the fertiliser was free. *1966* Championship Semi-Final: St Helens 14 Hull KR 6 at Knowsley Road. All points were scored by wing legend Len Killeen. There was already bad blood between the teams as a result of Rovers' Challenge Cup exit at Knowsley Road and things boiled over again. Near the end, skipper Alex Murphy put up a huge, what can only be described as 'provocative' up-and-under. I can see full-back Frankie Barrow now, among others, chasing after it full pelt. The result was total mayhem. It could have started World War Three.

15 MAY

1988 Premiership Final: Widnes 38 St Helens 14 Old Trafford, Manchester. Injury-hit Saints were well-beaten by a strong-running Widnes outfit. *2004* Challenge Cup Final: St Helens 32 Wigan Warriors 16 at the Millennium Stadium, Cardiff. A brilliant victory for the Saints, avenging their loss to the same opponents two years before. Scrum-half Sean Long won his second Lance Todd Trophy and he would win another two years later.

Skipper Paul Sculthorpe lifts the Challenge Cup aloft after beating Wigan Warriors at Cardiff in 2004 [Bernard Platt]

16 MAY

1959 Championship Final: St Helens 44 Hunslet 22 at Odsal. One of the most entertaining finals in rugby league history, full of fast, open rugby. After a slow start, the Saints grasped the nettle, inspired by a fantastic hat-trick of tries from winger Tom van Vollenhoven, who was carrying a hamstring injury. What if he had been fully fit? In this marvellous image, centre Duggie Greenall passes to Vollenhoven, with the vast Odsal crowd forming an impressive backdrop. What a magnificent sight it really was. [Robert Gate]

1964 Western Region Championship Final: St Helens 10 Swinton 7 at Central Park, Wigan. Saints inflicted another defeat on the Lions, just like they did in the Lancashire Cup at the same venue on several occasions. A big rap to second-rower Ray French, who dived over for a match-winning try. Coach Stan McCormick was so jubilant he jumped up in the concrete dugout and knocked himself out in the process. The Eastern and Western Region Championships were introduced after the move to two divisions the previous season, to provide more local fixtures. They were scrapped with the return to one division for 1964–65.

Left: Tom van Vollenhoven chases his opposite number John Stopford of Swinton in the 1964 Western Championship Final; right: loose forward Doug Laughton is tackled by Swinton's Ken Gowers in the same match. Stan Owen and Albert Blan (Swinton) are also in the picture.
[Alex Service]

1970 Championship Final: St Helens 24 Leeds 12 at Odsal. This was a real cracker between the two 'Roses' rivals. Frank Myler won the Harry Sunderland Trophy and there was no shelter for the fans in the giant Yorkshire bowl after a torrential rainstorm near the end of the game.

1979 Loose-forward Bob Harrison died aged 75. A rough-and-ready player who made 21 appearances for the club, his last being the 1930 Challenge Cup final at Wembley, he injured his knee in a Testimonial match for Recs' Frank Bowen that ended his career. A great shame.

1993 Premiership Final: St Helens 10 Wigan 4 at Old Trafford. A great win, preventing a Wigan grand-slam of trophies and revenge for the previous year's demise at the hands of the same opposition. Remember Paul Loughlin's four-pointer at the Stretford End? Unfortunately, it was star centre Gary Connolly's last game in a Saints' jersey. A great pity. Star stand-off Tea Ropati played in every match during the campaign too.

17 MAY

1934 Front-rower Albert Terry was born in St Helens. Abe made 216 appearances for the club, scoring 27 tries, and although he was a big unit, he amazed Australian crowds during the 1958 Great Britain tour with his speed and side-step. Abe, whose younger brother Fred also played for the club, joined Leeds in 1962. *1947* Northern Rugby League: St Helens 35 Featherstone Rovers 0 at Knowsley Road. According to the *St Helens Newspaper*: "The innovation of the day, however, was the sight of twenty German Prisoners of War, swinging along towards the Main Stand. Capt. Atherton, Welfare Officer, was connected with their visit. The idea was a good one and should help to bring friendship or reduce boredom." Talking of the German connection, Manchester City goalkeeper Bert Trautmann was allowed to do extra training at Knowsley Road during the early 1950s. *1975* Premiership Final: St Helens 11 Leeds 26 at Central Park. After a bad start, 16–0 down at half-time, the First Division Champions pulled themselves back into contention with tries from wingers Les Jones and Roy Mathias. Jeff Heaton added another, plus a goal from Kel Coslett, but it wasn't enough on the day. *2005* Former New Zealand Warriors and New Zealand Kiwis coach Daniel Anderson was appointed by the Saints. He was to oversee a fabulous 'treble' of trophies in the 2006 campaign, and the club's second World Club Challenge title in 2007.

18 MAY

1935 Jan Prinsloo was born in South Africa. A powerful, blockbusting winger, before such a species existed, I suppose, Jan scored 70 tries in 89 appearances from 1958 to 1961, generally in concert with fellow countryman Tom van Vollenhoven on the other flank. He was later transferred to Wakefield Trinity as part of the £11,000 deal that took Wigan winger Mick Sullivan to Knowsley Road. He died aged just 31 in July 1966 in South Africa, after playing rugby union, from which he was officially banned as a former League player. *1974* Club Merit Championship Final: St Helens 12 Warrington 13 at Central Park. It was that man Alex Murphy again, coming back to haunt us. Saints lost in a game of tight margins, despite two tries from left centre Frank Wilson and three Coslett goals. *2001* Super League Round 11: St Helens 66 Salford City Reds 16 at Knowsley Road. Scrum-half Sean Long booted over 11 goals – the highest he scored for the club in a single match. And there's more: Longy scored a hat-trick trick of touchdowns, together with Paul Wellens operating at stand-off.

19 MAY

1951 Festival of Britain celebrations – two matches were played on the same day: Great Britain 20 Australasia 23 at Headingley. Saints for the British: Eric Hesketh (6) George Parsons (12); for Australasia: Max Garbler (13) who scored a try. Meanwhile, over in South Wales: Welsh XIII 16 Empire XIII 29 at Steboneath Park, Llanelli. For Welsh XIII: Reg Blakemore (9) Ray Cale (11); For Empire XIII: Alan Prescott (8). **1999** Super League Round 10: Castleford Tigers 14 St Helens 33 at The Jungle. Former Castleford winger Chris Smith scooted over for a brilliant hat-trick, to the obvious disgust of the home crowd, who certainly proceeded to give him a bit of 'stick'. Only natural, I suppose.

20 MAY

1972 Championship Final: St Helens 5 Leeds 9 at Station Road. The Yorkshiremen, with front-rower Terry Clawson finding his kicking form after the previous week's defeat against Saints at Wembley, prevented a glorious double for the red vee. Hooker Les Greenall scored the only try that gave us hope in a game of tight margins.

Hooker Les Greenall scores against Leeds in 1972. John Stephens [left] and Eric Chisnall are the other Saints in the picture. [Alex Service]

2008 Councillors gave a massive thumbs up for the new Saints' stadium at Peasley Cross. It was set to transform the derelict 46-acre former United Glass site in St Helens into a £25-million 18,000 capacity stadium and a multi-million pound supermarket as part of the development. The club's Knowsley Road site was to become by a housing scheme. **2013** Super League Round 15: Leeds Rhinos 22 St Helens 30 at Carnegie Stadium, Headingley. A marvellous result – it always is to win there – with a searing break from centre Mark Percival in front of the strangely muted South Stand before sending Tommy Makinson over in the corner. One to treasure. **2017** Magic Weekend: St Helens 45 Hull FC 0 at St James Park, Newcastle. Ha'way the Saints. Where did that one come from? Were we so good? Were they so bad? Plump for the former and a superb all-round team performance. New coach Justin Holbrook's very recent arrival certainly seemed to have had a galvanising effect too.

21 MAY

1932 Eric Ledger was born in St Helens. A real flier, whose cameo of 32 tries in 35 appearances from 1954 to 1956 delighted the fans on the terraces at Knowsley Road. He later joined Rochdale Hornets and his son, Barry would later take one of the wing berths at the Saints with equal success. *1949* Challenge Match: St Helens 16 Huddersfield 25 at Abertillery, South Wales. The third and final match of Saints' tour of the Principality. The 25,000 crowd were delighted to see their former player, winger Steve Llewellyn, fly over for a brace of touchdowns. *1966* Challenge Cup Final: St Helens 21 Wigan 2 at Wembley Stadium. What's not to like? Saints were well on their way to a four-trophy haul, with Len Killeen's marvellous long-distance penalty goal leaving commentator Eddie Waring almost lost for words. Wigan let us have one of their hookers, Bill Sayer before the cup run and ended up with 'stand in' Tom Woosey at Wembley. C'est la vie! Altogether now: "Ee-aye-addio, we've won the cup!"

Apart from his brilliant place-kicking achievements, Len Killeen did not see much of the ball in his hands during the 1966 Challenge Cup final. Yet he did manage to score a fantastic try by chasing Billy Benyon's pin-point chip into the corner in the 54th minute, which made the score 14–2 and Challenge Cup glory – plus the Lance Todd Trophy for himself – was virtually assured.
[Alex Service]

22 MAY

1965 Championship Final: St Helens 7 Halifax 15 at Station Road. League leaders and Lancashire Cup winners Saints lost to a team from 8th place in the league. Tom van Vollenhoven played at right centre that afternoon, with Peter Harvey outside him. Revenge would be exacted in 12 months time. Same venue: different result. ***1971*** Championship Final: St Helens 16 Wigan 12 at Station Road. This was the one and only final of its type against the two old rivals. Billy Benyon's last-gasp try was the toast of St Helens after victory looked to have passed 12-man Saints by, but the lads claimed back-to-back League Championships for the first time. Happy days.

1976 Premiership Final: St Helens 15 Salford 2 at Station Road. It was 1–0 at half-time to the Red Devils, but Saints surged to victory after the break with tries from Peter Glynn, Tony Karalius and Eric Chisnall. Full-back Geoff Pimblett kicked 3 goals in the game.

2011 Challenge Cup Round 5: St Helens 70 Featherstone Rovers 0 at the Stobart Stadium, Widnes. Saints run riot, with winger Jamie Foster banging over 11 goals. Despite the heavy defeat, Rovers played some good rugby on occasions.

St Helens RFC: BBC 2 Floodlit Trophy, Challenge Cup and Premiership winners 1976
line up in front of the main stand at Knowsley Road.
Back: Ken Henthorne (physio), Dave Hull, Harry Pinner, Roy Mathias, Peter Glynn, George Nicholls,
John Mantle, Derek Noonan, Mel James, Eric Chisnall, Eric Ashton (coach).
Front: Graham Liptrot, Geoff Pimblett, Billy Benyon, Jeff Heaton, Kel Coslett, Les Jones,
Tony Karalius, Eddie Cunningham, Ken Gwilliam, Frank Wilson.
[Alex Service]

23 MAY

1966 Saints' victorious Challenge Cup winning squad return from London to a tumultuous welcome in Town Hall Square. "Calm down now!" Mayor Arthur Luther appeals for relative quiet so that skipper Alex Murphy (left) could thank the fans. Ray French is next to him. What a memorable evening it was. [Alex Service] **1999** Super League Round 11: St Helens 57 Warrington Wolves 20 at Knowsley Road. The impenetrable fortress, as far as Warrington were concerned in the Super League era.

24 MAY

1923 Charles Joseph Bishop, half-back in Saints' first-ever match against Liverpool Royal Infirmary, in 1874, and (flint) glassworks owner, died aged 72. He was Mayor of St Helens on two occasions. **1967** Farewell to a kicking legend. Len Killeen flew to Australia to join Balmain in the Sydney competition for a transfer fee of £5,750. Len went on to win a Premiership with the Tigers in 1969, one of a special band of players to win honours in both countries. **2002** Super League Round 12: St Helens 56 Widnes Vikings 6 at Knowsley Road. A try and seven goals for stand-off Paul Sculthorpe as the Vikings were put to the sword in convincing fashion by the future Champions.

25 MAY

1968 Test Match #161 (World Cup) Australia 25 Great Britain 10 at Sydney Cricket Ground. The British began their World Cup campaign with a defeat on the end of an 18–7 penalty count and eight goals from Australia's Eric Simms. Tommy Bishop was scrum-half; Cliff Watson in the front row. John Warlow was the named forward substitute, but remained on the bench. 62,256 fans packed into the famous old arena. **2017** Super League Round 15: St Helens 22 Wigan Warriors 19 at the Totally Wicked Stadium. Just when the Warriors thought they had won, up came centre Mark Percival with a brilliant try at the Wigan end to snatch victory virtually on the final hooter. Cue sheer ecstasy in three parts of the stadium.

26 MAY

1962 Loose forward or stand-off Shane Cooper was born in St Helens Hospital, Auckland. Coincidence? Well, he did play 271 matches for the Saints, after all. But there is another link. Some specially-built maternity hospitals were built in New Zealand early in the 20th Century to help reduce maternal and infant mortality rates and were called 'St Helens hospitals' after New Zealand Premier Richard Seddon, who was born in the Lancashire town. **1997** Super League Round 12: St. Helens 12 Wigan Warriors 65 at Knowsley Road. In our defence we had a horrendous injury crisis. It was the highest points against in any home match.

27 MAY

1964 Northern Rugby League: Castleford 11 St Helens 10 at Wheldon Road. Alex Murphy (7) and Tom Pimblett (right wing, on debut) scored the tries; Kel Coslett kicked two goals, in front of just 3,841. After the match, on the journey back home, Stan McCormick was relieved of his position as coach by chairman Harry Cook. Yet the decision had been made at a Board meeting earlier in the month. Joe Coan, a local schoolmaster, was his replacement.
2005 Super League Round 15: St Helens 38 Leeds Rhinos 24 at Knowsley Road. A try apiece for the two Andersons – England international Paul (10) and Kiwi second-rower Vinnie (12). The crowd: 13,236, loved every minute if they came from St Helens.

28 MAY

1966 Championship Final: St Helens 35 Halifax 12 at Station Road. Len Killeen (5) and Albert Halsall (8) each scored a hat-trick of tries: the first time this 'double' had happened in a major final. We also witnessed probably one of the worst all-in 'brawls' ever seen in a major final, as tempers got somewhat frayed on both sides. *1977* Premiership Final: St Helens 32 Warrington 20 at Station Road. The last final for legendary centre Billy Benyon who, ironically, joined the Wire as player-coach early in the following campaign. It was full-back Geoff Pimblett's day however, with a try, seven goals and the Harry Sunderland Trophy for good measure.

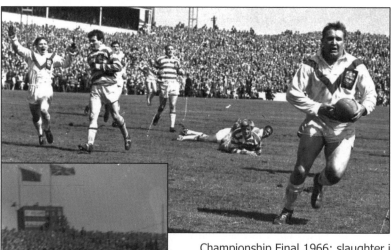

Championship Final 1966: slaughter in the sun! Two Saints players scored hat-tricks as Halifax were put to the sword. Albert Halsall (above) flies over for a marvellous try under the sticks. Tommy Bishop has his arms raised in acclamation. This image was put onto a glass slide, originally, as opposed to a negative, with cracks in the glass apparent; on the left Len Killeen wings his way over in the corner, with Colin Dixon unable to stop him. Notice the old scoreboard at Station Road and the packed crowd. What a season and sporting year. We never wanted it to end.
[St Helens Local History & Archives/*St Helens Reporter*]

90

Championship Final 1966. Above: tempers get frayed, with Saints' full-back Frankie Barrow and Halifax stand-off Barry Robinson slugging it out, amongst others with St Helens fan Minnie Cotton also being escorted off the field after another pitch incursion. Below: Right winger Tony Barrow scores after 56 minutes to give the Saints an unassailable lead, with the 30,000 crowd packed onto the terraces at Swinton. [St Helens Local History & Archives/*St Helens Reporter*]

29 MAY

1959 The strains of *Sweet Georgia Brown* echoed around Knowsley Road as the famous Harlem Globetrotters, including star turn Meadowlark Lemon and Wizard of Dribble Curly Lee, played an exhibition game against the San Francisco Chinese team on a specially-constructed court. The 'Trotters' won 60–51 and according to the *St Helens Reporter*, the undoubted star of the game was: "A colourful character called Meadowlark Lemon. The clown of the side, Lemon had the crowd in stitches and the Chinese players in knots with his incredible ball dribbling and passing." The travelling show was also preceded by a special table tennis match. *1985* New Zealand tour: Waikato 34 St Helens 24 at Waikato. Saints lost out in a free-scoring encounter in front of 4,000 fans. Full-back Kevin Wellens scored two tries. *2004* Super League Round 12: St Helens 35 Bradford Bulls 30 at Knowsley Road. Australian stand-off Jason Hooper ran in a hat-trick of tries; scrum-half Sean Long kicked seven goals. Interestingly, none of the threequarters scored for Saints in what was a free-scoring encounter.

Left: Jason Hooper is congratulated by Paul Sculthorpe during his hat-trick performance against the Bradford Bulls in 2004 [Bernard Platt]

30 MAY

1904 Committee Meeting Talbot Hotel: "Resolved: That the 1st Team players be entertained to dinner on Saturday June 11 '04 at the Talbot Hotel." A fine gesture by the club in those early days. *1928* Arthur Glyndwr 'Glyn' Moses was born in Nant-y-Moel, South Wales. The former Newbridge full-back originally came north to join Salford, but went back to Wales, somewhat disillusioned. Signed by the Saints late in 1952, his resolute defence and mobility was a revelation and he went on to win every honour at club level and was a regular with Great Britain and Wales. *1982* County Championship: Cumbria 8 Lancashire 46 at Derwent Park, Workington. Saints' young flyer Kevin Meadows scored a superb hat-trick for the Red Rose county from the right wing.

31 MAY

1947 Northern Rugby League: St Helens 36 Barrow 7 at Knowsley Road. This was a comprehensive victory for the Saints on a veritable 'dustbowl' of a pitch, in front of over 9,000 fans. The highlights? Flying winger Albert 'Sonny' Doyle zoomed in for a hat-trick; back-rower Len Aston scored two and Tom Stott kicked six goals. It was almost Super League, with the timing. Blame the bad winter. *1998* Super League Round 8: St Helens 18 Leeds Rhinos 31 at Knowsley Road. On the crest of a slump. Saints never really got their mojo back until a 68–18 victory over Huddersfield Giants at Knowsley Road on 2 August. *2015* Magic Weekend: St Helens 20 Warrington Wolves 16 at St James Park, Newcastle. Our on-off love affair with the concept was rekindled after an encouraging victory against tough opponents. The next year, against Huddersfield Giants, was to be a different story once again.

June
Winding down and warming up?

Two members of the great Saints teams from the early Super League days and good friends to boot. Paul Newlove (left) and Chris Joynt celebrate their induction into the Saints' Players' Association Hall of Fame on 30 June 2006 at Knowsley Road. [Alex Service]

Pre-Super League it was rare to find matches played in England in this particular month, unless there had been particularly bad winters, such as in 1947, when the latest finish occurred. Then, players, officials and supporters would start to wind down. Time for reseeding pitches, repainting grounds and generally tidying up for the pre-season friendlies in August. The Great Britain tourists would have already begun their programmes in earnest, but it was time for reflecting on the season just departed and wondering if the club would be making any inroads into the transfer market. Interestingly, the St Helens club were strong advocates of 'summer' rugby in May and June 1969 and prepared a report, circulated to member clubs. Secretary Basil Lowe later recalled that at least 20 clubs were in support of a season to extend from March to October.

1 JUNE

2003 Super League Round 12: Warrington Wolves 30 St Helens 30 at Wilderspool. The Wire went close to breaking their Super League hoodoo over the Saints in this magnificent contest at the ground known – before Castleford, although unofficially – as the 'Jungle'. Definitely no place for fainthearts. *2007* Super League Round 16: St Helens 27 Salford City Reds 26 at Knowsley Road. Former Oldham St Annes junior Kyle Eastmond made an encouraging debut at stand-off; Leon Pryce was at full-back. Yet it was his scrum-half Matty Smith who sealed the two points with a 79th minute drop-goal. Matty did it again just over a decade later against the same opponents, in the last few seconds, at the Totally Wicked Stadium, on 23 June 2017 in a 25–24 spectacular. *2008* Challenge Cup Round 6: Hull KR 18 St Helens 24 at New Craven Park. This proved to be a fantastic backs-to-the-wall performance from the future cup winners. The scores were level, 12–12, at half time and it was a real rollercoaster affair – exactly why most of us cherish this Blue Riband of rugby league competitions. Sean Long kicked four goals and scored a try, as captured by Bernard Platt's lens below. James Roby is the first to congratulate him.

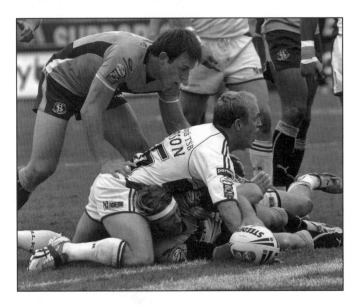

2 JUNE

1996 Super League Round 10: St Helens 52 Paris St Germain 10 at Knowsley Road. The visitors were the first team from France to take part in a league match in St Helens. Former Balmain second-rower Derek McVey scored a brace of tries for the Saints at a sun-baked Knowsley Road. *2001* Super League Round 13: St Helens 38 Bradford Bulls 26 at Knowsley Road. 23 years old Paul Sculthorpe scored two tries and kicked five goals. Little wonder his all-round displays earned him the prestigious Man of Steel award at the end of the campaign. And he won it again in 2002. The complete footballer. *2013* Anthony Sullivan was inducted into the St Helens Players' Association Hall of Fame during their Annual Luncheon at Langtree Park. And why ever not? His 213 tries from 305 appearances, together with numerous club honours and international selection for both Wales and Great Britain made it a veritable 'no-brainer' really for the selection of the former left-wing flyer.

3 JUNE

1925 Frank Beesley was born in St Helens. A county rugby union player, who was signed from St Helens RUFC, he was like quicksilver around the scrum-base and loved to run at the opposition. He made 46 appearances from 1947 to 1949. *2016* Super League Round 17: St Helens 4 Warrington Wolves 26 at Langtree Park. A disappointing reversal for the Saints against one of their new stadium 'bogey teams'. Ominously, it was 16–0 to the Wolves at half-time. Full-back Jonny Lomax was our sole try-scorer.

4 JUNE

2010 Super League Round 16: Hull FC 27 St. Helens 26 at KC Stadium, Hull. A great game and a marvellous come-back from the visitors after their 22–6 deficit at half-time. Saints' star? Francis Meli, with four tries from the left wing berth. His centre was Chris Flannery. *2017* Super League Round 17 Castleford Tigers 16 St Helens 12 at Mend a Hose Jungle, Castleford. Mark Percival and Louie McCarthy-Scarsbrook scored tries; Tommy Makinson kicked two goals. A narrow defeat, but a much improved performance from the last visit: a 53–10 walloping in the Challenge Cup on 13 May. The next encounter was at the same venue in the Grand Final Play-Off and 23-22 extra time heartbreak for the Saints. But what a fantastic match.

5 JUNE

1971 European Championship second leg: St Helens 62 St Gaudens 0 at Knowsley Road. Oooh la la! The Saints inflicted a resounding defeat on the visitors, who 'warmed up' on the pitch for half an hour before the match, when nobody did warm-ups. Could it have been too much of the good life during their visit? Our lips are sealed.

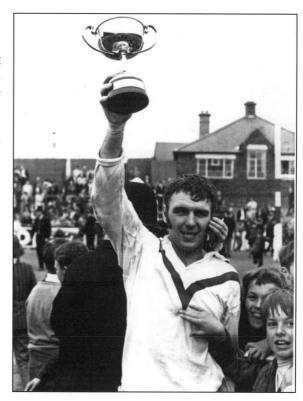

Left: Skipper Kel Coslett shows the European Cup to the fans after the St Gaudens game at Knowsley Road in 1971. [Alex Service]

95

2005 Super League Round 16: Bradford Bulls 4 St Helens 66 at Odsal Stadium. Easy, easy. Vinnie Anderson got a hat-trick of tries. Walking out of Odsal, you wouldn't have given a bean for Bradford's chances of end-of-season glory after this cakewalk, even though they ended up with 12 men after Leon Pryce's dismissal. But they beat injury-hit Saints, minus Long and Albert, in particular, 23–18 in the Elimination Final at Knowsley Road on 7 October and went on to win the Grand Final. Funny old game.

Left: Saints-and sinners at Odsal in 2005. Leon Pryce (3) of Bradford Bulls is about to get the proverbial early bath after a mistimed challenge on Jamie Lyon. Result – game over.
[Bernard Platt]

2009 Super League Round 15: Hull FC 6 St Helens 30 at KC Stadium. Interesting times. Sean Long, who three days before had announced that he was to play for the Black and Whites of Hull in 2010, gave a masterly display. Paul Wellens also scored a brilliant hat-trick, with two assists from Long, just days after being dropped from the England squad. After Saints' record-equalling 15th successive away victory in Super League, they were three points ahead of second-placed Hull KR.

6 JUNE

1932 Test Match #45: Australia 6 Great Britain 8 at the Sydney Cricket Ground. A world record crowd of 70,204 saw Alf Ellaby score a try, together with his centre, Arthur Atkinson. The gates were closed on police instructions. Thousands swarmed onto the grandstands of the adjacent Sydney showgrounds and attempted to watch the game from there. *1944* Saints' winger Albert 'Sonny' Doyle was a navigator in the RAF and flew to France on D Day (Operation Overlord) in an aircraft pulling one of the many gliders that were part of the Normandy invasion. Troops in this glider had the objective of holding Pegasus Bridge, one of the things crucial to the success of the whole operation in that part of Normandy. Brave men indeed. *1997* World Club Championship: St Helens 14 Auckland Warriors 42 at Knowsley Road. As the inaugural Super League Champions, we hosted the first game in the new Anglo-Australasian competition, but Saints were beaten by a much superior side on the day. Former favourite Tea Ropati made a popular return to Knowsley Road with the Warriors.

7 JUNE

1927 Saints' centre extraordinaire Duggie Greenall was born in St Helens. His star sign was Gemini and as such he could be expected to be sociable, chatty and knowledgeable. Spot on. Duggie always delighted in telling his opposite number what he was going to do to him in the forthcoming 80 minutes.

Left: Centre supreme Duggie Greenall in action against Huddersfield at Knowsley Road. Despite his fearsome reputation, he could play a bit too and was the perfect winger's centre; right: Paul Sculthorpe and Alan Hunte at their Hall of Fame induction in 2015. [Alex Service]

1947 Northern Rugby League: St Helens 26 Rochdale Hornets 4 at Knowsley Road. As a result of one of the worst winters on record, there was an enormous backlog of fixtures. This game was, in fact, the latest conclusion to a winter season for the Saints. Centre supreme Jimmy Stott – who would have probably preferred to be playing cricket – scored a try and kicked four goals. *2015* Two of Saints' finest were inducted into the St Helens Player Association's Hall of Fame: double Man of Steel Paul Sculthorpe and international wing flyer Alan Hunte. Wise choices indeed.

8 JUNE

1996 Super League Round 11: Sheffield Eagles 32 St Helens 43 at Cardiff RFC's Cardiff Arms Park. Sheffield's stadium was being used for athletics, so a game on the road was implemented and a thoroughly enjoyable affair it was. Full-back Steve Prescott kicked seven goals. Alan Hunte and Welsh international Anthony Sullivan roared in for a brace of tries apiece. *2006* Super League Round 16: St Helens 26 Hull FC 27 at Knowsley Road. This should not have happened to the future 'treble' winners, but it did. Paul Cooke's towering drop-goal flew between the posts amid disbelieving looks from Saints' fans – a brilliant piece of opportunism, it has to be said.

2012 Super League Round 17: St Helens 54 Bradford Bulls 0 at Langtree Park. Left centre Josh Jones, an Academy tourist with the club to Australia in 2009, notched a fine hat-trick. The Saints backline read: Makinson, Shenton, Jones and Meli.

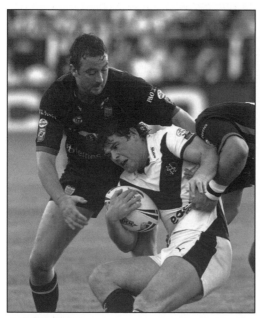

Paul Cooke (left, tackling Paul Wellens) whose drop-goal for Hull FC stunned the Saints at Knowsley Road in 2006; below: three-try Josh Jones terrorises Bradford Bulls in 2012. [Bernard Platt]

9 JUNE

1931 Josh Gaskell was born in the central area of St Helens known as the 'Bruk'. A forceful forward, who could play in the front or second row, he was later transferred to Warrington, although no surprises where his heart remained. *2013* Super League Round 18: St Helens 30 Bradford Bulls 18 at Langtree Park. 11,385 saw on-loan half-back Gareth O'Brien kick five goals. The sad decline of the Bulls was becoming apparent by this time, leading to ultimate relegation and dire straits.

10 JUNE

1975 World Championship: England 7 Wales 12 at Lang Park, Brisbane. Saints' forceful centre, Eddie Cunningham played his first game for his adopted country. By our reckoning he is the 283rd Welshman to make his debut at international level. He was later followed in the scarlet jersey by brothers Tommy and Keiron, both hookers, of course. *2005* Super League Round 17: Salford City Reds 22 St Helens 33 at The Willows. A good reason for the Sky Sports commentary team to eulogise over the performance of centre Jamie Lyon, whose brilliant hat-trick won the game, when things threatened, potentially, to go belly-up.

11 JUNE

2004 Super League Round 14: St Helens 52 Castleford Tigers 8 at Knowsley Road. Three players scored a brace of tries: Paul Wellens, Darren Albert and Chris Joynt. This was the Saints truly living up to their 'Great Entertainers' tag. It was also centre Martin Gleeson's last game for the club, before his transfer to Warrington Wolves. **2017** Former hooker Graham Liptrot was inducted into the St Helens Players Association Hall of Fame at a packed luncheon at the Totally Wicked Stadium. A great player, who could dominate the scrums and dictate around the ruck, Graham also played in 387 matches for the club. A worthy incumbent.

Left: All smiles! Harry Pinner (left) presents Graham Liptrot with his framed image during his induction into the Players' Association Hall of Fame [Alex Service];

12 JUNE

1920 Front-rower Norman Thompson was born in St Helens. The flaxen-haired powerhouse played 96 games for Saints before joining Oldham and was one of Saints' first Lancashire representatives post-war, together with team-mate Frank Riley. They played in the 17–16 victory over Yorkshire at Swinton on 11 November 1945. **1992** Test Match #271: Australia 22 Great Britain 6 at the Sydney Cricket Ground. An unequal balance of power? Perhaps a sign of the times. There were 10 Wiganers in this Great Britain team, with left centre Paul Loughlin the sole Saints' representative. Mal Meninga scored twice for the Green and Golds.

2015 Super League Round 18: St Helens 30 Wigan Warriors 14 at Langtree Park. Let the come-back begin. Saints were 10–8 down at half-time in front of 16,692 fans before taking the spoils.

Right: Jason Hooper crosses the whitewash during the convincing win against Castleford in 2004.
[Bernard Platt]

13 JUNE

1946 Centre John Walsh was born in St Helens. Geminis are characterised by a quicksilver mind and the ability to analyse. Little wonder that Hull University graduate John became a successful insurance actuary and went to live in Ontario, Canada. *2003* John Arkwright, the father of Chris, died aged 70. A former goalkeeper and a real fiery character, like his father, Jack, we remember him getting sent off in the 1962 Lancashire Cup Final against Swinton at Central Park and, as such, could not be presented with his medal on the day and was not on the celebratory team picture. A great pity. *2008* Super League Round 17: St Helens 58 Bradford Bulls 20 at Knowsley Road. A one-and-only hat-trick for durable front-rower Bryn Hargreaves during his Saints' career, who, ironically, later joined the Bulls on a two-year contract before he moved to the USA.

14 JUNE

1920 Back rower Len Aston was born in St Helens. A fabulous ball-player, he was once pulled up for a forward pass by one disbelieving referee after one of his trademark 'dummies'.

No dummies this time. Len Aston in defensive mode at Knowsley Road. He was a terrific footballer until he had to give up the game somewhat early in his career with a heart condition. [Alex Service]

1958 Test Match #108: Australia 25 Great Britain 8 at the Sydney Cricket Ground. It was the debut of Alex Murphy at scrum-half, although not the start, result-wise, that he would have wanted. Dave Bolton of Wigan was his stand-off and scored a try in front of 68,777 screaming Australian fans. *2002* County of Origin: Lancashire 22 Yorkshire 18 at Wigan. A record-equalling number of Saints' players for the Red Rose county who were coached by Ian Millward: Martin Gleeson, Paul Wellens (two tries), Anthony Stewart, Paul Sculthorpe, Chris Joynt and John Stankevitch. John was the last St Helens player to debut for Lancashire.

Up for the Red Rose in 2002. Left to right: Paul Sculthorpe, John Stankevitch, Tony Stewart, Paul Wellens, Chris Joynt. Front: Ian Millward (coach), Stan Wall (kitman) Martin Gleeson. [Bernard Platt]

15 JUNE

1957 World Cup (Test Match #102): France 5 Great Britain 23 at Sydney Cricket Ground. Glyn Moses played full-back; Alan Prescott skippered the side from number eight. There were just over 50,000 at the famous old ground. *1974* Test Match #192: Australia 12 Great Britain 6 at Lang Park, Brisbane. A dour affair, with just one try scored. George Nicholls was loose forward, with David Eckersley on the bench. The Australians eventually won the rubber 2–1, although by relatively close margins. The other two scores were: a 16–11 British win and 22–18 Australian win in the decider.

16 JUNE

1939 Centre Ken Large was born in St Helens. Famous for his part in the 1961 Vollenhoven 'epic' three-pointer at Wembley, he is fondly remembered as the licensee of the Victoria Hotel in Rainhill. He was quick, too. *1996* Super League Round 12: St Helens 60 Workington Town 16 at Knowsley Road. Durable front-rower Jon Neill played his last game in the red vee before moving to Huddersfield Giants. His other front-row compatriots were Keiron Cunningham and budding thespian Adam Fogerty. Skipper Bobbie Goulding kicked eight goals and reached his century in just 17 games. He also broke the 800 point barrier in less than three seasons as a Saint – simply phenomenal. *1997* World Club Challenge: St Helens 8 Cronulla Sharks 48 at Knowsley Road. Injury-wracked Saints were forced to bow to a much superior outfit, who were 36 points up at half-time. Sean Long, signed from Widnes Vikings shortly before the match, made his debut at scrum-half and kicked two goals. A great career in the red vee was about to begin.

17 JUNE

1902 At a meeting of the Northern League, applications were accepted for places in the newly-proposed Second Division. The Northern League, an early 'Super League' if you like, began in 1901–02. Saints applied and after another meeting on 1 July St Helens, Widnes and Hull KR actually found themselves voted into the First Division. St Helens officials were delighted, but it was a step too far. The club was relegated at the end of 1902–03. *2007* Super League Round 17: Hull KR 0 St. Helens 40 at New Craven Park. Wowsers! Saints on fire with a try and six goals from young Steve Tyrer. He improved on that performance in the next match against Huddersfield at Knowsley Road, with a two try and seven goal cameo.

Young Gun Steve Tyrer shrugs off a tackle against Hull KR in 2007 on his way to a personal points haul of 16. [Bernard Platt]

18 JUNE

1977 Test Match #200: Australia 19 Great Britain 5 at Lang Park, Brisbane. This was in the World Championship and the Brits had qualified for the final before a virtual dead rubber against the Australians. Second-rower George Nicholls was the sole Saints' player on view and was badly concussed during the match, missing the Final seven days later in Sydney, which was lost 13-12. *1985* Hooker Mark Lee was signed from St Helens Colts. A clever player, Mark found opportunities limited at Knowsley Road and later enjoyed a brilliant career at Salford. *2015* Super League Round 19: Castleford Tigers 25 St. Helens 24 at the Mend-a-Hose Jungle. Hard to take, because Castleford gradually crept into Saints' half and stand-off Ben Roberts delivered a last-gasp one-pointer. Sheer desolation.

19 JUNE

1936 Loose forward George Case was born in St Helens. This former Blackbrook amateur had the toughest of first team debuts when he was drafted in on the left wing to mark Wigan`s Billy Boston, at Central Park on 28 April 1962. Despite a 12–3 defeat, Case did his job well and the big Welshman did not score. Two days later, at the Willows, Boston scored seven tries against Salford. George played mostly with the 'A' team until he damaged his ankle in a club pre-season trial match in 1963, which ended his career. ***2015*** Former powerhouse All Black rugby union wing legend Jonah Lomu passed away after battling illness for some time. He gained the respect of all 'rugby' folk with his tremendous strength and power. Saints' all-time great Keiron Cunningham named his own son in his honour. Praise indeed.

20 JUNE

1902 Winger George Cotton was born in St Helens. The winger had pace and finishing ability to score 25 tries in 39 appearances in 1924-25 but he was plagued by shoulder trouble which unfortunately ended his career shortly after. George retained his links with St Helens RFC and became a valued member of the Saints' Supporters' Committee for many years. His wife, Minnie, made national headlines by trying to 'sort out' Dewsbury forward Trevor Lowe with an umbrella in the 1966 Challenge Cup Semi-Final at Swinton. The ultimate enforcer!

2010 Super League Round 24: Wigan Warriors 24 St. Helens 26 at the DW Stadium, Wigan. So much for the fans to savour in this Sunday evening 'derby' clash in front of over 20,000. Saints led 16–2 at one stage and held on to secure the points in a nervy finale. It was Paul Wellens' 400th career appearance and he duly capped it with a try, captured by Bernard Platt, below, later tackling Wigan's George Carmont when all seemed lost. 19 year old left winger Jamie Foster kicked three goals and scored a try in a game that could have gone either way. His team-mates in the threequarter line Gidley, Flannery and Meli, were all aged 30 years or more.

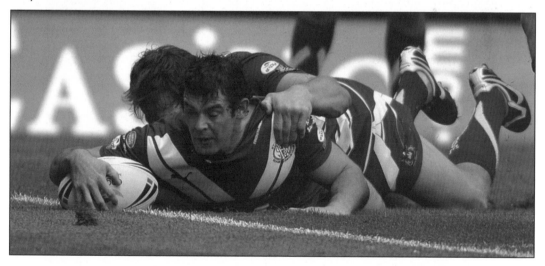

21 JUNE

1948 Second-rower Eric Prescott was born in St Helens. A superb, mobile forward, who later joined Salford for £13,000 a record transfer fee received by the Saints at the time. ***1996*** Super League Round 13: Wigan Warriors 35 St Helens 19 at Central Park. This was a potential blow for Saints' title hopes, with both clubs in close contention. Yet London Broncos, with Terry Matterson's goal, had given the Saints a crucial one point advantage in the league table with their draw at the same venue on 9 June that was never relinquished. Rock on, Terry.

22 JUNE

1937 Mighty second-rower Dick Huddart was born in Flimby, Cumberland. For his debut for Saints at Workington on 18 October 1958, a 10–10 draw, he merely caught the train from his home to Derwent Park. Aaah, the trappings of superstardom. ***1976*** Challenge Match: Queensland 21 St Helens 15 at Lang Park, Brisbane and a real 'ground-breaker' - the first-ever match played by an English club side in Australia. Notice the opposition: *Queensland.* Not a club side. Saints did really well in context. ***2001*** Super League Round 16: St Helens 28 Wigan Warriors 29 at Knowsley Road. Saints' 'you score one, we'll score two' mantra backfired a little here. A game of fine margins, with a brace of tries from Australian front-rower David Fairleigh, seen from Bernard Platt's image below in the same match, taking the ball up with his usual determination and skill. Wigan's Australian forward Furner waits for the collision. Scrum-half Adrian Lam, hopefully, would have wanted a watching brief.

23 JUNE

1924 Test Match #26: Australia 3 England 22 at Sydney Cricket Ground. Wigan's Welsh full-back Jim Sullivan made his debut and kicked five goals, the first a 55-yard penalty. A legend was born as a player and he became a legendary coach at Knowsley Road some 30 years later. *1928* Test match #35: Australia 12 England 15 at the Exhibition Ground, Brisbane. This was flying winger Alf Ellaby's debut in an Ashes test, when he also scored a debut try. Fellow Saint Leslie Fairclough also notched a three-pointer – the first tries scored by Saints' players against Australia in test match rugby was a marvellous milestone.

24 JUNE

2006 Super League Round 18: St Helens 28 Salford City Reds 6 at Knowsley Road. Current Man of Steel Jamie Lyon chipped in with two tries and two goals with his usual poise and panache. A natural footballer. A footnote: Saints were flying at top of the table, with 30 points from 18 matches. Wigan Warriors were bottom, with eight points to their name. *2011* Super League Round 19: Warrington Wolves 35 St Helens 28 at the Halliwell Jones Stadium. A high-scoring affair, with Saints just falling short. These 'derby' clashes were always full of open rugby.

A marked man. Jamie Lyon cops a high tackle against Salford City Reds [Bernard Platt]

25 JUNE

1957 Test Match #104 (World Cup): Great Britain 21 New Zealand 29 at Sydney Cricket Ground. Austin Rhodes, a fantastic player, made his Test debut at stand-off. Leeds Scrum-half Jeff Stevenson was his partner in the halves. *2010* Super League Round 19: St. Helens 58 Salford City Reds 34 at GPW Recruitment Stadium Knowsley Road. In a real 'points fest' full-back and Man-of- the-Match Paul Wellens scored four tries. Jonny Lomax kicked nine goals from 10 attempts too.

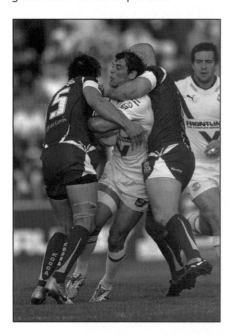 

Left: Stop him at all costs. Paul Wellens gets a high one against Salford City Reds in 2010.
Right: The grave of Cecile Herman at Christ Church, a sad reminder of the days without antibiotics.
[Alex Service]

26 JUNE

1889 Cecile Herman, the second child of Club Founder William Douglas Herman and his wife Alice, succumbed to the dreaded typhoid at the age of just 17 months. She is buried at Christ Church, Eccleston, to the right of the main entrance in a tiny grave, with an unusual, almost pyramidal design. Heart-breaking stuff. *1965* Mobile front-rower Andy Bateman was born in Leeds. A fireman, he joined Saints from Hunslet and his debut was the memorable 27–26 victory against the visiting Kiwis at Knowsley Road on 1 October 1989. Andy made 27 appearances, although was somewhat blighted by injuries. *1984* Test Match #224: Australia 18 Great Britain 6 at Lang Park, Brisbane. Any hope of Ashes glory duly disappeared with this loss in the second test, but on a club level, Saints' fans watched the performance of the big Australian centre Mal Meninga, who scored a try and kicked three goals. Rumours were that he was to 'winter' at Knowsley Road, which he duly did. The rest, as they say, is history. Scrum-half Neil Holding was the Saints' representative for the Lions that day.

2005 Challenge Cup Round 6: St Helens 75 Wigan Warriors 0 at Knowsley Road. St Helens. This did much to help us forget the disastrous league match in 1997 – and how. This was Wigan's worst-ever loss. Enough said? Well, no: Saints scored 13 tries, with interchange forward Mark Edmondson notching a hat-trick and stand-in kicker Paul Sculthorpe booting over nine goals. Sean Long was injured. His replacement? Jon Wilkin.

The aftermath of **that** 75–0 Challenge Cup game against the Old Enemy at an ecstatic Knowsley Road. Keiron Cunningham gives the thumbs up for a job well done. n the background the 'Scaff' roars its approval. [Bernard Platt]

27 JUNE

1933 Annual General Meeting at the Town Hall: "A special resolution proposed by E. Howard and seconded by J.W. Sweeney 'That a portion of the Popular Side Stand opposite the centre line be railed off for members only' was agreed." *2003* Super League Round 16: Bradford Bulls 0 St Helens 35 at Odsal. A great victory. How did they control the ball in the pouring rain? Veritable monsoon conditions at Odsal Top. Some would say: 'no change there, then!'

28 JUNE

1962 Second row star John Fieldhouse was born in Wigan. A fine player, John joined Saints from Widnes and it is a shame that his time at Knowsley Road tended to be blighted by injuries, even though he remained a regular at international level with Great Britain. *2002* Super League Round 16: St Helens 34 Bradford Bulls 26 at Knowsley Road. A breath-taking affair, with Paul Sculthorpe scoring two tries and kicking five goals. Paul Wellens, at scrum-half, also chipped in with two four-pointers. It was great entertainment. Mind you, Saints, the 'great entertainers' scored more tries than any other team in Super League VIII – 169.

29 JUNE

1976 World Club Challenge: Eastern Suburbs (Sydney) 25 St Helens 2 at Sydney Cricket Ground. Geoff Pimblett was the Saints' sole points scorer in this match Down Under, watched by 16,000 fans. It was a 'game too far' for the team, who had lost momentum after the English season finished on over a month before with the Premiership Final victory over Salford. *2008* Super League Round 19: St Helens 46 Huddersfield Giants 16 at the GPW Stadium. A convincing win for the homesters, with centre Willie Talau and Maurie Fa'asavalu scoring two tries apiece. Maurie in particular played like a man possessed.

Wish you were here. Saints players and officials are photographed at the famous Sydney Cricket Ground before the 1976 clash against the Roosters of Eastern Suburbs.
Back row: Stan Ince (director), Derek Noonan, Eddie Cunningham, Billy Benyon, George Nicholls, Roy Mathias, Eric Chisnall, Kel Coslett, Graham Liptrot, Eric Ashton (coach).
Front row: Ken Gwilliam, Jeff Heaton, Geoff Pimblett. [Alex Service]

30 JUNE

1945 Second-rower Don Stillwell, the son of an engineer, was born in India. The family later returned to Blighty, although it is believed that Don is the only 'Saint' to have been born on the sub-continent. *2001* Super League Round 17: Hull FC 34 St Helens 28 at the Boulevard. It was 16–16 at half time. The 'quiet man', Chris Joynt made his 87th successive appearance for the club, breaking hooker Harold Smith's 72-year-old club record from the late 1920s. Kiwi legend Sean Hoppe was his partner in the second row. It appeared that the team always needed his steadying influence on the field. If he came off to the bench for a bit of a rest, he was often recalled into the fray quite quickly, when it looked like the wheels were about to come off without his steadying influence. *2004* Australian flyer Darren Albert clinched the inaugural Powergen Fastest Man in Rugby League title in a time of 11.37 seconds over 100 metres on the track at Robin Park, Wigan. Former 1950s winger Stan McCormick was a Powderhall sprinter and Barry Ledger of the 1980s could give anyone a run for their money.

Left: Yorkshireman Harold Smith (obviously a hooker – look at those cauliflower ears, magnificent scars of battle) was once Saints' record successive appearance maker, until Chris Joynt came along! [Alex Service] Right: Whoosshh! Like a well-tuned Rolls Royce, Darren Albert glides in effortlessly to become rugby league's fastest man. [Bernard Platt]

July

Holiday mood?

Geoff Pimblett was a natural cricketer, the fastest bowler **never** to play for Lancashire, they reckon, who topped the Manchester Association's averages in 1970. He was no slouch with the bat, either.
[Alex Service]

In the 'good old days' of winter rugby, this would traditionally be the time when players and supporters would be enjoying an extended break from the game and thoughts turned to family holidays. Got the sun tan lotion then? Some would turn to other sports in the balmy English summer, like cricket. Apart from the redoubtable Pimblett, Jimmy Stott [UGB], Tom van Vollenhoven, Alan Hunte and New Zealander 'Jum' Turtill, before the First World War, were no mugs at all when it came to the leather and willow. Mind you, pre-season training would commence shortly. As for the days of Super League, it is mid-term in the race for honours – a time when clubs are beginning to gird their loins for the perceived 'business end' of the campaign just on the horizon, ending in glory at Old Trafford or, as in recent years, Wembley as well.

1 JULY

2011 Super League Round 20: St Helens 28 Hull FC 14 at the Stobart Stadium. A fine win for the red vee in their temporary home. Francis Meli with two, Chris Flannery, Tommy Makinson and Jonny Lomax scored tries, with Jamie Foster kicking four goals. There was an unfortunate twist, however, with Australian front-rower Josh Perry picking up the hamstring injury which ended his inaugural season. *2015* Full-back crisis at Langtree Park. Saints signed talented Australian full-back Adam Quinlan from Parramatta Eels to bolster the squad after an unfortunate series of circumstances left them struggling for a last line of defence. On 29 April New Zealand international Lance Hohaia, a former Kiwi legend in the number one jersey, had announced his retirement; another Australian, Shannon McDonnell snapped his Achilles at Castleford on 18 June and less than a week later club legend Paul Wellens was forced to retire himself through a hip problem. Tough old game, rugby league.

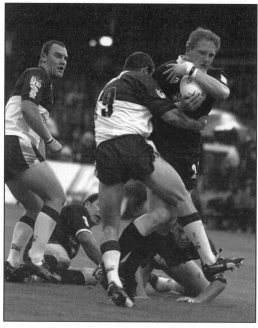 

Left: Young front-rower James Graham in action against Wakefield Trinity Wildcats in 2004;
Right: Jonny Lomax runs in a belter against Hull FC at the Saints' temporary home at Widnes in 2011.
[Bernard Platt]

2 JULY

2003 County of Origin: Yorkshire 56 Lancashire 6 at Odsal. Three Saints' players represented Lancashire in what was, effectively the last 'Roses match' of its kind: Paul Wellens at full-back; Martin Gleeson (right centre) and Keiron Cunningham (interchange). *2004* Super League Round 17: Wakefield Trinity Wildcats 41 St Helens 22 at Belle Vue. In unseasonably damp and cold conditions, the Saints looked rather jaded and, quite simply, just failed to ignite.

3 JULY

1981 Former Blackbrook junior Tim Jonkers was born in Amsterdam. The only Dutch Saint. A real workaholic second-rower, who scored a try in the 2000 Grand Final. It was such a pity that injuries eventually took their toll on his career. *1982* Former 'will o' the wisp' stand-off Jimmy Honey died aged 58. A fine finisher for the Saints in the late 1940s and early 1950s, he later joined Warrington and won Championship honours. *2006* Former Newcastle Knight, State of Origin and Australian international centre Matt Gidley signed on an initial two-year contract. He was to replace fellow countryman Jamie Lyon. Not a bad swap. *2016* Super League Round 20: Wakefield Trinity Wildcats 32 St Helens 44 at Belle Vue. Good game, this one, with Saints ahead 22–16 at the interval. Full-back Jonny Lomax scored two tries, with other four pointers spread between Morgan Knowles, James Roby, Jordan Turner, Greg Richards, Matty Fleming, and Mark Percival. The latter kicked six goals.

4 JULY

1961 From the boardroom: It was confirmed at the meeting that: "A selected panel of 18/20 players to train together as the first team, with special sprinting instruction from Tom van Vollenhoven." Who better? *1970* Test match #168: Australia 17 Great Britain 21 at Sydney Cricket Ground. Oh yes. The Ashes were won back after three successive series losses. The Skipper Frank Myler and Vice-Captain Cliff Watson came back to a warm welcome at Knowsley Road. Fully justified. *1976* Challenge Match: Auckland 20 St Helens 13, at Carlaw Park, Auckland. The end of an era in some ways. The last of the club's ground-breaking three-match tour to Australasia was the last game for four great Saints' players: Jeff Heaton, Frank Wilson, John Mantle and skipper Kel Coslett. Few clubs could afford to lose such talent en masse, even though anno domini was clearly a factor. *1999* Super League Round 17: St Helens 22 London Broncos 24 at Knowsley Road. This was Saints' first home defeat against a London-based side since a 3–2 loss to Streatham & Mitcham on 28 November 1936.

The Master and his method. Saints hooker Keiron Cunningham gets the attack rolling at The Boulevard in 2002. Hull's Lee Jackson, Paul King and Steve Prescott attempt to cover.
[Bernard Platt]

2002 Super League Round 17: Hull FC 30 St. Helens 32 at the Boulevard. A real roller-coaster encounter, this was our last visit to one of rugby league's most 'atmospheric' grounds before its eventual demolition. Our first visit? A 9–0 defeat on 1 February 1896.

5 JULY

1903 Peter 'Micky' Dale, a fine local-born forward and a great character who played in both the rugby union and Northern Union days for the club, died of consumption, aged 34. In the 1901 census, his employment was given as 'labourer at the manure works.' Tough job, but somebody had to do it. **1923** Wing wizard Stan McCormick was born in Oldham. A record £4,000 signing from Belle Vue Rangers early in 1949, Stan was a genius at interceptions – always a potentially risky business, but he had the knack and it paid off, more often than not. A member of Saints' Championship-winning team from 1953, he later went to Warrington, with equal success. A real character, Stan also coached the Saints in the early 1960s and was eventually replaced by Joe Coan. **1958** Test match #109 Australia 18 Great Britain 25 at the Exhibition Ground, Brisbane. Saints players Murphy, Prescott (broken arm) and Karalius (on Test debut) star in a fantastic backs-to-the-wall victory for the injury-ravaged tourists. Future Saint Dick Huddart, who was with Whitehaven at the time, was also in the second row. Karalius once described test match football as "like nuclear war – there are no prisoners, only survivors!" After hearing some of the graphic tales of Anglo-Australian test match battles, we can definitely see where he was coming from.

2008 Super League Round 20: Harlequins 0 St Helens 54 at The Stoop, Twickenham. The Saints team of 2008 was one of the most entertaining of all time – fact. We watched 'em and couldn't wait for the next match to come around. The visitors blew away the Quins in brilliant fashion, with nine players scoring the 10 tries. James Roby scored twice; Sean Long kicked six goals and Paul Sculthorpe added one. A stunning all-round performance.

Bernard Platt's image shows 'wrecking ball' centre Willie Talau adding to the carnage at The Stoop.

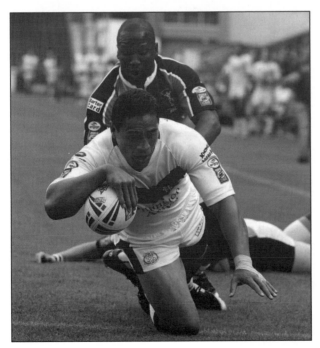

6 JULY

1971 From the Boardroom: "The Chairman reported that we had received the payment of £6,000 for the transfer of Cliff Watson from the Cronulla club." He had previously been presented with a testimonial cheque for £3,111–32d by Acting Club Chairman Cec Dromgoole (left) on 1 June in the Social Club at Knowsley Road. [Photo: Alex Service]

1974 Test Match #193 Australia 11 Great Britain 16 at Sydney Cricket Ground. An often brutal encounter, that ended with the series levelled. Saints' representatives Eckersley, Chisnall and Nicholls did us proud. In fact, 'Chissy' on his test debut scored a crucial try on 36 minutes and helped to create one for Colin Dixon just before half-time. Great stuff. *1994* Former centre and Captain Jimmy Stott died aged 74. Idolised by many who watched him in the early post-war years, Jimmy was a superb all-round footballer. His philosophy was indeed a Corinthian one: "If my opponent was better than me on the day, so be it." He played the game fairly and honestly, something to respect in such a tough professional sport as rugby league.

Codebreakers! Rugby league players who took part in rugby union internationals during the Second World War included Private Jimmy Stott (far right) who played for England. Others in the picture are (from left): Sergeant Trevor Foster, Lance Corporal Ted Ward and Sergeant Instructor Roy Francis. [Alex Service]

7 JULY

2001 Super League Round 18: St Helens 70 Warrington Wolves 16 at Knowsley Road. The Wire failed to win at Knowsley Road during the Super League era and there was little chance of breaking the hoodoo in this encounter. Paul Sculthorpe put his usual stamp on proceedings with two tries and 11 goals. *2006* Super League Round 20: St Helens 52 Catalans Dragons 26 at Knowsley Road. A real 'dragon-slaying' performance for the Saints, despite the absence of Willie Talau, Paul Sculthorpe, Lee Gilmour and Francis Meli. Right centre Jamie Lyon scored two tries and kicked eight goals, a 24-point haul, almost for the sheer fun of it. His future had, by this time, been decided: a four-year contract with Manly Sea Eagles in Sydney, but he ended the season on a high with Grand Final glory against Hull FC. What a great player. *2013* Super League Round 21: Castleford 24 St Helens 40 at the Jungle. Right winger Tommy Makinson scored three tries in fine style. What a superbly-entertaining encounter it was too.

8 JULY

1904 In Morley Street, St Helens, Albert Graham first saw the light of day. One of 11 siblings, two of his brothers lost their lives in the Great War, unfortunately not an uncommon occurrence at the time. Albert was a reliable utility back, who was asked to stand down for one match to give a new lad a chance to see what he could do in the seniors. Just Albert's luck – it was Alf Ellaby. *2012* Super League Round 20: Widnes Vikings 23 St Helens 24 at the Stobart Stadium. Stand-off Lee Gaskell kicked a fantastic last-minute conversion from the touchline to give the Saints what seemed to be an unlikely victory at one stage. It made one Saints' supporter, Katz, from Japan, a very happy man indeed.

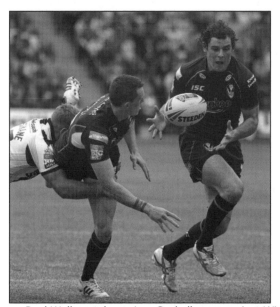 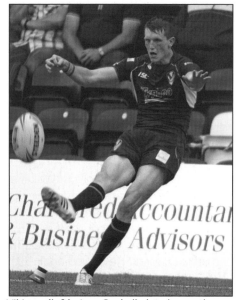

Paul Wellens takes a Lee Gaskell pass against Widnes Vikings (left); Lee Gaskell slots home the last-gasp winning goal [Bernard Platt]

9 JULY

1988 Test Match #248 (World Cup rated) Australia 12 Great Britain 26 at Sydney Football Stadium. Redemption Day. Left centre Paul Loughlin kicked three goals. Remember his half-break and pass for Henderson Gill's try? Party time for all Brits in Sydney that afternoon, even though the series had slipped away. *2000* Super League Round 18: Wigan Warriors 28 St Helens 30 at the JJB Stadium, Wigan. What a game, the epitome of a true 'derby' clash, with Tommy Martyn's late winning try, to complete a memorable hat-trick, verified by the video referee. Waiting for the decision seemed like an eternity, but when it appeared on the Big Screen, cue absolute bedlam in the West Stand. [Alex Service]

10 JULY

1883 Rumbustious second rower James 'Butcher' Prescott was born in St Helens. Two of his brothers played for Saints, although Butcher was the most prominent. His mobility enabled him to get on the scoresheet with reasonable regularity for a forward, with 66 tries in 254 appearances for the Saints. A Sergeant in the St Helens Pals during the First World War, he later became a member of the Committee over at local rivals St Helens Recs. *2004* Super League Round 18: St Helens 30 London Broncos 10 at Knowsley Road. Saints' tries were scored by John Stankevitch, Keith Mason, James Roby, Paul Wellens and a one for Samoan wingman Dominic Feaunati. Loose-forward Paul Sculthorpe kicked five goals. *2015* Super League Round 21: St Helens 35 Huddersfield 34 at Langtree Park. An amazing game in some ways, with a sensational hat-trick of tries on debut for former Paramatta player Adam Quinlan from full-back. Not many have done that in the red vee! Then this veritable 'cliff-hanger' was eventually settled by Australian scrum-half Luke Walsh's brilliant one-pointer. Breathless stuff indeed.

11 JULY

1970 Alan Hunte was born in Wakefield. He combined strength and speed to become one of the most effective wingers in the game in the early 1990s and represented Great Britain with fellow-Saint Gary Connolly in the centre. Alan was a good cricketer too, an aspect of his sporting life which was cut short with the advent of the Summer Super League. *2008* Hooker Dave Harrison died aged 69. A local lad, he found opportunities limited at Knowsley Road and joined Halifax. He played against the Saints in the 1966 Championship Final at Swinton. *2009* Super League Round 20: Warrington Wolves 26 St Helens 40 at Halliwell Jones Stadium. 'Young Gun' front-rower James Graham made his mark on the proceedings with a brace of tries.

12 JULY

1972 From the boardroom: Playing terms for 1972–73 were decided as follows for league matches: "£23 for a win at home. £26 for a win away. £10 for losing and £30 for the win against Wigan at home. £35 for a win against Wigan away. The above payments to include playing Sunday matches. Cup matches to be dealt with as a separate item." Beating Wigan has always been a priority – especially for the fans! *2002* Test Match #300 Australia 64 Great Britain 10 at Aussie Stadium, Sydney. This was no way to celebrate Great Britain's 300th test match. Why, oh why did this 'one-off' international have to take place in the first instance? Madness. The result, given jet lag and short preparation time, was predictable, to say the least. Paul Wellens – at centre, Paul Sculthorpe and Keiron Cunningham were in the starting line-up, with Chris Joynt and Martin Gleeson on the bench, who all bore the inevitable mental and physical scars of defeat during the long flight home.

13 JULY

1997 Super League Round 17: St Helens 38 Halifax Blue Sox 20 at Knowsley Road. After an injury-hit and generally 'up and down' few months, the Saints gave us something to cheer about. Star of the show? Speedster Anthony Sullivan, who scored a brilliant hat-trick of touchdowns. No-one could get near him on the day.

Anthony Sullivan flies towards the try-line against Halifax Blue Sox. Visiting hooker Paul Rowley can only try and force him wider for the conversion. [Alex Service]

2001 Super League Round 19: St Helens 46 Leeds Rhinos 24 at Knowsley Road. Paul Sculthorpe, the reigning Man of Steel led the way with three tries and seven goals. He was the best around in Super League at the time, wasn't he?

14 JULY

1962 Test Match #132 Australia 18 Great Britain 17 at Sydney Cricket Ground. The series was already won and Australia prevented a first-ever whitewash on their own soil in a full Ashes series with a last-gasp try from Ken Irvine, who scored in the corner and converted it shortly afterwards. Saints' representatives were Mick Sullivan, Alex Murphy and rampaging second-rower Dick Huddart.

1969 From the Boardroom: "The Chairman [Harry Cook] opened the meeting and asked all the members to rise and observe a few moments silence as a token of respect for a former member of the Board, Mr Joe Harrison, who died during the season". A long-standing member of the club, right from the pre-war days, he was Chief Executive of the UGB glass company in the town. *1996* Super League Round 16: St Helens 58 Halifax Blue Sox 20 at Knowsley Road. Saints' young number 9, Keiron Cunningham, scored three seemingly unstoppable tries. All told, he scored three hat-tricks for the club during his long career. *2006* Welsh hooker Reg Blakemore died in St Helens aged 81. Reg signed from Newport RUFC and became a fixture at Knowsley Road, with his ability to hook the ball and dominate in the loose. For three seasons, 1949–50, 1952–53 and 1953–54, he played in over 40 matches. He was part of the Welsh connection which served Saints so well over the years.

St Helens RFC 1948–49. Back: Jack Grundy, Reg Blakemore, Jimmy Lowe, Alan Prescott, Bill Whittaker, Len Aston, Walter Norris. Front: Jimmy Honey, Steve Llewellyn, Jimmy Stott (Capt), Stan McCormick. On ground: Ray Huyton, Doug Greenall. [Alex Service]

15 JULY

1958 Evenin' all! Fred Leyland, a durable front-rower joined the Saints from St Helens RUFC. A police officer, he made 55 appearances in the red and white jersey from 1958 to 1962. *2005* Super League Round 21: St Helens 40 Wigan Warriors 18 at Knowsley Road. No respite for Wigan, following the 75–0 Challenge Cup tie. Saints were comfortable winners on the day, with James Roby [aged 19] and Jon Wilkin [21] dominating in the halves.

No stopping him! Hooker supreme Keiron Cunningham adds to Wigan's woes in 2005. Later-to-be-Saint Bryn Hargreaves is in the hooped jersey behind him. [Bernard Platt]

16 JULY

1944 Lest we forget. At the age of 29, Flying Officer Billy Hough's plane, part of 44 Rhodesian Squadron, crashed over the North Sea. His name is commemorated on the RAF memorial at Runnymede. Billy made 37 appearances for the club, his last on 11 September 1937 at home to Broughton Rangers in the Lancashire Cup. *1969* One small step for man. One *giant* step for the Saints. Apollo Perelini, born in Auckland, New Zealand, was later named after the first manned spacecraft that landed on the moon on 20 July. He always used to joke that he was lucky the Russians didn't get there first. 'Sputnik' certainly does not have the same ring, somehow. Nicknamed 'The Terminator' from his days in rugby union, he became a Saints' great, making 193 appearances before taking up the reins as fitness conditioner at the club and now has a rugby academy in Dubai. Good on him. *2000* Super League Round 19: St Helens 40 Huddersfield/Sheffield Giants 24 at Knowsley Road. The one and only home clash against the 'awkwardly-merged' entity. A non-starter. End of. *2015* Super League Round 22: Warrington Wolves 14 St Helens 20 at Halliwell Jones Stadium. Giant interchange forward Mose Masoe came off the bench to score a crushing four-pointer, with the impetus of a runaway dumper truck. *2017* Super League Round 22: St Helens 46 Catalans Dragons 28 at the Totally Wicked Stadium. A try and nine goals for 'young gun' centre Mark Percival, soon to be selected for the England World Cup squad later in the year.

Unstoppable! Mose Masoe leaves Warrington's Ben Westwood (left) and Stefan Ratchford in his wake to score a brilliant four-pointer under the sticks at Halliwell Jones in 2015. [RLPhotos.com]

17 JULY

1988 Test Match #249 New Zealand 12 Great Britain 10 at Addington Showgrounds, Christchurch. A crucial match for both teams; New Zealand had to win to qualify for the World Cup Final in October; The Brits just needed a draw. Paul Loughlin scored a first-minute try, although he found that place-kicking in the cloying mud was not easy. Shane Cooper ('of Mangere East and St Helens' said the match programme) was at stand-off for New Zealand and had a fine match with his superlative handling skills. *2016* Super League Round 22: Huddersfield Giants 18 St Helens 34 at the Galpharm Stadium, Huddersfield. Saints' fourth win in succession lifted them into fourth place in the table. It was the first game for new Huddersfield – and former Newcastle Knights – coach Rick Stone. Another former Knight, scrum-half Luke Walsh, who had returned from injury, was in superb form for the visitors.

18 JULY

1922 Former dual code international loose forward Ray Cale was born in Usk, South Wales. A crunching tackler, former Chairman Harry Cook would often visibly wince at his some of his devil-may-care challenges. A greengrocer, he was a popular character during his spell at Knowsley Road before moving back to Wales. *1999* Super League Round 19: St Helens 74 Hull Sharks 16 at Knowsley Road. Despite rumblings about coach Ellery Hanley's suspension as a backdrop, the Saints ran riot, with a try and 11 goals from stand-off Tommy Martyn. It all came right in the end and Saints won the Grand Final. *2003* Super League Round 19: St Helens 22 Huddersfield Giants 18 at Knowsley Road. Saints came from 14–0 down at half-time to win, in front of 9,288 fans. Never write them off at any price.

19 JULY

1948 Flying winger Les Jones was born in St Helens. After his memorable interception try against Wigan at Central Park on his debut, he certainly endeared himself early to the Saints' faithful. He does tend to go 'under the radar' somewhat. Why? He is the club's second-highest try-scorer: 282 from a staggering 485 appearances – above the great Ellaby. Only Vol scored more. A genuine bloody legend. *1958* Test Match #110: Australia 17 Great Britain 40 at Sydney Cricket Ground. A game rated as one of his finest by scrum-half Alex Murphy, whose long-distance solo effort was the second-half game-breaker for the British as they clinched the Ashes in stupendous style. No foot off the accelerator for the rampaging Brits, who ran up their biggest score in an Ashes test to date and won the series for the first time on Australian soil for the first time since the 'Indomitables' of 1946. Happy days. *1996* Super League Round 17: Oldham Bears 18 St Helens 54 at Boundary Park. Saints maintained their challenge for an inaugural European Super League title at the town's football ground.

20 JULY

1974 Test Match #194: Australia 22 Great Britain 18 at Sydney Cricket Ground. Heartbreak for the Brits as the Australians win the rubber 2–1 in front of 55,505 fans. Saints' Eric Chisnall and George Nicholls were in the back row. *2007* Super League Round 21: St Helens 19 Wigan Warriors 12 at Knowsley Road. 10–6 to Wigan at half-time. Saints' try-scorers included Jason Cayless, Leon Pryce and Francis Meli. Sean Long came off the bench to kick two goals

and a drop-goal. Paul Wellens also added a further two-pointer.

The immaculate James Roby off-loads against Wigan Warriors in 2007 at Knowsley Road. Full-back Paul Wellens awaits the outcome on the left. [Bernard Platt]

21 JULY

1928 Test Match #37 Australia 21 England 14 at Sydney Cricket Ground. Saints' stand-off Les Fairclough scored two tries in a memorable individual performance. He was one of the first English players to be 'noticed' by several Sydney clubs and was offered the tenancy of some public houses Down Under, among other possible inducements. Yet he stayed with the Saints and eventually became a director of the club in the late 1940s.

1933 From the *St Helens Newspaper*: "The Saints have made a business-like start. Their leading players were up for practising training on Tuesday and on Wednesday Mr Edward Massey, the international rugby union player was appointed manager and coach to the team. Mr Massey played for England, Lancashire County and Leicester County and his name was a famous one in the international teams for 1920 to 1925. He has a practical knowledge and experience of the game that should be of very useful service to the St Helens club. He will commence his duties next week." An interesting and in some ways forward-thinking appointment, although financial restrictions were already starting to bite at Knowsley Road and his tenure was not a particularly long one. **1997** World Club Challenge: Cronulla Sharks 28 St Helens 12 at Shark Park. Andy Leathem played a fine game in the front row, despite being bitten by a poisonous spider some time before during his stay Down Under. Apparently the spider survived the experience too.

22 JULY

2006 Super League Round 22: Leeds Rhinos 14 St Helens 18 at Headingley. Saints pulled off a marvellous win in the summer drizzle, despite having Jamie Lyon dismissed, for the only time in his career. Maybe it was an awkward challenge but trying to tackle Robbie Burrow was the stuff of nightmares for anyone. He subsequently escaped suspension. **2013** Super League Round 22: St Helens 22 Wigan Warriors 16 at Langtree Park Stadium. Young second-rower Joe Greenwood scored a memorable try as Saints defeat the Old Enemy for the first time at their new home of the Red Vee in Peasley Cross. Couldn't have a better Christening. Yeeeeessssss!

Up against it now in the rain at Headingley. Bernard Platt's dramatic image shows referee Ashley Klein brandishing the dreaded red card to fellow Australian Jamie Lyon (far right).

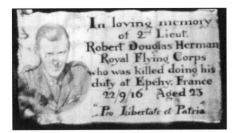

23 JULY

1893 Robert Douglas Herman, son of the club's founder William, was baptised at Christ Church, Eccleston. A First World War casualty, a superb stained-glass window can be found in the church itself in his image. [Alex Service]

1999 Super League Round 20: Leeds Rhinos 12 St Helens 28 at Headingley. Saints got caught up in traffic and are asked if they wanted the kick-off delayed, despite the presence of television. "My boys are ready" insisted coach Ellery Hanley – and how right he was. The stuff of legend. **2004** Super League Round 20: Leeds Rhinos 70 St Helens 0 at Headingley 16,635. More tales from the home of the Rhinos. Ooops apocalypse. 38–0 down at half-time as the Saints embark on a mini crisis results-wise, having been battered 34–6 at Hull the previous week. Three further defeats followed in the next four matches, as the momentum for league success stalled somewhat after Challenge Cup glory.

24 JULY

2011 Challenge Cup Round 6: St Helens 54 Hull KR 6 at the Autoquest Stadium, Widnes. Winger Jamie Foster kicked seven goals with metronomic precision in this comprehensive thrashing of the visitors from Humberside at the Saints' temporary home. Young winger Tommy Makinson (right) in his debut season as a Saint, scored a brace of touchdowns. [Bernard Platt]

2015 Super League Round 23: St Helens 52 Hull KR 12 at Langtree Park. A fine team performance picked up the points. In the backs, Adam Swift with two, Adam Quinlan and Matty Dawson scored tries; forwards Joe Greenwood with two, Atelia Vea and Mark Flanagan did the same. And what about the halves? The Australian duo of Travis Burns with a try and Luke Walsh, who kicked eight goals, also got into the act.

Before the Challenge Cup game against Hull KR in 2011, chief executive Tony Colquitt (centre) presented special commemorative pennants on behalf of the Saints' Heritage Society to members of the 1961 Challenge Cup winning team who, 50 years before, helped to beat Wigan 12–6 at Wembley. Players are, from left to right: Abe Terry, Brian McGinn, Austin Rhodes and Wilf Smith. [Bernard Platt]

25 JULY

1997 World Club Championship: Auckland Warriors 70 St Helens 6 at Erikson Stadium, Auckland. Jet-lagged, battered and blue, the Saints succumbed, perhaps predictably, in this return match. Alan Hunte scored our only try, but no consolation whatsoever. *2014* Super League Round 22: St Helens 44 Widnes Vikings 22 at Langtree Park. Right winger Tommy Makinson flew in for a memorable hat-trick of touchdowns. On his day he was the epitome of the modern winger: fast, a competent kick-returner and could score tries from seemingly impossible situations by the corner flag.

26 JULY

1998 Super League Round 14: Wigan Warriors 36 St Helens 2 'On the Road' at Vetch Field, Swansea. Arguably the end of the initial Super League impetus of success was becoming apparent. This was also Bobbie Goulding's last game in the red vee before joining Huddersfield Giants. A great pity. A truly effervescent character, Bobbie is forever revered by Saints' fans for his ability to get the backline moving and his captaincy of the famous 1996 'double' team in particular. *2008* Challenge Cup Semi-Final: St Helens 26 Leeds Rhinos 16 at the Galpharm Stadium. One of James Graham's most memorable matches. "They were saying they were going to do this and that to us and we beat them in the end in one of the hottest games I ever played in. A great performance." Jammer's right; it was really hot.

Front-rower Bryn Hargreaves turns up the heat for the Saints against Leeds Rhinos in the 2008 Semi-Final clash with his brilliant touchdown. [Bernard Platt]

27 JULY

1970 Henry Greenall, Saints' left-winger in the 1915 Challenge Cup Final, died aged 79. A member of a famous sporting family, both his younger brothers found fame in the halves – for rivals St Helens Recreation. Henry, who worked in the export department at Pilkington Brothers glass works lived in Leslie Road, Thatto Heath for most of his life and spent a few evenings a week in his local, the British Lion, where he would always have two gills of bitter – nothing more. *1996* Super League Round 18: London Broncos 28 St Helens 32 at Charlton Athletic FC's The Valley. The Video Referee's decision to award a four-pointer to Apollo Perelini – quite rightly, in our opinion and Apollo's – ensured that Saints' inaugural Super League title aspirations remained well on course. Pure theatre. We thought it was always nailed on. But what a contest – typical of the games between these two sides during a momentous opening campaign of summer rugby league.

28 JULY

1906 Quicksilver winger Roy Hardgrave was born in Auckland, New Zealand. Small, though powerful, with great acceleration, this guy was a real fans' favourite at Knowsley Road when he came over with the other two Kiwis – Lou Hutt and Trevor Hall – before the start of the 1929–30 season. Dare I say, it: the Jason Robinson of his day?

Roy Hardgrave in typical hand-off mode in New Zealand club rugby league and in his Saints' jersey.
[Alex Service]

1951 The *Brisbane Courier-Mail* reported that Alf Ellaby hoped to acquire a farm property and settle in Australia. Alf did want to settle in Australia and initially 'sold up' in this country and had actually gone out there for that reason. Yet family needs came first and he returned to become a very popular and successful licensee in Garforth, near Leeds. **1966** Centre and goal-kicker supreme Paul Loughlin was born in St Helens and followed his father Terry by playing for the Saints – but not in the front row like his dad.

2007 Challenge Cup Semi-Final: St Helens 35 Bradford Bulls 14 at the Galpharm Stadium, Huddersfield. This can be summed up as a comprehensive victory. Job done. Bernard Platt's image of Mike Bennett after scoring a try in this game (left) shows the tremendous adrenaline rush in helping to get your team to Wembley and, of course, the sheer joy of playing for the Saints.

126

29 JULY

1896 Half-back Jack Halsall was born in St Helens. A powerful footballer, although not the biggest, he played 40 matches for the club in the War Emergency League, together with 99 senior games when competitive rugby resumed after the First World War. Alas, he crossed the Rubicon and joined rivals St Helens Recreation in 1923. *1962* Shock-horror for Saints' fans. Vince Karalius, the one and only Wild Bull of the Pampas, was 'open to transfer' for a fee of £8,000. He would join his hometown club Widnes soon afterwards and captained them to Wembley glory in 1964. *2001* Super League Round 21: Salford City Reds 18 St Helens 56 at the Willows. A brilliant performance from the visitors, typified by a clinical hat-trick from full-back Paul Wellens, with Paul Sculthorpe booting over eight goals and scoring at try himself for good measure. What a player – in his 'pomp' then. *2006* Challenge Cup Semi-Final: St Helens 50 Hull KR 0 at the Galpharm Stadium, Huddersfield. Rockin' Robins indeed. Second tier Rovers were no match for the Saints in this mood. Jamie Lyon scored a try and kicked seven goals and, just to rub it in somewhat, former Rover Jon Wilkin helped himself to a brace of touchdowns. Twickenham – and Old Trafford – and a famous 'treble' beckoned.

It's that man again! Willie Talau crashes over for a four-pointer in the 2006 Challenge Cup Semi-Final against Hull KR. He was unstoppable on the day. [Bernard Platt]

30 JULY

2002 Super League Round 18: Wigan Warriors 22 St Helens 8 at the JJB Stadium, Wigan. Despite a try from Tommy Martyn and two goals from Paul Sculthorpe, it wasn't enough for second-placed St Helens against the team in third. All relative, as the Saints went unbeaten for the remainder of the campaign. Next up? Warrington Wolves at Knowsley Road and a 72–2 flogging for the unfortunate visitors.

2005 Challenge Cup Semi-Final: St Helens 8 Hull FC 34 at Galpharm Stadium, Huddersfield. The Black and Whites derailed Saints' Wembley hopes in somewhat comprehensive fashion – and eventually lifted the trophy itself in Cardiff. Would the Old Faithful ever win at Wembley? Well, yes they did, in 2016 and beat Saints along the way once again.

31 JULY

1954 Test Match #87: New Zealand 20 Great Britain 14 at Wingham Park, Greymouth. Saints' Alan Prescott was a stalwart in the front row as he had been during every international of the tour. It was also centre Duggie Greenall's one and only international in Australasia, although he did have a hand in two of the tries for the visitors in front of a 4,250 crowd on the West Coast at what must be one of the smallest venues ever for such a prestigious match. The Lions went on to secure the rubber 2–1, with a 12–6 win at Carlaw Park in Auckland a fortnight later. **1965** Second-rower George Mann was born in Auckland. A superb running forward, George was always one who other players wanted 'in the trenches' with them. His first try at Knowsley Road, against Featherstone Rovers, was a real belter. **2011** Super League Round 23: Castleford Tigers 26 St Helens 46 at the Jungle, Wheldon Road. Arm wrestles? Who needs 'em! A high-scoring affair, this one, as these matches often were, with Saints out-scoring their opponents, as they often did, in fine style. Pure entertainment. Full-back Paul Wellens scored a fine brace of touchdowns.

On the fly at Castleford in 2011. James Roby (left) and Jon Wilkin enjoy acres of space at the Jungle as the Saints come away with the points. [Bernard Platt]

August

Friendly Fire and Wembley Glory.

2007 Challenge Cup Final: St Helens 30 Catalans Dragons 8. Simply unforgettable! James Roby (left) the first-ever try-scorer at the 'new' Wembley and Mal Meninga – are photographed with the gleaming trophy in a jubilant dressing room. [Bernard Platt]

In the 'good old days' August was quite a benign month, starting with friendly clashes against opponents such as Barrow (Ward Cup) and Liverpool City (Gallie Trophy) as the squad flexed their muscles for the early Lancashire Cup rounds and league openers against traditional opponents, such as Widnes for many years before the Second World War. Yet the prospect of good weather made watching games quite pleasurable, home and away, with several midweek matches thrown in with the good light. In the Super League calendar, there has been a switch of emphasis, with the Wembley showpiece switched to the August Bank Holiday weekend. A good move? Given recent transport complications, perhaps not. The idea was to make both cup and league reach a conclusion towards the end of the campaign, rather than the Challenge Cup be a 'pre-season' competition. Saints have won three Challenge Cups since the change: 2006 at Twickenham and a Wembley double in 2007 and 2008. Will it ever return to May? There is now, of course, the Magic Weekend thrown into the mix and it seems unlikely. A great shame. Yet pre-Super League, the Championship Final followed the Wembley showpiece, so that, presumably, is the rationale in the modern era, despite the logistics being ever more complicated. Don't overspend on your summer holidays – we might be going to Wembley.

1 AUGUST

1907 Saints' loose-forward Tom Griffin was born in Garryowen, Limerick – a fine rugby-related place name if there ever was one. A master carpenter, he made 34 appearances before his transfer to Warrington in 1934.

Talking of Tom Griffin, his stay at Saints was relatively short before his transfer to Warrington. He is second from the right on this magnificent image of St Helens players in more formal garb. This could well be a testimonial event for the great Alf Ellaby, stood next to Tom on the left. Others in the picture are, left to right: Bob Atkin, Leslie Fairclough, Jack Garvey, Bob Jones and Ben Halfpenny far right. [Alex Service]

2014 Super League Round 23: Hull FC 19 St Helens 12 at the KC Com Stadium. Tries were scored by Paul Wellens and Tommy Makinson. Rising star Mark Percival kicked two goals. Injuries were starting to bite in the run-in to the League Leader's Shield and an ultimate Grand Final place. Were we worried? Yes, to be honest, but it all came right in the end.

2 AUGUST

1996 Super League Round 19: Castleford Tigers 16 St Helens 20 at Wheldon Road. Anthony Sullivan scored two tries, but the match is best remembered for brilliant cover tackling by Steve Prescott and Joey Hayes when, in the last few seconds, Castleford full-back Jason Flowers looked certain to score and clinch the spoils - and with it, Saints' hopes of an inaugural Super League title. "Desperate situations call for desperate men," said a somewhat relieved Saints coach Shaun McRae afterwards. How right he was. *1998* Super League Round 15: St Helens 68 Huddersfield Giants 18 at Knowsley Road. Given their recent patchy form before this game, this was a 'must-win' scenario. Three tries from redoubtable full-back Paul Atcheson took the eye; Sean Long kicked 10 goals, watched by just 4,227 fans, a measure of how the team's recent form had slumped.

3 AUGUST

2003 Super League Round 21: London Broncos 18 St Helens 30 at Brentford FC's Griffin Park. Australian front-rower Darren Britt played his 50th game for the club on a sweltering day in London. Even he thought it was hot. Six days later his career was over after an accidental clash of heads with fellow Australian Barry Ward, against Hull FC at Knowsley Road.

Phew what a scorcher! Darren Britt (left) feels the heat in Brentford, while (right) second-rower Tim Jonkers is about to bite the dust in the same game. [Bernard Platt]

2007 Super League Round 22: St Helens 31 Hull FC 20 at Knowsley Road. Our first look at former Sydney Roosters and Queensland Origin star Chris Flannery, who could operate either at centre or in the back row. A really quality signing from Down Under. Left winger Francis Meli also roared in for a hat-trick of tries. His centre was fellow Kiwi Willie Talau. Francis scored 145 tries in over 200 matches for the Saints and this was one of his five hat-tricks in the red vee.

4 AUGUST

1890 the new Theatre Royal was opened under the distinguished patronage of his worship the Mayor (and former Original Saint) CJ Bishop and the Aldermen and councillors of the Borough of St Helens. The Theatre, in Corporation Street was given a makeover in 1964 and has hosted several Saints-related events over the years since then. *1997* World Club Championship: Penrith Panthers 32 St Helens 24 at Penrith Football Stadium. In what proved to be a bizarre finale, Penrith went out of the competition. Saints lived to fight again, facing a play-off against PSG at Knowsley Road and a future quarter-final in Brisbane and total annihilation. *2006* Super League Round 23: St Helens 56 Huddersfield Giants 8 at Knowsley Road. Towering New Zealand international front-rower Jason Cayless scored one of his team's tries. He was to repeat the performance in the Challenge Cup final several weeks later at Twickenham against the same opponents.

5 AUGUST

1957 Front-row legend Kevin Ward was born in Wakefield. We thought he was made from girders, but not born in Scotland. The classic example of a player who enjoyed an 'Indian Summer' to his career. In the 'Noughties, Paul Anderson, from Bradford Bulls was another case in point. Two cracking players in their own way. *2005* Super League Round 23: Warrington Wolves 10 St Helens 30 at Halliwell Jones. Another superb victory for the rampant Saints and a case, almost, of 'business as usual'. They really seemed to enjoy their matches against the Wire – for obvious reasons.

6 AUGUST

1982 Testimonial match: St Helens 57 Pilkington Recs 7 at Knowsley Road. A match in aid of the Roy Mathias testimonial. Was this a 'friendly'? Didn't seem to be at the time, with local pride at stake. It was almost a throwback to the raucous clashes between the wars, when both teams were in the Northern Rugby League and families were often divided in their affiliations. *2011* Challenge Cup Semi-Final: St Helens 12 Wigan Warriors 18 at Halliwell Jones Stadium, Warrington. A bitter blow, with Wigan coach Michael Maguire ensuring they did their utmost to secure a Challenge Cup Final place. Saints duly lost their third successive semi-final. Winger Jamie Foster scored all the points, with two tries and two goals.

Rip-roaring Kevin Ward takes the ball up against former club Castleford at Knowsley Road. No wonder he was such a fans' favourite. [Sportsphoto Ltd]

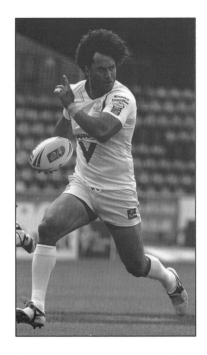

Heartbreak on both counts. Left: Powerhouse winger Francis Meli on the charge against Leeds Rhinos in the 2010 Challenge Cup Semi-Final at Huddersfield; right: Jonny Lomax about to execute his own special 'galloping side-step' during the 2011 Challenge Cup Semi-Final at Warrington. Wigan's Ryan Hoffman tries to work him out. [Bernard Platt]

7 AUGUST

1879 Scrum-half James Peters was born in Queen Street, Salford. James became the first player of Afro-Caribbean descent to represent England at rugby union, before joining Barrow RLFC, where he was signed by the Saints. *2010* Challenge Cup Semi-Final: St Helens 28 Leeds Rhinos 32 at the Galpharm Stadium, Huddersfield. Saints were 18–8 ahead at the interval, yet the Rhinos triumphed in the end. A real disappointment.

8 AUGUST

1959 Ward Cup: St Helens 50 Barrow 3 at Knowsley Road. South African flyer Jan Prinsloo scored six tries in this charity encounter. Jan had a marvellous strike rate of 70 tries in 89 appearances for the Saints. *2004* Super League Round 22: Salford City Reds 30 St Helens 20 at The Willows. Two tries from right winger Ade Gardner, with his centre, Darren Albert, also getting on the scoresheet with a four-pointer. Yet it was Salford's first Super League victory against the Saints in seven years.

2015 Super League Super 8s Round 1: Catalans Dragons 26 St Helens 16 at the Gilbert Brutus Stadium, Perpignan. Our first match in the new 'unknown' league re-organisation concept. Most supporters, given the short notice, just couldn't get there, as they normally might have done, at the height of the holiday season.

Quicksilver winger Jan Prinsloo in action against Swinton at Station Road [Alex Service]

9 AUGUST

1897 Saints' centre and captain from the 1920s, George Lewis (right), was born just outside Pontypool at Pentrepiod. George, who was Alf Ellaby's favourite centre partner, was a fantastic servant to the St Helens club, making 428 appearances, scoring 45 tries and kicking 850 goals. He was the first Saints captain to lift the League Championship Trophy too, in 1932. [Photo courtesy Dave Makin]

1910 The *St Helens Newspaper* talked about Saints' new playing strip for the forthcoming campaign: "The Saints will not this season be dubbed the All Blacks for they are to appear in all the splendour of new jerseys, which will be blue and

black hoops with a black saddle round the shoulders, padded, leather-edged and laced up front. The new rig out will be on view at [full-back] Turtill's shop this week." Hundreds went to see it when it was displayed too. Those were the days. **1943** At a Committee meeting in the Pavilion at Knowsley Road, RH (Rex) Winter (Chairman) and Henry Tomlinson (Vice-Chairman) were re-elected to their positions of responsibility until the commencement of the 1945–46 season. **2009** Challenge Cup Semi-Final: St Helens 14 Huddersfield Giants 24 at Halliwell Jones Stadium, Warrington. Coach Nathan Brown's Huddersfield team out-wrestled (ugh!) and out-thought a below-par St Helens. Francis Meli scored a brilliant hat-trick of tries but scant consolation in the circumstances.

Big Tony Puletua charges through the Huddersfield Giants defence at the Halliwell Jones in the 2009 Challenge Cup Semi-Final. James Graham, John Wilkin, Paul Wellens and James Roby are the other Saints in the photo. [Bernard Platt]

10 AUGUST

1957 Ward Cup: St Helens 79 Barrow 13 at Knowsley Road. Scrum-half Alex Murphy scored a hat-trick as Saints ran riot in this pre-season charity romp. *1971* Strike centre Paul Newlove was born in Pontefract. The signing that confirmed Saints' future Super League ambitions in 1995, he was so nimble on his feet for a big man. Sometimes agility, just as much as size and power is a real bonus.

11 AUGUST

1928 Powerhouse centre Bill Finnan was born in St Helens. The former Rivington Road schoolboy left Knowsley Road in the early 1950s to join Salford, but returned to win a Challenge Cup winner's medal in 1956 in the club's inaugural Wembley victory against Halifax. Bill liked to run with the ball held out in front of him on the flat of his hand.

2007 Super League Round 23: Catalans Dragons 21 St Helens 0 at the Stade Gilbert Brutus. Mon Dieu! A long way to go to see a big fat zero. There was consolation exactly two weeks later, when the Saints beat them 30–8 at the 'new' Wembley Stadium, to lift the Challenge Cup for the second successive year.

12 AUGUST

2005 Super League Round 24: St Helens 60 Wakefield Trinity Wildcats 4 at Knowsley Road. A hat-trick from flying winger Australian Darren Albert, the last of his 88 for the Saints before moving back to the NRL in Australia with the Cronulla Sharks. One of the four-pointers has been captured below by Bernard Platt.

2012 Academy tour: Australian Schoolboys 40 England Academy 14 at Wynnum Manly. England lined up with four St Helens players: Greg Wilde (full-back), Mark Percival (left centre) and Dom Speakman and Luke Thompson on the interchange bench. From small acorns, as they say. *2016* Super League Super 8s Round 2: St Helens 39 Catalans Dragons 16 at Langtree Park. Gamestar? Undoubtedly left winger Adam Swift, who roared in for four stunning touchdowns. Half-back Luke Walsh was also outstanding with his distribution and kicking game against the club he would later join for the 2017 campaign.

13 AUGUST

1997 World Club Challenge Play-Off: St Helens 26 Paris St Germain 4 at Knowsley Road. Despite not winning any matches, the Saints had to play a qualifier for the quarter-finals. What lay ahead? A trip to play Brisbane Broncos. Incentive enough, you might think. Needless to say, it was a bridge too far, Saints losing 66–12. *2006* Super League Round 24: Castleford Tigers 4 St Helens 72 at the Jungle. Legendary centre Jamie Lyon scored two tries and kicked 12 goals in this one-sided affair. His 32 points is third in the all-time list behind Sean Long against UTC in 2003 and Paul Loughlin against Carlisle in 1986. It was also the team's third-best 'away' win in their history, but let's not get carried away.

14 AUGUST

1954 Northern Rugby League: St Helens 31 Widnes 3 at Knowsley Road. A bit of a one-sided affair. The Saints opened their new scoreboard and clock in the corner of the Popular Side and Dunriding Lane End, which became a feature of the ground for many years afterwards. Unfortunately, a mechanical problem stopped it from working on the day. Now, how many points have we scored so far? *2015* Super League Super 8s Round 2: St Helens 22 Hull FC 32 at Langtree Park. 10,203 fans watched the Saints defeated by their 'bogey' team at the new stadium. The electronic scoreboard functioned fully this time, unfortunately.

15 AUGUST

1967 From the Boardroom: "Mr Martin reported that it had not been possible to enclose completely the Boys Pen. It was therefore decided to allow boys access to all parts of the ground and to open a second entrance at the Edington End of the ground." Situated directly behind the posts at the Pavilion End, the Boys Pen holds special memories for hundreds of supporters in their younger days. *1985* Australian Brett French was signed from Wynnum Manly for the 1985–86 campaign. This guy was quick for sure, and formed a dynamic centre partnership with Kiwi Mark Elia. His brother, Ian, a back-rower, later played for Castleford.

Left: Australian centre Brett French in his Saints jersey [Brian Peers]. Right: 'Maybe you'll play for Saints one day like me.' Nick Fozzard enthrals a group of youngsters during a coaching Open Day at Knowsley Road on 13 August 2005. [Bernard Platt]

16 AUGUST

1901 The *St Helens Newspaper* talked about personnel for the forthcoming season and said that Saints would have one of their best forwards available: "Carney has come back from fighting the Boers". Rather him than me. Fix bayonets and stand fast.

1928 Scrum-half Harry Frodsham, (left courtesy Dave Makin) brother of Great Britain threequarter Alf, signed for the Saints. He went on to make 197 appearances from 1928 to 1936 before joining Liverpool Stanley.

1969 Northern Rugby League: St Helens 27 Castleford 3 at Knowsley Road. Former Wakefield Trinity and Bradford Northern winger Berwyn Jones made his debut and scored a try. Jones was a former sprinter and British record holder for the 100 metres – 10.3 seconds, so he could trap a bit. When he first played for Wakefield, it was under the pseudonym 'A. Walker'. Brilliant.

17 AUGUST

1889 The *St Helens Newspaper* wrote that Saints' first opponents for the new season were originally Wakefield Trinity at Knowsley Road, but explained that "the Trinitarians were discovered to have been advancing the welfare of one of their team in an illegal manner and they are being hung up to dry till the end of October." Warrington took their place. *2012* Super League Round 25: St Helens 44 Castleford Tigers 12 at Langtree Park, St Helens. Saints had bedded themselves down in their new stadium and produced a convincing performance with seven players scoring tries. Third place was assured.

18 AUGUST

1891 Utility back Teddy McLoughlin was born in St. Helens and first played for the club in early January 1914. On 4 September 1914, a month after war was declared, he enlisted with the famous 11th Service Battalion South Lancashire Regiment – the St Helens Pals. Four days later, another Saint, 'Butcher Prescott' also joined the same regiment. Brave men indeed. *1909* According to the *St Helens Newspaper*: "The committee on Wednesday were so pleased with the earnestness and ability of Berlin Barnes of the Denton's Green FC that they signed this enthusiastic young forward after the Practice." How he got his first name is a mystery. *1928* Test Match #39. New Zealand 5 England 13 at Caledonia Ground Dunedin. Saints' utility back Alf Frodsham made his long-awaited Test match debut. *1951* Northern Rugby League: Widnes 11 St Helens 20 at Naughton Park. A brace of tries for Welsh powerhouse centre Don Gullick, who certainly wanted some stopping. He thought nothing of swimming across the big lake in Taylor Park – carrying son Dave on his back. *1962* Western Division Championship: Salford 24 St Helens 35 at the Willows. Wow! South African left winger Len Killeen, on debut, notched a brilliant hat-trick. Not to be out-done, so did Tom van Vollenhoven! Another debutant, Kel Coslett, kicked four goals from full-back. It was 11–10 at half-time too. *1965* Representative match: Commonwealth XIII 7 New Zealand 15 at Crystal Palace, London. Australian centre Dave Wood and Welsh powerhouse Mervyn Hicks played for the home team. *1996* Super League Round 21: St Helens 68 Sheffield Eagles 2 at Knowsley Road. Saints ran absolute riot and had a number of tries disallowed by the Video Ref, otherwise it would have been a real landslide.

Left: 'That's a 9.9 without doubt!' An outdoor PE lesson with bare chested Saints' legend Don Gullick at Rivington Road school was always interesting, or, on second thoughts, quite challenging. Right: Len Killeen scores a vital try against Dewsbury in the 1966 Challenge Cup Semi-Final. [Alex Service]

19 AUGUST

1984 Friendly: St Helens 54 Mansfield Marksmen 12 at Knowsley Road. A comfortable win for the Saints against this fledgling club. Australian half-back Paul Hamson, from North Sydney, made his debut in the red vee. *2006* Super League Round 25: Catalans Dragons 26 St Helens 22 at Stade Michel, Canet Plage. Stand-off Craig Ashall made his debut for the seniors and scored a memorable try as a weakened St Helens outfit – the Challenge Cup final was the following week – really took the game to the homesters. Frightened the life out of 'em, in fact.

20 AUGUST

1932 Hooker Frank McCabe was born in the Thatto Heath district. Must be something in the air there that seems to produce good number nines, like Sammy Daniels, Bob Dagnall and Keiron Cunningham! A great pity his career was ultimately ended by a knee injury sustained at the beginning of the 1956 Challenge Cup campaign. *1961* Ray French was signed from St Helens RUFC. Ray was a workaholic second-rower, who won every honour at club level with the Saints and was a crucial member of the back row during the club's 'four trophy' campaign in 1965–66. Ironically, he earned international recognition later, when he joined Widnes. *2000* Super League Round 24: St Helens 58 Warrington Wolves 18. Tommy Martyn scored a mesmerising hat-trick – his second for the club. How the Wire hated coming to Knowsley Road in the Super League years.

21 AUGUST

1914 The *St Helens Newspaper* gave the following sporting news update: "Immediately on the declaration of war by Great Britain, Arthur Kelly, the popular captain of the 'A' team, joined the Corps of colonials which had been formed by the overseas and colonial residents in England and he is now stationed in Shepherds Bush."

Left: Scrum-half Arthur Kelly was one of the first players to 'sign up' for the Military in the First World War [Alex Service]; right: Tommy Martyn (far left) appearing as one of three legends in the Sean Long Testimonial match in January 2007. The others, with Sean, are, of course, Chris Joynt and Paul Newlove [Bernard Platt]

1928 Former Unos Dabs front-rower Edward 'Ebor' Hill signed for the Saints. A member of Saints' first ever League Championship-winning team, in 1932, he later joined Bradford Northern. **1954** Northern Rugby League: Blackpool Borough 2 St Helens 34 at Borough Park. Left centre Bill Finnan scored four tries. He repeated the feat in the next match, at home to Swinton in a 28–9 success. Follow that.

1976 Lancashire Cup Round 1: Wigan 37 St Helens 5 at Central Park. The Saints' First team were on strike for improved terms. A reserve team turned out at and were duly taken to the cleaners. Wigan's ebullient South African winger Green Vigo scored seven tries. **1983** First Division: St Helens 30 Hull KR 11 at Knowsley Road. Barnstorming Geordie front-rower Paul Grimes scored a typically bustling try for the homesters. Winger Barry Ledger went one better with a brilliant near-length of the field effort which brought the house down! **1994** First Division: St Helens 20 Doncaster 29 at Knowsley Road. Centres Simon Booth, a signing from Leigh, and Scott Gibbs, who had switched codes from Cardiff RUFC, made their debuts in what turned out to be a shock reversal against newly-promoted Doncaster.

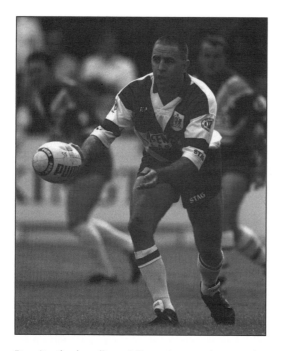

Despite the handling skills and general promptings of skipper Shane Cooper (left), Saints still suffered an unexpected defeat to Doncaster on the opening day of the 1994–95 campaign. It was also a debut day for a new Saint, Simon Booth. [Sportsphoto Ltd]

22 AUGUST

1913 The *St Helens Newspaper* announced the signing of Bert Roberts from Barnsley RUFC who 'gained a reputation last season as a full-back and was expected to gain his county cap this season'. *1972* Division One: St Helens 15 Warrington 11 at Knowsley Road. New signing Roy Mathias (5) scored a typically bustling try on his debut. We had got a good 'un for sure. *1995* Mike Bennett was signed from Golborne Parkside ARLFC. A tremendously durable forward, with a high work rate, Mike always played with a smile on his face – the tougher, the better for him.

23 AUGUST

1919 Northern Rugby League: St Helens 28 Broughton Rangers 2 at Knowsley Road. Normality – of sorts – returned after the carnage of the First World War. This was a crushing victory for the Saints, with a brace of tries from centre Billy Lavin and five goals from full-back Tom Barton. *1958* Northern Rugby League: St Helens 32 Featherstone Rovers 9 at Knowsley Road. The new Main Stand, designed by local architect Clive Robinson, was opened. Tom van Vollenhoven scored two tries. Centre Peter Fearis kicked seven goals and would eventually lead the goalkicking charts. *1969* Northern Rugby League: St Helens 31 Workington Town 11 at Knowsley Road. After re-joining Saints after a five-year spell with Liverpool City/Huyton, scrum-half Jeff Heaton played again for his hometown club. His last match was on 4 July 1976 in Auckland, after a glittering return to the club he loved.

Left: Any excuse to see Tom van Vollenhoven in action, even though he has the Popular Side at Knowsley Road behind him. Both Popular Side and Main Stands were designed by Clive Robinson, one clever guy. Above: this try was a veritable match-winner. Jeff Heaton scores against Widnes in the 1976 Challenge Cup final [Alex Service]

1992 Charity Shield: St Helens 17 Wigan 0 at Gateshead International Stadium. A statement of intent. Saints were 17 points up at the interval and that's how it stayed. Captain Shane Cooper and the boys showed that they could compete with their deadliest rivals for trophies.

24 AUGUST

1963 Northern Rugby League: St Helens 7 Huddersfield 10 at Knowsley Road. Peter Harvey 'the Redhead with Fire in his Boots' made his Saints' debut at stand-off. *1964* Northern Rugby League: St Helens 28 Rochdale Hornets 4 at Knowsley Road. Full-back Kel Coslett kicked seven goals from nine attempts and later had to leave the field with a broken ankle. *1994* First Division: Warrington 31 St Helens 10 at Wilderspool. A tough debut for young hooker Keiron Cunningham, but really nothing ever seemed to faze him.

25 AUGUST

1923 Northern Rugby League: St Helens 5 Widnes 3 at Knowsley Road. Saints play in their new white jerseys with a red chest and arm bands for the first time. Previous colours were blue and white hoops a la Halifax. *1945* Northern Rugby League: Widnes 20 St Helens 8 at Naughton Park. The first post-war match did not go the way of the visitors. Ernie Mills and Frank Tracey scored Saints' tries; Stan Powell kicked a goal.

1990 Confirmation was given by the club of the signing of centre or stand-off Tea Ropati, from the Mangere East club in New Zealand. The First Division Player of the Year in 1992–93, Tea later returned to New Zealand to play for the Auckland Warriors club. He was a fantastic footballer. **2007** Challenge Cup Final: St Helens 30 Catalans Dragons 8 at Wembley Stadium. It is a tremendous source of pride that the Saints were the first winners at the rebuilt stadium – and that interchange hooker James Roby scored the first try. How good is that? Talking of number nines, skipper Keiron Cunningham was the only survivor from the club's last Challenge Cup success 10 years before.

Right: Wembley 2007: Sean Long makes a break; skipper Keiron Cunningham is on the right
[Bernard Platt]

26 AUGUST

1933 Northern Rugby League: St Helens 29 Widnes 14 at Knowsley Road. Thatto Heath-born Les Garner made his debut at loose-forward. Ben Halfpenny and Jack Arkwright made up the back row. Les was a fine crown green bowler and was also a gateman at Knowsley Road for a spell. **1996** Super League Round 22: St Helens 66 Warrington Wolves 14 at Knowsley Road. It was all hail Bobbie Goulding and the boys as Saints won the inaugural Super League title. It was their first such triumph for 21 years. Let the party begin.

2006 Challenge Cup Final: St Helens Huddersfield Giants at Twickenham. Saints justified their favourites tag with a dominant performance. Remember Jon Wilkin and his broken nose? Or was it Adam Ant? Then there was Jamie Lyon, with a try and seven goals, plus the inevitable Sean Long, who won a record third Lance Todd Trophy. Magnificent memories.

Above: Jamie Lyon scores against Huddersfield at Twickenham in 2006, with Huddersfield's Robbie Paul unable to prevent the inevitable. [Bernard Platt]

27 AUGUST

1921 Northern Rugby League: St Helens 3 Oldham 10. Scottish full-back John McCallum played his one and only game after signing from Hawick RUFC. He returned to Scotland, followed by members of the Saints' Committee, trying to re-claim his signing-on fee. What a commotion. *1926* Second-rower Jack Grundy was born in St Helens. The son of a former St Helens Recs' player, Harry, he was transferred to Barrow and played in three Challenge Cup Finals, 1951, 1955 and 1957, winning one – 1955. *2000* Super League Round 25: St Helens 50 Salford City Reds 28 at Knowsley Road. Keiron Cunningham bludgeoned his way over for a brace of tries; Apollo Perelini also scored a four-pointer, his 44th and last for the club. Sean Long scored 18 points, making his seasonal total 328, surpassing the Super League record of 326 held by Iestyn Harris, then of Leeds Rhinos.

28 AUGUST

1937 Northern Rugby League: St Helens 11 Widnes 7 at Knowsley Road. A landmark for the club: it's first as a Limited Liability Company. The new shareholders must have been pleased as the Saints, wearing brand new jerseys with two thin red bands above and below the broad red band – a gift from the lady supporters – scored tries from winger Harold Forsyth, front-rower Stan Hill and Welshman Emlyn Hughes. It was a much-needed opening day victory. *1967* Northern Rugby League: St Helens 13 Wakefield Trinity 11 at Knowsley Road. John Mantle, normally a second-rower, played on the right wing in place of the injured Tom van Vollenhoven. The backline read: Mantle, Douglas, Benyon and Jones. *2009* The Steve Prescott Foundation undertook a dragon boat challenge down the River Thames, from Windsor to Teddington Lock, including many prominent former players, such as Gary Connolly, Anthony Sullivan and Paul Sculthorpe. They were joined for a spell by comedian Johnny Vegas, pictured with Steve Prescott. [Alex Service]

29 AUGUST

1895 The meeting to form the breakaway professional Northern Union took place at the George Hotel, Huddersfield. Secretary Fred Dennett represented the Saints and the 21 clubs present adopted the following resolution: "That the clubs represented decide to form a Northern Rugby Football Union, and pledge themselves to push forward, without delay, its establishment on the principle of payment for bona-fide time only." A seminal moment! *1899* The *St Helens Newspaper* wrote about a new rule: "The play the ball rule has been eliminated and the rule has been altered to read: 'If a player, while holding or running with the ball, be tackled, and the ball firmly held, the referee shall at once order a scrummage.'"

1949 When Saints lost 7–0 to Workington Town in a first round, first leg, Lancashire Cup tie at Knowsley Road, there was an unusual occurrence during the game that could only happen to Saints' legend Duggie Greenall. Two days later, The *Daily Mirror* took up the story: "The top of the goalpost was lost when Pepperell, one of the three famous Cumberland brothers weaved his way over for the only try of the game. Pepperell was being chased so closely by Greenall that when he swerved, Greenall tackled the goal post. Greenall went down first and the top of the pole came down after him, but Greenall did not feel it. He was out to the world, whilst Risman was adding a goal to the try."What a marvellous tale.

30 AUGUST

1890 According to the day's *St Helens Newspaper*: "The Saints are in operation of their new field in Knowsley Road and on Saturday last they had a practice match, a twelve-a-side game being played." And there they stayed for the next 120 years! ***1943*** From the Boardroom: "The meeting discussed the position of W. P. Lyon [sic] who had coached the players since the commencement of the season and agreed that he had given every satisfaction in the discharge of his duties." This was former Widnes trainer Peter Lyons. The meeting then appointed Jimmy Stott as captain for the 1943–44 season, with George 'Porky' Davies as vice-captain. ***1950*** Friendly match: St Helens 74 Turin (Italy) 38 at Knowsley Road. A real points fest, with Saints' wingers scoring nine tries between them: Steve Llewellyn five, Stan McCormick four. The Italians, hoping to get experience for establishing the game on a solid footing in their country had been beaten 49–28 by Wigan the previous Saturday and had an English Player-Coach, Dennis Chappell, formerly of Wakefield Trinity, who served in Italy during the war and married an Italian girl.

Welsh centre Viv Harrison splits the Italian defence in the friendly encounter at Knowsley Road, with the old Main Stand in the background. [Alex Service]

1962 Western Division Championship: Liverpool City 9 St Helens 16 at Knotty Ash. Jack Arkwright (jr) son of 'Old' Jack Arkwright from the 1930s, made his debut in the front row with Cliff Watson and hooker Bob Dagnall. *1998* Super League Round 19: St Helens 36 Halifax Blue Sox 6 at Knowsley Road. Young Paul Wellens, essentially a half-back, came off the bench for his senior debut. *2008* Challenge Cup Final: St Helens 28 Hull FC 16 at Wembley Stadium. Three in a row. In some ways a hard-fought victory as Hull hit back strongly after the interval, but Saints' firepower and flair triumphed in the end. Remember Francis Meli's 'tap' restart and subsequent four pointer? Breathless stuff.

Blame it on the Walney Express. Ade Gardner causes mayhem in the Hull defence at Wembley in 2008 [Bernard Platt]

31 AUGUST

1929 Northern Rugby League: St Helens 0 Widnes 3 at Knowsley Road. A large crowd flocked to see three New Zealanders – the Three Hs – Roy Hardgrave and forwards Lou Hutt and Trevor Hall, make their eagerly-anticipated debuts. Widnes ruined the party, however, but Saints' investments paid off as the season unfurled. *1936* Welsh forward Emlyn Hughes, former Llanelli and Llanelli Dock Stars forward, signed for the Saints. He was the uncle of Liverpool football legend Emlyn Hughes, whose father was also a professional rugby league player. *1959* County Championship: Cumberland 14 Lancashire 8 at Derwent Park, Workington. Four Saints appeared for the Red Rose: Austin Rhodes at full-back, Alex Murphy (scrum-half), Albert Terry (front-row) and loose-forward Vince Karalius.

A signed photograph of Kiwi front-rower Lou Hutt, who made his debut in 1929. [Alex Service]

146

September

First and Last!

St Helens versus Huddersfield Giants, Super League Qualifying Semi-Final, 24 September 2010.
An emotional time for everyone connected with St Helens RFC. The last-ever Saints' team lined up for
the camera at soon-to-be-demolished Knowsley Road. [Bernard Platt]
Back: Bryn Hargreaves, Andrew Dixon, Keiron Purtill (assistant coach), Jake Emmitt, Sia Soliola, Paul
Clough, Matt Gidley, Jamie Foster, James Graham, Stan Wall (kit), Jon Wilkin, Alan Clarke (kit) Mick
Potter (Head Coach), Mike Rush (CEO); Front row: Matt Daniels (Conditioner) James Roby, Matty
Smith, Francis Meli, Chris Flannery, Keiron Cunningham, Paul Wellens, Tony Puletua

Still one of the most interesting months for rugby league fans. The weather remains relatively warm and in the Super League, matters are drawing to a heady climax, with Old Trafford the ultimate goal. But historically, there are a number of key dates that show the development of St Helens RFC over the years: the first and last matches at Knowsley Road, spanning 120 years; the first match on the new ground against Manchester Rangers in 1890; the first time the team played in the fledgling Northern Union against Rochdale Hornets in 1895. Then, fast forward 115 years to the final league game and all the drama that went with it – against Castleford Tigers in 2010. Keiron Cunningham's late try just seemed to fit the script perfectly, but there was more to come. The final match was in the Super League Qualifying Semi-Final against Huddersfield Giants. Fitting that this should be against a fellow foundation club from 1895. It was, however, a great pity that this was not to be followed by Grand Final glory at Old Trafford a week later.

1 SEPTEMBER

1883 from the *Prescot Reporter and St Helens General Advertiser:* "The annual meeting of the members of this club was held on Thursday evening last week, for the election of officers and the transaction of other business. A full list of matches has been arranged, including the following clubs: Southport Olympic, Glodwick (Oldham), Wigan, Newton, St Helens Recs, Edge Hill, Blundellsands, Widnes Wasps and Birkenhead." Interesting times for the 10-year-old club. *1906* Northern Rugby League: St Helens 6 Swinton 10 at Knowsley Road. No place for flankers. The club's first-ever game in the new XIII-a-side format produced a victory for the visiting Lions. Billy Briers and Jack Pope scored Saints' tries. *1962* Western Division Championship: St Helens 59 Salford 0 at Knowsley Road. Whitehaven-born second-rower John Tembey, who became a ball-handling prop, scored his first two tries as a Saint. He became captain of St Helens and played international rugby league for Great Britain. A real good 'un. *1969* Lancashire Cup Round 1: St Helens 58 Maryport 5 at Knowsley Road. Stand-off Frank Myler displayed his silky skills with a club record-equalling six tries. But wait, there's more. Cumbrian rugby league expert Harry Edgar explains: "A couple of amateur teams were invited to play in the Lancashire Cup that season. Maryport were one of those representatives, but the truth was that it wasn't a Maryport team at all which took the field at St Helens, but a Cumbrian County Amateur XIII. Players were not selected just from the Maryport and District club, but also included several from the Whitehaven clubs like Kells, Hensingham and nearby Wath Brow." *2017* Super 8s Round 4: St Helens 16 Wigan Warriors 26 at the Totally Wicked Stadium. Australian full-back Ben Barba made his long-awaited debut for the Saints and scored their first try.

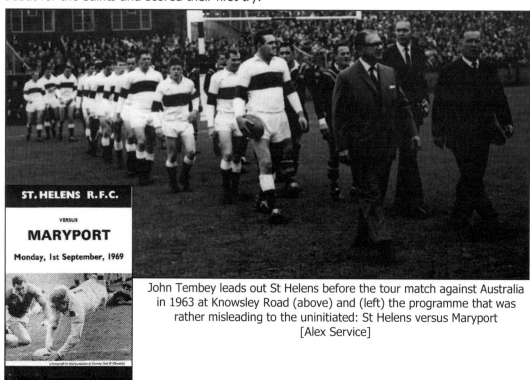

ST. HELENS R.F.C.

VERSUS

MARYPORT

Monday, 1st September, 1969

John Tembey leads out St Helens before the tour match against Australia in 1963 at Knowsley Road (above) and (left) the programme that was rather misleading to the uninitiated: St Helens versus Maryport
[Alex Service]

148

2 SEPTEMBER

1909 Northern Union: Hull KR 30 St Helens 7 at Craven Park. Full-back Hubert Sydney 'Jum' Turtill made his debut. The New Zealander went on to make 140 appearances and kick 200 goals before eventual retirement in February 1914. Sad to relate that the high-profile licensee of the Nelson Hotel in Bridge Street became a casualty in the Great War. *1916* War Emergency League: St Helens 0 St Helens Recreation 24 at Knowsley Road. "Military Search for Slackers" exclaimed the *St Helens Newspaper*. "At the end of the game, spectators were held at the exits by a number of members of staff of the recruiting officer, assisted by several police officers. Those who were obviously over the age limit were allowed to go at once and those who had taken the precaution to carry their registration form and their attestation or exemption card with them treated the matter as something in the nature of a joke. Those however who were not so fortunate had to give the officers their names and addresses, a course which took some little time. We understand that a considerable number of names and addresses were taken and a few absentees were detected…. Captain McPhail strongly advises those whose names and addresses were taken on Saturday and did not go to the Town Hall on Monday morning, to report at once, and thus obviate further trouble."

St. Helens Rugby Football Club Ltd.

OFFICIAL PROGRAMME

ST. HELENS

versus

NEW ZEALAND

SATURDAY, SEPTEMBER 2nd, 1939
Kick-off 3-30 p.m.

PRICE - ONE PENNY

This space is reserved for the

St. Helens R.F.C. Supporters' Club

Come and Join the Supporters'
Club **NOW**

1939 Tour match: St Helens 3 New Zealand 19 at Knowsley Road. A significant date, with Germany invading Poland the previous day. On 3 September, Britain and France declared war on Germany. The Kiwis played one more match, against Dewsbury, before sailing home as a result of the emergency. The programme is a real collectors' item. [Alex Service] *1984* First Division: St Helens 25 Featherstone Rovers 10 at Knowsley Road. The front row had an unusual ring to it, with second-rower Andy Platt as hooker. One name was an ever-present on the team sheet throughout the season: Tony Burke, whose durability and consistency as 'first man in' number eight was legendary.

3 SEPTEMBER

1965 Full-back Dave Lyon was born in Billinge. The son of Wigan forward Geoff Lyon, he joined Saints from Warrington in the early 1990s and became a popular player with the fans, who warmed to his attacking flair. Dave won a Premiership Final against Wigan in 1993. *1989* First Division: Sheffield Eagles 20 St. Helens 36 at Hillsborough, Sheffield. Two tries on debut for Welsh rugby union convert scrum-half Jon Griffiths. He looked like a player with strength and pace, for sure, that later earned him caps for Wales and Great Britain.

4 SEPTEMBER

1933 Northern Rugby League: St Helens 21 Hull KR 11 at Knowsley Road. Arthur Lemon, from Neath with 13 Welsh international rugby union caps, made his debut at loose-forward. He was joined in the back row by Jack Arkwright and former St Helens Recs' stalwart Frank Bowen. After racking up 79 games for the Saints, Arthur was later transferred to the Streatham & Mitcham club in London. *1943* War Emergency League: St Helens 15 Keighley 23 at Knowsley Road. A disappointing start to the season for Saints' fans, who went on to witness a further seven straight losses at home during the campaign. A somewhat un-wanted club record. *2005* Super League Round 26: Leigh Centurions 4 St Helens 78 at the Coliseum. Leigh were thrown to the lions, so to speak. Rampant Saints registered their highest-ever score in Super League and their widest margin of victory in an away match. It really was one-way traffic. *2010* Super League Round 27: St Helens 40 Castleford Tigers 30 at GPW Stadium, Knowsley Road. As if 'Wide to West' was enough. The scenario was this: Saints had to win by nine points to clinch second-place and another home game at the old ground. By the third quarter, they were coasting, 30–10, but things went a bit pear-shaped, as the

Tigers, desperate for their own play-off aspirations – eighth place was up for grabs – levelled things up. Centre Matt Gidley got the lead back with three minutes remaining and then, a sensational finale, as Keiron Cunningham, the King of Knowsley Road, forced his way over with just nine seconds to spare. (See Bernard Platt's image left) Jamie Foster's conversion made the margin 10 points: Saints were second; Castleford were out; North Wales Crusaders were 'in'. Unbelievable stuff.

5 SEPTEMBER

1914 Northern Rugby League: St. Helens 26 Runcorn 0 at Knowsley Road. The dreadful Battle of the Marne started on this day, when William Jackson, a strong-running forward, made his debut. In the Royal Engineers some time later he was one of the first to suffer the effects of mustard gas. He recovered and became a PTI in the South Lancashire Regiment. William played in every round of the 1914–15 Challenge Cup run, when Saints reached the Final, only to lose to the overwhelming favourites Huddersfield. He made 52 appearances overall for the Saints before joining the fledgling Wigan Highfield club. *1933* At the Committee Meeting in the Pavilion, it was agreed to pay the groundsman, former player William Whiteley, three guineas (£3.15) towards the cost of a new overcoat. A very wise purchase indeed.

6 SEPTEMBER

1890 Friendly match: St Helens 2 goals 1 try 4 minors Manchester Rangers 1 try 4 minors at Knowsley Road. The first-ever game at the new 'out of town' ground in Eccleston. The first points were scored by fly-half Billy Cross, with a drop-goal. Joseph Brownbill scored a try and Alex Borthwick kicked a goal in the second half. *1943* From the Saints' Committee meeting at Knowsley Road: "Councillor G. Marsden said that he had received a number of bags from Mr Devanney to make towels for the players and had passed them on to the Secretary to be made up. The Secretary was requested to forward to Mr Devanney a letter of thanks." It was really a case of 'make do and mend' in those austere days. *1971* Tour match: St Helens 18 New Zealand 8 at Knowsley Road. Les Jones, Frank Wilson, Jeff Heaton and Eric Chisnall were the try-scorers. Kel Coslett kicked three goals. *1981* First Division: Castleford 17 St Helens 32 at Wheldon Road, Castleford. Right winger Les Jones played the last of his 485 matches for the club, a fantastic servant, whose 283 tries put him second behind the legendary Tom van Vollenhoven. Two reasons for supporters to be proud of the achievements of this local-born player.

1992 First Division: St Helens 24 Wakefield Trinity 12 at Knowsley Road. Chris Joynt [image courtesy Bernard Platt] came off the bench for his senior debut. A Saints institution after 382 matches and 121 tries in the red vee, plus a shed full of silverware, the mobile running forward was nailed on as a member of the club's Greatest 17 selected before the leaving of Knowsley Road.

7 SEPTEMBER

1895 Northern Union: St Helens 8 Rochdale Hornets 3 at Knowsley Road. The first match in the new professional competition. Saints' first try-scorer was Cumbrian 'pocket battleship' winger Bob Doherty. Local-born forward Peter Dale added a second almost immediately. Skipper and stand-off Billy Cross added the conversion. It was 8–0 at the interval. Speedy winger Tom Sudlow didn't play for Saints in the first Northern Union match. He took on local sprint star Jacky Banks at the Starr Inn Race Grounds, Merton Bank, for the Championship of St Helens. Banks won by two yards and claimed the £50 prize! Should have stuck to rugby, Tom. *1952* Scrum-half Ken Kelly was born in St Helens. A teenage prodigy, like Alex Murphy, Ken was like lightening in his early games for the club and won a Challenge Cup winner's medal against Leeds in 1972 when he produced an outstanding defensive display too.

8 SEPTEMBER

2006 Super League Round 26: St Helens 36 Warrington Wolves 16 at Knowsley Road. Hull FC beat the Rhinos at Headingley and the Saints were duly awarded their third consecutive League Leaders' Shield, a great testimony to their consistently high standards on the field.

2017 Ron Hoofe, the voice of the Saints' video for many years passed away after a short illness. A local institution, who instigated such phrases as "a real Sister Duffy," when a player got belted – She was the famous nurse in the casualty department at the Providence Hospital in St Helens – and the euphoric "lick 'em and stick 'em" when a game was won among others! But his eternally famous quip is a last-minute four-pointer by Cumbrian winger Les Quirk at Knowsley Road: "A try of orgasmic proportions!" Ron certainly had a way with words!

Ron Hoofe pre-match at Knowsley Road [Bernard Platt]; Les Quirk (right), the Cumbrian Express, hurtles towards the line for another brilliant try at Knowsley Road. [Brian Peers]

9 SEPTEMBER

1924 Centre and back-rower Tommy Stott was born in Parr. A goalkicker like his elder brother Jimmy, he was a reliable member of the squad and made 79 appearances from 1942 to 1951, scoring 14 tries, before his transfer to Swinton. After his retirement from playing he was also a regular spectator on the popular Side at Knowsley Road for the rest of his life. A salt of the earth character. *2005* Super League Round 27: Wigan Warriors 12 St Helens 38 at the JJB Stadium. Maurie Fa'asavalu scored a typically forceful – downright belligerent – try to help to secure the League Leaders Shield for the rampant Saints. The sheer elation of his achievement was there for all to see. *2006* Super League Round 27: St Helens 58 Leeds Rhinos 18 at Knowsley Road. Front-rower Paul Anderson set the seal on a memorable victory with a last-try conversion from the touchline, the sheer nonchalance of which still has fans talking to this day. Brilliant.

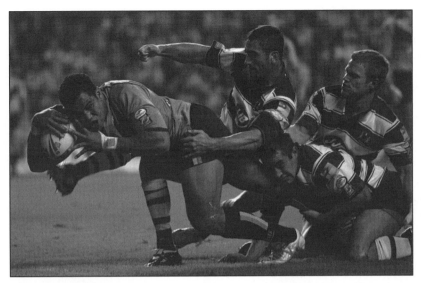

Maurie Fa'asavalu heads for the try line against Wigan Warriors in 2005 and no-one on earth, including this posse of Wigan defenders, is going to stop him. [Bernard Platt]

10 SEPTEMBER

1906 Committee Meeting at Headquarters [Talbot Hotel]: "Resolved – that Secretary write Chief Constable complaining of want of attention on part of constables to their duties at the football ground and asking that they be compelled to follow instructions imposed on them." *1989* First Division: St Helens 24 Castleford 26 at Knowsley Road. Welsh scrum-half Jon Griffiths scored a marvellous long-distance solo try on his home debut, a memorable highlight despite his new team's demise on the day. *2010* Super League Qualifying Play-Off: St Helens 28 Warrington Wolves 12 at GPW Stadium. The Saints' proud record in the Super League era at Knowsley Road against the Wire remained intact. Second-rower Sia Soliola played his second game since injuring his knee against the same opponents on 19 March.

11 SEPTEMBER

1874 The second Annual General Meeting of the St Helens Rugby Football Club was held at the Fleece Hotel, Church Street. The new organisation was gradually gathering support and strength in our coal mining and glass making town. *1905* Committee Meeting at Headquarters, Talbot Hotel, Duke Street: "Resolved that C. Creevey be paid 10/- insurance for damaged fore-finger." *1909* Northern Rugby League at Knowsley Road: St Helens 5 Runcorn 5. England international forward Frank Lee scored the try; Charlie Creevey kicked a goal. The Saints wore their new all-black kit for the first time. The influence of the New Zealanders was apparent with this choice. There was a record crowd of almost 10,000 spectators. Runcorn in myrtle jerseys, known as the Linnets, were a strong side in those days. *1954* Northern Rugby League: St Helens 27 Whitehaven 6 at Knowsley Road. Right winger Eric Ledger flew in for four tries. He repeated the dose against Wakefield at Belle Vue seven days later.

Eric Ledger (above) and son Barry were superb on the flanks for the Saints in the 1950s and 1980s respectively. [Alex Service]

1977 First Division: St Helens 39 Castleford 17 at Knowsley Road. Scrum-half Ken Gwilliam, more renowned for his graft around the scrum-base scored a memorable hat-trick of tries. *1985* County Championship: Lancashire 10 Yorkshire 26 at Central Park, Wigan. Left winger Barry Ledger and workaholic front-rower Paul Forber were the Saints' representatives. Wigan's Sean Wane was the substitute forward that day.

12 SEPTEMBER

1962 County Championship: Lancashire 28 Cumberland 8 at Naughton Park, Widnes. Saints' Red Rose representative was back-rower Ray French; John Tembey was in the back row for Cumberland. *1964* Northern Rugby League: St Helens 37 Blackpool Borough 5 at Knowsley Road. A dazzling hat-trick of tries from stand-off Keith Northey. He had a marvellous side-step that bamboozled opposing defenders one-on-one. *1967* County Championship: Cumberland 6 Lancashire 19 Derwent Park, Workington. Another strong Saints' contingent representing the Red Rose county: Frank Barrow at full-back, Frank Myler at left centre who scored a try, Tommy Bishop at scrum-half was also a try-scorer and Albert Halsall in the front-row. *2014* Super League Round 27 Huddersfield Giants 17 St Helens 16 at Galpharm Stadium, Huddersfield. Big Alex Walmsley was sent off after a late tackle on Luke Robinson, as Saints' chances of finishing top of the table remained in the balance. 24 hours later, however, Castleford Tigers lost against Catalans Dragons in France and the relieved Saints' players celebrated on their sofas in front of the television. Merci beaucoup, mes amis.

Get ready to be bamboozled: Keith Northey takes on the Workington defence at Knowsley Road. Ken Large runs in support. [Alex Service]

13 SEPTEMBER

1987 Lancashire Cup Round 1: Leigh 27 St Helens 21 at Hilton Park. Welsh international rugby union forward Stuart Evans, from Neath made his debut in the front row. Paul Forber and hooker Dave Harrison started with him up front. *1998* Super League Round 21: St Helens 32 Castleford Tigers 32 at Knowsley Road. An amazing game, equalling the record for the club's highest drawn match. It was 14–14 at half-time too. Sean Long kicked six goals. *2002* Super League Round 27: St Helens 64 Hull 10 at Knowsley Road. File under 'wholesale slaughter'. Saints were in irresistible form, racing to a 36–0 advantage by half-time and running in nine tries overall. They scored more, 169, than any other team during the campaign. Paul Sculthorpe was Man-of-the Match with 10 goals and just a solitary touchdown. What a season he had: the most carries, clean breaks, metres gained and tackle busts for his club in the OPTA stats.

14 SEPTEMBER

1963 Northern Rugby League: St Helens 40 Hull KR 12 at Knowsley Road. Rampaging second-rower Dick Huddart scored his last try for the Saints before his £10,000 move to Australian rugby league with St George in Sydney.

Left: Dick Huddart tackled by Swinton's Ken Gowers at Station Road; former Saints' second-rower Jimmy Measures meets with his hero, Dick Huddart (right) at Knowsley Road in 2004. [Alex Service]

1984 Lancashire Cup Round 1: St Helens 58 Runcorn Highfield 14 at Knowsley Road. Young second-rower Paul Round ran in an impressive hat-trick of tries, one of two such feats in his career as a Saint. *1986* Lancashire Cup Round 1: St Helens 112 Carlisle 0 at Knowsley Road. More county cup action and this time club records were well and truly shattered. The scoreboard could not cope with the veritable avalanche of points. It was the club's highest-ever score in any competition; centre Paul Loughlin kicked 16 goals and finished the match with 40 points, establishing probably an unassailable individual record – who knows?

15 SEPTEMBER

1961 Disaster at Knowsley Road! Strong gales broke one of the 'trembling' wooden posts at the Eccleston End. The club was forced to put in an order for new tubular steel posts, but in the meanwhile the temporary replacements were, according to the local press: "well below the proper height ... it will be a month or two before the new posts are delivered and in the meantime, the Saints will manage with the old posts, which will have a metal tube to support the upper portion." *1964* From the Boardroom: "A letter from Manchester City Football Club asking if we had any interest in purchasing four 90' towers with 24 lights on each at a price of £2,500 was turned down by the Board." Saints were well on the way towards having their own floodlight system at the ground and four 'corner pylons' would not have been given planning permission, together with the logistical expense of transporting and installing the towers. Don't ask, you don't get, though. *1965* Tour Match: St Helens 28 New Zealand 7 at Knowsley Road. Welsh scrum-half Bob Prosser enjoyed a fantastic debut at scrum-half. The Kiwis were duly 'Prosserised' according to the local press. Peter Harvey was his partner at stand-off and was full of praise: "What Bob brought with him – and it was revolutionary at the time – was the spin pass. Playing stand-off to Bob, I was guaranteed a long, flat pass from the base of the scrum. Also, because he did not attempt to break, it was provided either on the right or the left as had been called."

1970 Northern Rugby League: St Helens 22 Halifax 7 at Knowsley Road. Young hooker Billy Barrow played his one and only game for the seniors, joining his elder brothers Tony and Frank, who also played for the first team on that afternoon. They duly joined the three Creevey brothers from Pocket Nook, Jimmy, Charlie and Matt, who played together in the same team in the pre-First World War days. The image shows Tony (left), Billy (with his Lancashire schoolboys' blazer badge) and Frank, in his Saints' blazer. [Alex Service]

16 SEPTEMBER

1922 Northern Rugby League: St Helens 21 Wigan Highfield 5 at Knowsley Road. The first away game for the recently-formed Wigan club ended in defeat. The club signed several St Helens-born players in their early days to boost their playing roster. **1953** International tournament: England 24 Wales 5 at Knowsley Road. Four Saints on view equally split for the crowd to savour: right centre Duggie Greenall and left-winger Stan McCormick scored tries for England. For Wales Don Gullick marked Greenall in the centre and George Parsons was in the second-row. **1968** From the Boardroom: "It was agreed to invite Lord Pilkington to become President of the St Helens Rugby League Club." Lord and Lady Pilkington were great supporters of the Saints and also had a soft spot for their own works team, Pilkington Recs! **1979** John Player Trophy Round 1: Barrow 13 St Helens 18 at Craven Park. Two tries from Welsh winger Roy Mathias, playing in the un-accustomed role of

loose-forward. Yet he had a successful spell in the back row when he played in the other code, hence his powerful running style. **2003** Former front-row legend Apollo Perelini was appointed strength and conditioning coach at Knowsley Road. He had previously left Saints for a spell in rugby union with Sale Sharks.

Apollo Perelini as a valued member of Saints' backroom staff in 2007. [Bernard Platt]

17 SEPTEMBER

1932 Northern Rugby League: St Helens 33 Leigh 10 at Knowsley Road. Young stand-off Jack Garvey scored a brilliant hat-trick of tries. He was highly rated by star winger Alf Ellaby too, so he must have been a good 'un. *1978* First Division: Barrow 16 St Helens 16 at Craven Park. Never an easy assignment, even though Barrow were relegated at the season's end. Left centre Eddie Cunningham scored a brace of tries and Saints had two 'Smiths' on the bench: Johnny [14] and Malcolm [15]. *2004* Super League Round 28: Bradford Bulls 64 St Helens 24 at Odsal Stadium, Bradford. A high scoring extravaganza in the last league match of the campaign. Saints finished in fifth place and travelled to Wigan in the Elimination Play-Off, where they lost 18–12. At least their defence was rather more solid on that evening.

18 SEPTEMBER

1905 Committee meeting Headquarters "Resolved – That 2doz jerseys, amber and black broad stripes – with bands at neck instead of collars be provided by JH Houghton." Secretary Houghton, a fine administrator, later became President of the Northern Union, in which capacity he led the 1910 Australasian tour party. *1939* Board meeting in the Pavilion at Knowsley Road. "The club secretary read a letter from Pilkington Bros. Ltd. Stating that owing to the emergency the stand [at their City Road HQ] was not for sale. The steel etc. might possibly be required for other purposes." St Helens Recreation, who played there originally, had disbanded at the end of the 1938–39 campaign, although the stand itself lasted well into the 1960s. *1948* Northern Rugby League: St Helens 8 Workington Town 2 at Knowsley Road. This was the final game for front-row 'enforcer' Jonty Pilkington, who packed down with hooker Ike Fishwick and Jack Aspinall. Incidentally, one of Ike's hobbies was ballroom dancing and he was good at it too. John 'Mick' Lawrence, a former West Park schoolboy player, also made his debut on the left wing. Another local lad, Frank Brown, was his centre.

left: Centre Jimmy Stott shared a benefit with Ike Fishwick in the late 1940s; right: Strictly speaking? Ike (left) as a well-respected ballroom dancing judge. [Alex Service]

158

19 SEPTEMBER

1929 Northern Rugby League: St Helens 22 Leeds 7 at Knowsley Road. This comfortable victory included a first try for New Zealand front-rower Lou Hutt, who scored a total of 6 during his Saints' career. He was a superb scrummager and tackler. A real hard man. *1933* The Committee Meeting in the Pavilion carried this final missive: "It was resolved that players who desire their Lady friends to occupy the V.P. Stand may do so on payment of ten shillings." No freeloaders at Knowsley Road! *1951* International match: England 35 Wales 11 at Knowsley Road. Saints' Welsh contingent included centre Viv Harrison who scored one goal, with George Parsons and Ray Cale in the back row. *2000* The Super League Dream team contained three Saints: hooker Keiron Cunningham, together with half-backs Sean Long and Tommy Martyn. They were the best in the competition, by far.

20 SEPTEMBER

1902 Jimmy Garrity, Saints' first mascot, who was a person with dwarfism, died aged 27. He was buried in a pauper's grave in St Helens cemetery. *1975* World Championship: Wales 16 England 22 at Wilderspool, Warrington. Four members of the Welsh pack played for St Helens: John Mantle (8), Mel James (10 on debut), Eddie Cunningham (12) and a try-scorer, Kel Coslett (13). Eckersley and Nicholls were the two Saints who represented England. *1998* Saints and Great Britain front-row legend (George) Alan Prescott died aged 71. Famous for playing on despite a broken arm in the crucial second test match at Brisbane in 1958, he had the distinction of captaining his club, county and country in 1955–56. A true rugby league icon. *2013* Super League Play-Off Semi-Final: Leeds Rhinos 11 St Helens 10 at Headingley. A brave effort from the Saints to get to Old Trafford. Second-rower Willie Manu scored two tries, but it just wasn't enough.

21 SEPTEMBER

1973 First Division: Whitehaven 7 St Helens 26 at the Recreation Ground. Left winger Roy Mathias scored three tries and repeated the achievement in his next three games, at Dewsbury and at home to Hull KR, for a hat-trick of hat-tricks. *2017* Super 8s Round 7: Salford Red Devils 4 St Helens 30 at AJ Bell Stadium, Salford. Saints produced a fine second half display to qualify for a semi-final date with Castleford Tigers.

Fans' forums have always been well-attended at the Totally Wicked Stadium. On 21 September 2016, (from left to right) Bernard Dwyer, Phil Veivers, Alex Walmsley and Sean Long fielded questions from the audience, with Radio Merseyside's Allan Rooney as popular MC. [Alex Service].

22 SEPTEMBER

1916 A sad day indeed. The son of the club's founder, Robert Douglas Herman, died of wounds 'in enemy hands' and was buried at Epehy Communal Cemetery on the Somme. It is a village between Cambrai and Peronne. Robert was a member of the 5th South Lancs Regiment and at the time was attached to the Royal Flying Corps. His name is inscribed on the war memorial at Rainhill. *2000* Super League Qualifying Play-Off: St Helens 16 Bradford Bulls 11 at Knowsley Road. The stuff of legend. 8,864 fans witnessed the most dramatic finish in the club's history, captured for posterity by the 'Sky' cameras. Saints, the defending champions, were 11–10 down until the famous 'overtime' cameo unfolded, with Chris Joynt's try triggering all sorts of joyful mayhem. Commentator Eddie Hemmings's famous 'Wide to [substitute Dwayne] West' call has become enshrined in rugby league folklore. Even today, when the clip is shown, we burst into spontaneous applause. Saints went on to win back-to-back Grand Finals by beating Wigan Warriors at Old Trafford. It should be noted that the week before the legendary Bradford Bulls game, Wigan had inflicted a 42–4 defeat on their great rivals. Talk about payback time. Footnote: it was also loose-forward Paul Sculthorpe's 23rd birthday too.

Dwayne West, the man who spawned a famous catchphrase, in action against London Broncos (left) and is on the far left (above) as Anthony Sullivan is about to celebrate Chris Joynt's wonder try against Bradford Bulls at Knowsley Road. The attendance was under 9,000 but many more would claim to be there. You just had to be.
[Bernard Platt]

160

23 SEPTEMBER

1944 War Emergency League: Oldham 6 St Helens 27 at Watersheddings. A rare wartime win for the Saints, largely thanks to three tries from guest international centre Stanley Brogden. The classy Yorkshireman put his winger, Aubrey Gregory, in for a try too. He was certainly one of the great players in England between the Wars. *1961* Northern Rugby League: Barrow 2 St Helens 34 at Craven Park. Centre Brian McGinn scored a fine hat-trick of tries. *2016* Super League Super 8s Round 1: St Helens 32 Wakefield Trinity 12 at the Totally Wicked Stadium. Australian and Irish international Shannon McDonnell, playing on the wing instead of his normal full-back berth scored a hat-trick in his final game for the club.

24 SEPTEMBER

1949 Northern Rugby League: St. Helens 43 Workington Town 10 at Knowsley Road. A first Saints' hat-trick for left-winger Stan McCormick, the 'Interception King' in front of over 18,000 rapturous fans. All the threequarter line scored tries: Mac's centre Duggie Greenall scored twice. On the other flank, centre Jimmy Stott scored and put his winger, Steve Llewellyn in for another hat-trick. Happy days *1955* Northern Rugby League: St Helens 66 Barrow 15 at Knowsley Road. Scrum-half Austin Rhodes booted over 12 goals in this one-way landslide. Always a prodigious points scorer, Rhodes amassed 141 goals and 10 tries from 39 appearances during the 1955–56 campaign. Saints fans will remember his typical 'golfers' approach to goal kicking with his head well over the ball. *1976* Scrum-half Sean Long was born in Billinge Hospital. A member of the Greatest 17, Sean was the complete half-back. What more can you say? *2010* Super League Qualifying Semi-Final: St Helens 42 Huddersfield Giants 22 at Knowsley Road. The unplanned end to Saints' tenure on the famous old ground. Paul Wellens and Bryn Hargreaves scored a brace of tries; other four pointers were notched by Francis Meli, Tony Puletua and, inevitably, the great Keiron Cunningham. Jamie Foster booted over seven goals. An impressive finale.

Left: A great player from Thatto Heath: goalkicker supreme Austin Rhodes [Alex Service]

25 SEPTEMBER

1937 Northern Rugby League: St Helens 18 Bramley 9 at Knowsley Road. A try for former Llanelli scrum-half Glan Prior in this straightforward victory, who made a total of 9 appearances for the club, scoring two tries. *1947* Tour match: St Helens 5 New Zealand 11 at Knowsley Road. The first tourists to visit after the terrible conflict. Saints included Welsh hooker Reg Blakemore for his debut. He was previously dubbed 'Mr X' by the local press. *1983* First Division: St Helens 50 Wakefield Trinity 12 at Knowsley Road. Stand-off Steve Peters scored a hat-trick of tries. Steve was a talented player who never let the side down, whether in the halves or at centre. *2001* Great Britain Academy winger Adrian (Ade) Gardner signed for the Saints from Barrow Border Raiders. Despite his height, he developed the knack of diving low into the corner to avoid last-ditch tackles to score many vital tries: 173 in 286 appearances in the red vee. A true legend. *2016* Academy Grand Final: St Helens 22 Wigan Warriors 20 at the Totally Wicked Stadium. A fascinating encounter, settled by young stand-off Danny Richardson's extra time penalty. This marvellous victory maintained their unbeaten status throughout the season. How good was that?

The legendary Mr X, later identified as Welshman Reg Blakemore, scores another try for the Saints; Steve Peters (right) was renowned for his defensive toughness, but also had his moments in attack. [Alex Service]

26 SEPTEMBER

1885 Friendly match: St Helens 2 tries (1 disputed), 2 minors Aspull 2 goals 4 tries and 8 minors. According to the *Wigan Observer*: "St Helens have recently amalgamated with the cricket club and strengthened their forces by several new men." This ensured the on-going existence and development of St Helens RFC at a crucial stage. *1925* Northern Rugby League: St Helens 15 Batley 3 at Knowsley Road. Front-rower Ivor Hopkin, a Police Officer, born in Caerphilly made his senior debut as 'P. Williams' and signed on after the match. *1991* Lancashire Cup Round 2: St Helens 39 Oldham 26 at Knowsley Road. Livewire scrum-half Paul Bishop scored two tries, kicked three goals and a drop-goal. New Zealand star Tea Ropati was his stand-off – a great combination.

27 SEPTEMBER

1952 Tour match: St Helens 26 Australia 8 at Knowsley Road. A fantastic victory against the powerful Kangaroos, who were blitzed with tries from 'Todder' Dickinson, Stan McCormick and George Langfield, who also added seven goals. Uncompromising centre Duggie Greenall frightened them to death that day with his verbal and physical intimidation – and he was only a slip of a lad.

The caption of this happy image reads as follows: "Mr T. Brooks, Chairman of St Helens Supporters' Club, presents a set of pens and propelling leads to Duggie Greenall, St Helens Captain, on behalf of St Helens Supporters Club." Essential items, if, like Duggie, you were always signing autographs.
[Alex Service]

1965 Northern Rugby League: Widnes 4 St Helens 9 at Naughton Park. Saints christen the new floodlights at Widnes with a hard-fought victory. Kel Coslett (2) and Len Killeen kicked goals. Back rower Duggie Laughton – a Widnes lad – scored a try. *1966* Ooops apocalypse! 'Four Cups' captain Alex Murphy was transfer listed at £12,000. This was the start of a protracted and sometimes bitter divorce from the St Helens club, of truly Brexit proportions. *1972* County Championship: Lancashire 26 Cumberland 16 at Wilderspool Stadium, Warrington. Five Saints: Billy Benyon (3), John Walsh (4), Ken Kelly (6), Tony Karalius (9) and John Stephens (10). Other Saints' connections were future coach Eric Hughes (5), then of Widnes and former players Albert Halsall (8) Swinton and Eric Prescott (11) Salford. Second-rower George Nicholls [12] of Widnes would soon also become a Saint himself. *1987* First Division: St Helens 38 Bradford Northern 10 at Knowsley Road. This comprehensive victory included two well-taken tries from former UGB winger Dave Large.

28 SEPTEMBER

1963 Tour match: St Helens 2 Australia 8 at Knowsley Road. A Kel Coslett goal was the only thing to show for a really tough encounter against the Kangaroos. Aussie loose forward Johnny Raper was at his most mobile and dangerous, while the crowd seemed to take an almost instant dislike to the rugged Australian centre Peter Dimond. Saved time, after all. Another interesting fact: winger Arthur Johnson was named on the team-sheet as substitute. They were allowed as agreed on the tour itself, some 12 months before they became officially recognised. *1997* Premiership Final: St Helens 20 Wigan Warriors 33 at Old Trafford, Manchester. The back-to-back Challenge Cup winners just had little left in the tank after an exhausting campaign to beat the Warriors, who were victorious in what was the last-ever final of this competition. The Grand Final concept came in the following season. *2017* Super League Semi-Final: Castleford Tigers 23 St Helens 22 at the Mend-a-Hose Jungle. Defeat from the jaws of victory, as one supporter succinctly put it. Saints looked to have clinched it with a Ryan Morgan try, from a fantastic break from James Roby. Just 90 seconds remained and Castleford equalised with a penalty from Luke Gale, who kicked the one-pointer in 'golden point'. A kick in the guts, but what a performance: five tries to three for the Saints on the night! So close.

We might be Grand Final-bound here. The big screen at the Mend-a-Hose Jungle signals Saints' marvellous comeback when the game seemed beyond them. Such a shame it was all to end in 'golden point' heartache.
[Alex Service]

29 SEPTEMBER

1972 Northern Rugby League: St Helens 33 Swinton 12 at Knowsley Road. Stand-off Dave Eckersley, signed from Leigh, scored twice on debut. *1991* First Division: St Helens 25 Castleford 14 at Knowsley Road. Former Widnes Tigers product Mike Riley made his debut on the wing and scored a try. Mike was a fine club winger and a reliable defender as well as a capable try-scorer. *1995* Former club secretary Basil Lowe died aged 71. Appointed in September 1956 to replace Bert Murray and dubbed the 'Foreign Secretary' by Stan McCormick, he was the integral right hand man to Chairman Harry Cook. They presided over some great times from the early 1950s to the early 1970s, a real golden era for the club.

The 'Foreign Secretary' in France. Basil Lowe (bottom right) has his cine camera at the ready to record highlights of the European Championship game between St Gaudens and Saints in Toulouse on 5 December 1970. Stan Magowan (Gavin Murray's coach proprietor) is next to him on the left. Behind him are: Cliff Watson, Jim Challinor (coach), Harry Cook (chairman), Bill Sayer and Kel Coslett. [Alex Service]

30 SEPTEMBER

1902 Stand-off Leslie Fairclough was born in St Helens. Originally from Sutton, Leslie was a superb schemer on the field at club and representative level. In 355 matches for the Saints, he scored 84 tries and kicked three goals. And he was the first Saint to captain a team at international level too. *1904* Special Committee Meeting at Club Headquarters, the Talbot Hotel: "Resolved – That 15 or 18 pairs of galoshes be purchased for team practising".

Running shoes ['spikes'] were also a standard requisite for training well into the 1960s for sprinting practice. There was an indoor running track under the old Grandstand, great for those cold winter training nights. *1966* Northern Rugby League: St Helens 35 Whitehaven 12 at Knowsley Road. In a comprehensive victory, former Blackbrook forward Brian Hogan scored his first try for the club. Right-winger Peter Harvey ran in another four; Welsh centre Cen Williams crossed the whitewash and the irrepressible Len Killeen scored a try and kicked seven goals for good measure. *1979* John Player Trophy Round 2: Widnes 31 St Helens 20 at Naughton Park. Thatto Heath-born Roy Haggerty made his senior debut at left centre and a cult hero of the Popular Side is born. Fellow Thatto Heathen Kevin Meadows, also on debut and a real speedster on the flanks, was outside him.

One of our favourite images of Roy Haggerty, scuttling under the posts for a marvellous try against Widnes in the 1988 Premiership Final. Although in vein after defeat against a stronger Widnes side, Roy had given his usual 110 percent, like he always did.
[Alex Service]

October

A tale of two trophies.

Cup Kings of Lancashire. Skipper Harry Pinner (left) and winger Barry Ledger show the magnificent Lancashire Cup trophy to the fans after the 1984 Final against Wigan at Central Park. [Brian Peers]

Both county cups, Lancashire and Yorkshire, really added interest into the first part of the winter season and, more often than not, the finals were played in the last week of October. The Saints' record is: Played 20; won 11; drawn one; lost eight. This includes a marvellous sequence of five successive victories, from 1960 to 1964, when our opponents, with one exception – Leigh in 1963 – were Swinton, no mean team in their own right, who were League Champions in 1962–63 and 1963–64. Amazingly, there was only one final appearance in the 1970s and Knowsley Road did play host to several finals, including the very last one, a pulsating 'derby' clash against Wigan in 1992.

In the modern era, it is the time of the Grand Final and the ultimate conclusion to the Super League season. Up to 2017, the Saints played in 10 of these showpiece affairs, in front of huge crowds, winning five. There was, however, a truly gut-wrenching sequence of five straight losses from 2007 to 2011, four against our Yorkshire rivals Leeds Rhinos, who have embraced a 'winning culture' at the Theatre of Dreams, including their 2017 success against Castleford. Our best win? The one-point success against Bradford Bulls in 2002 was a belter, but for sheer drama and controversy, the 2014 clash against Wigan Warriors is right up there with them. The end of an eight year drought too.

1 OCTOBER

1949 Northern Rugby League: St Helens 39 Bramley 2 at Knowsley Road. All three front-row members, Walter Norris (8), Reg Blakemore (9) and Bill Whittaker (10) scored tries. "Don't we wish they could do it just once to Wigan, Widnes or Warrington", wrote one exasperated scribe. *1960* World Cup (Test Match #121): Great Britain 33 France 7 at Station Road, Swinton. Austin Rhodes, at right centre, scored two tries. The Brits won all three of their matches and lifted the coveted trophy. Happy days. *1986* Lancashire Cup Semi-Final: Wigan 22 St Helens 16 at Central Park, Wigan. In front of a packed crowd of 28,252, there was drama as the floodlights failed, just as Saints were starting to assert their ascendancy. Pure coincidence, of course. Video commentator Ron Hoofe had a suggestion: "Perhaps Saints' fans should wave their arms in the air, after all, many hands make light[s] work!" Genius! *2008* Front rower supreme James Graham was named Man of Steel, to go with his Player of the Year award from the Rugby League Writer's Association. James was also the top metre-maker too with 3,935 in Super League. He was best in the world then, in our opinion.

2 OCTOBER

1909 Northern Rugby League: Barrow 9 St Helens 21 at Craven Park. A stunning four try performance from local-born winger Jimmy Flanagan. Jimmy Greenwood was his centre and provider on the day. Four years later Flanagan became the first Saints' player to score a try for the Red Rose County in a rugby league match, when Lancashire beat Yorkshire 19–11 at Fartown, Huddersfield.

A family affair: Jimmy Flanagan (left) in his Lancashire county jersey; grandson Jim Flanagan with the same jersey in 2012. [Alex Service]

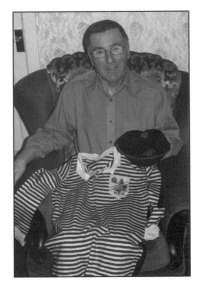

1951 St Helens Supporters' Club handed over a cheque for £1,000 to the St Helens RFC Committee. It was revealed that the Supporters' Club had given over £5,000 since 1945. This was a vital source of extra income as the Saints maintained their development into one of the leading clubs. *1963* County Championship: Cumberland 13 Lancashire 8 at the Recreation Ground, Whitehaven. On the right wing was flame-haired flyer Peter Harvey; at right centre was Keith Northey, both former pupils of West Park School.

1988 First Division: St Helens 30 Wakefield Trinity 14 at Knowsley Road. A try on debut for new signing Darren Bloor, from Salford. A tall, almost gangly figure, he seemed an unlikely number 7, but he certainly had ability. **2010** Grand Final: St Helens 10 Wigan Warriors 22 at Old Trafford. A horror story, as Saints never really fired on the day against the Old Enemy. Francis Meli and Andrew Dixon scored the tries; Jamie Foster kicked a goal. One to forget.

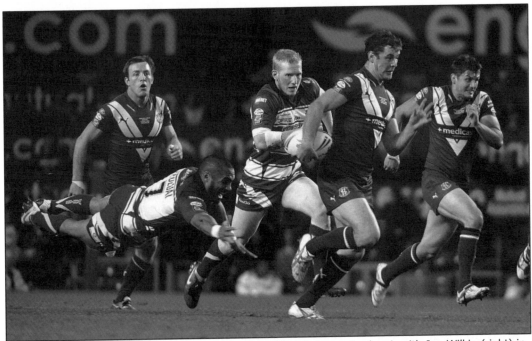

2010 Grand Final: Paul Wellens breaks away from Wigan's James Leuleuai, with Jon Wilkin (right) in support. [Bernard Platt]

3 OCTOBER

1919 Centre Jack Waring was born in St Helens. From a family of 11 from Doulton Street and one of four brothers who all played for Saints, Jack was a clever footballer. He played for England against Wales during the war at Oldham and scored the winning try, but not before an air raid warning interrupted proceedings for eight minutes. **1936** Northern Rugby League: St Helens 3 Warrington 3 at Knowsley Road. Walter Gowers, father of Swinton full-back of the 1960s Ken, played the first of his six matches for the club. The team's record: drawn three, lost three. **2003** Super League Elimination Semi-Final: Wigan Warriors 40 St Helens 24 at JJB Stadium. The last hurrah – and a final try – for centre supreme Paul Newlove. Naturally strong and powerful, he was a great try-scorer, but could set them up as well. Just ask Anthony Sullivan.

2009 Super League Qualifying Semi-Final: St Helens 14 Wigan Warriors 10 at Knowsley Road. Scrum-half Sean Long scored a try in his final appearance as a Saint on home turf. It was his 330th match and his try total increased to 156. He was quite some player. A pity he was not able to celebrate Grand Final success in his final match in the Red Vee.

Farewell to a legend. Chairman Eamonn McManus and the Saints' team pay tribute to star centre Paul Newlove after his final league game for the club, against Bradford Bulls on 9 September at Knowsley Road. One of the main 'triggers' for the club's initial success in Super League, he was later inducted into the Saints Greatest 17 in 2010. Richly deserved.

4 OCTOBER

1930 Northern Rugby League: St Helens 12 Dewsbury 10 at Knowsley Road. Albert Fildes, the international second-rower played his first game for Saints following his controversial transfer from local rivals St Helens Recreation. Light the blue touch paper. *1943* From the Committee Meeting at Knowsley Road: "An application from the Dewsbury club for the services of J. Stott on Saturday October 9th, was submitted. The meeting requested the Secretary to advise Dewsbury that when Stott was available to play, his services were required by St Helens and therefore permission could not be granted." If players were stationed close by to another club, they could play for them with written permission from the player's parent club. *1947* Test Match #66: Great Britain 11 New Zealand 10 at Headingley. Centre Jimmy Stott was joined by team-mate and second-rower Len Aston, who scored on his debut. *1958* Northern Rugby League: Blackpool Borough 19 St Helens 26 at Borough Park. As he surged to the try-line, Tom van Vollenhoven hit the rails separating the pitch from the dog track and needed treatment from Jim Sullivan. He scored two tries in the match.

5 OCTOBER

1929 Test match #41: England 8 Australia 31, at Craven Park, Hull. The selectors had dropped full-back Jim Sullivan, a real shock, so stand-off Les Fairclough captained England. Club mate Alf Frodsham played on the left wing. Australian stand-off Eric Weissel scored 13 points – then a record for an Ashes test. *1996* Test Match #287: Fiji 4 Great Britain 72 at Prince of Wales Park, Nadi. There were four Saints in the Great Britain line up: Alan Hunte (2), Anthony Sullivan (5), Bobbie Goulding (7) and Keiron Cunningham (9). Bobbie Goulding scored his first tries hat-trick and his 32-point haul is a record for a Great Britain test match.

6 OCTOBER

1895 County Championship: Cheshire 0 Lancashire 6 at Stockport. Right winger Bob Doherty became Saints' first representative in county rugby in the Northern Union. **1951** Test match #77: Great Britain 21 New Zealand 15 at Odsal. Doug Greenall, in the right centre position, scored a try on his international debut. Give 'em Mammy, Duggie. **1982** Lancashire Cup Semi-Final replay: Carlisle 5 St Helens 9 at Brunton Park, Carlisle. Saints won through to the final against Warrington with skipper and loose-forward Harry Pinner dropping three goals during a dogged encounter in Cumbria.

2001 Super League Elimination Final: Wigan Warriors 44 St Helens 10 at the JJB Stadium. The Saints ran out of steam after their early season successes in the World Club Challenge and the Challenge Cup. Young second-rower Tim Jonkers played in every match, coming off the bench on 24 occasions.

7 OCTOBER

1894 Loose-forward Ernie Shaw was born in Runcorn. A former Wigan international, Ernie joined Saints where he enjoyed great success, winning a Lancashire Cup winner's medal and Lancashire League title in 1926–27. Ernie made 259 appearances overall, from 1922 to 1930, scoring 57 tries and kicking 47 goals. A real good 'un, so they used to tell me.

1951 'Greatest 17' stand-off Les Fairclough died aged 49 after a short illness. The popular local licensee of the Liverpool Arms was also a member of the St Helens RFC Committee. A sad loss indeed. **1967** Lancashire Cup Final: St Helens 2 Warrington 2 at Central Park. Both teams lived to fight again. The replay was on 2 December, with Saints winning 13–10 at Swinton. **1984** First Division: St Helens 30 Castleford 16 at Knowsley Road. Australian international centre Mal Meninga and full-back Phil Veivers made their Saints debuts in front of an enthusiastic crowd of over 7,000 fans. It was to be a most memorable season for them too. **1990** Tour match: St Helens 4 Australia 34 at Knowsley Road. The RFL granted the Saints the first match of the Kangaroo tour as part of the 100th anniversary celebrations of the Knowsley Road ground. It was certainly a festive occasion, with a marquee on the training ground and a parade of former Saints' greats, including the return of Mal Meninga in the Green and Gold. Alas, the visitors proved too good on the day, with Les Quirk the sole try-scorer for the home team.

Enter the Wild Bull! Vince Karalius is inducted into the Saints' Past Players' Hall of Fame by former Chairman Harry Cook during the club's Ground Centenary celebrations in 1990.
[Alex Service]

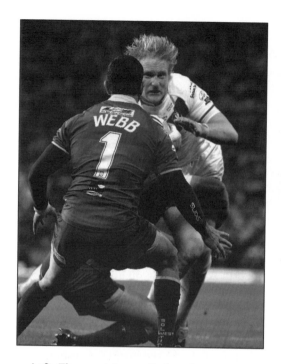

Left: The great James Graham in action against Leeds Rhinos in the 2011 Grand Final, the sixth successive appearance – and fifth loss – at the Theatre of Dreams. Right: Chairman Eamonn McManus offers words of support, but James, in his final game for the club, was lachrymose, beyond sorrow almost. [Bernard Platt]

8 OCTOBER

1952 County Championship: Lancashire 41 Cumberland 14 at Knowsley Road. Right centre Duggie Greenall, scored a try. Winger Stan McCormick and Alan Prescott were also in the Red Rose line-up for the local crowd of 12,000 to savour. Former Saints' hooker Ike Fishwick, then of Warrington scored two tries for the homesters. *1955* Test match #93: Great Britain 25 New Zealand 6 at Station Road Swinton. Popular Welsh full-back Glyn Moses made his test match debut. His Saints' team-mate Alan Prescott also captained his country for the first time. *2011* Grand Final: St Helens 16 Leeds Rhinos 32 at Old Trafford. We thought it was ours this time, despite a season 'on the road' in a temporary home at Widnes. Yet crucial injuries, particularly to centre Michael Shenton, added to the mix and it was further heartbreak. You really did feel for the lads though. They had given their all.

9 OCTOBER

1965 After the Saints versus Barrow league match, Kel Coslett and Len Killeen kicked a Canadian pigskin football, the idea of the *Toronto Telegram* newspaper. The crowd who stayed behind saw Killeen boot a 55-yard goal with his first shot. The Canadian Football league record was 58 yards. The feats from both players stirred the interest of the Argo club – a follow-up article talked about 'The Incredible Mr Killeen' – although thankfully for the Saints, nothing came of it. An unusual post-match event, for sure.

1999 Super League Grand Final: St Helens 8 Bradford Bulls 6 at Old Trafford, Manchester. The first success. What a cracking game it was – a fabulous spectacle – that could have gone either way. Kevin Iro's try and Sean Long's brilliant conversion are etched into the memory bank of every Saints' fan who witnessed them. *2017* Forwards Kyle Amor and Louie McCarthy-Scarsbrook were drafted into the Ireland Squad for the forthcoming World Cup in Australia and New Zealand. Former Saint Shannon McDonnell (Camden Rams) was also in the squad. The Irish squad certainly did not disgrace themselves in the competition.

10 OCTOBER

1933 At the Committee meeting in the Pavilion, the name of former South African Wigan winger Adrian van Heerden was added to the 'A' team at loose-forward. The team was to be captained by George Lewis at full-back. *1970* Lancashire Cup Semi-Final: Wigan 0 St. Helens 23 at Central Park. A convincing win for the visitors, who picked up a winning bonus of £45 per man. A great pity that Leigh proved to be such a stumbling block in the final itself. *2009* Super League Grand Final: St Helens 10 Leeds Rhinos 18 at Old Trafford. A game of fine margins and controversial Video Referee's call saw Saints' Grand Final heartache continue. It became a recurring nightmare on three more occasions.

2009 Grand Final: the fireworks have given Old Trafford a ghostly pallor as James Graham, Sean Long, Keiron Cunningham and Paul Wellens prepare for the battle to come.
[Bernard Platt]

11 OCTOBER

1962 Saints were watching the progress of a Welsh rugby union fly-half called David Watkins, from Newport who, according to the Minutes of the Board, "had an excellent scouting report". Up to date and reliable reports of rugby talent in the Principality was most important as far as the top clubs were concerned. *1978* County Championship: Cumbria 16 Lancashire 15 at Whitehaven. There was a record county representation from the Saints in this match: Peter Glynn, full-back, three goals, Les Jones, left wing, Dave Chisnall, front row, Graham Liptrot, hooker, George Nicholls, second row and Harry Pinner [playing substitute]. *2014* Super League Grand Final: St Helens 14 Wigan Warriors 6 at Old Trafford. The losing spell was broken at last. Remember the Flower-Hohaia controversy? Wigan were always up against it with 12 men, but cracked in the end. Try-scorers were Tommy Makinson and Sia Soliola, in his final game for the club, with three goals from Mark Percival. Seeing Paul Wellens lift the trophy remains one of the great moments from Saints' history. James Roby won the Harry Sunderland Trophy too – a fantastic day for two St Helens RFC legends.

2014 Grand Final: the fans' view from the Stretford End. Lance Hohaia receives treatment as mayhem ensues after **that** tackle. [Alex Service]

12 OCTOBER

1895 Northern Rugby League St Helens 3 Warrington 0 at Knowsley Road. New signing Billy Ewan, from Kendal, made his debut at scrum-half. Belfast-born Fred Little was his stand-off. Saints were quite a cosmopolitan lot in those early days. *1960* Tour match: St Helens 15 Australia 12 at Knowsley Road. The Kangaroos were defeated by tries from Wilf Smith, Alan Briers and Tom van Vollenhoven. Brian McGinn kicked three goals. At full-back was South African Percy Landsberg. *1963* Northern Rugby League: Leeds 2 St Helens 10 at Headingley. Hooker Les Greenall made his second appearance for the club. Several years later, via Wigan and Rochdale Hornets, he played again for the Saints when he came off the bench at home to Batley, on 25 April 1970. *1975* Tour match: St Helens 7 Australia 32 at Knowsley Road. Australian stand-off Les Mara, from Balmain, made his debut for Saints against his fellow-countrymen.

Two Saints from different continents: St Helens–born Brian Glover [left pic Alex Service], the veteran threequarter who joined Saints from Warrington. Ross Conlon, a specialist goal-kicker from the Balmain club in Sydney. [Brian Peers]

13 OCTOBER

1970 Northern Rugby League: St Helens 37 Warrington 6 at Knowsley Road. Right winger Brian Glover made his debut against his former Warrington team-mates. Glover had previously enjoyed a successful Testimonial season at Wilderspool. *1985* First Division: Castleford 32 St Helens 18. Australian international centre Ross Conlon made his debut and kicked 5 goals. He was partnered at centre by another Australian import, Brett French. Conlon was happy to be in the Old Dart to watch his favourite football team: Manchester United! *1995* World Cup Group 2: New Zealand 22 Papua New Guinea 8 at Knowsley Road. 8,679 fans watched this encounter, with legendary Silver Ferns' right winger Sean Hoppe scoring one of the tries. Four years later, he became a Saint. Another future signing, Kevin Iro, was on the bench. *2007* Grand Final: St Helens 6 Leeds Rhinos 33 at Old Trafford, Manchester. Several years of competitive rugby and major final successes caught up with the Saints, with only a fabulous James Roby try and a Sean Long goal to show for another terrific season. But beware. The nightmare was only just beginning.

14 OCTOBER

1905 Lancashire Cup Round 1: St Helens 0 Wigan 18 at Knowsley Road. A disappointing start for the Saints in this fledgling competition that meant so much to both players and fans over the ensuing years. ***1911*** Tour match: St Helens 5 Australia 16 at Knowsley Road. Saints were well beaten by the visitors and the sole try-scorer was forward James 'Butcher' Prescott, with a goal from Jimmy Greenwood. ***1953*** County Championship: Lancashire 18 Yorkshire 10 at Leigh. Stand-off Peter Metcalfe, in his sole county appearance, kicked six goals – more than any other Saints' player in one match for the Red Rose county. ***1961*** Tour match: St Helens 25 New Zealand 10 at Knowsley Road. A most entertaining spectacle. 21-year-old Keith Northey scored a try and kicked five goals from stand-off half in his sixth competitive match. Other scorers were McGinn, Abe Terry, Huddart and Tom van Vollenhoven.

International class! Front-rower Abe Terry smashes his way past three Kiwi defenders for a three-pointer at Knowsley Road in 1961. [Alex Service]

2000 Grand Final: St Helens 29 Wigan Warriors 16 at Old Trafford. Saints duly retained their Super League crown and lifted their fifth trophy in the first five years of Super League. Wigan-born skipper Chris Joynt – had to mention that, didn't we – lifted the trophy after playing in every match of a triumphant, but exhausting, campaign. He became the third player to win the Harry Sunderland trophy twice, joining Alan Tait (Widnes) and Wigan's Andy Farrell. Six years later, there was more to savour. ***2006*** Grand Final: St. Helens 24 Hull FC 4 at Old Trafford, Manchester. A comprehensive victory in every respect. Saints thus won all three domestic trophies to claim a genuine treble. What a team. It was also Jamie Lyon's final game for the club. What a player.

2006 Grand Final: Great to be here. Saints' players make their preliminary visit to the Theatre of Dreams: Jon Wilkin, Ade Gardner, James Graham, Paul Wellens, Jamie Lyon, Maurie Fa'asavalu, James Roby and Francis Meli. [Bernard Platt]

15 OCTOBER

1890 Young Saints' forward John Brownbill, from Eldon Street, died as a result of typhoid fever and was buried in St Helens cemetery. The former employee of Nuttall's Bottleworks was just 20 years of age. This was a real tragedy that hit his close friends at Knowsley Road particularly hard. *1932* Vince Karalius, later dubbed the Wild Bull of the Pampas by the somewhat amazed Australian press during the 1958 Great Britain tour, was born in Widnes. He played every match, at whatever level, like it was a shoot-out at the OK Corral. *1940* Tommy Bishop, the Mighty Atom scrum-half, was born in St Helens. Tommy had a roundabout route via Blackpool Borough and Barrow before he joined his home town club in 1966. He helped the Saints to four trophies and ended up with selection for the Australasian tour. The Australians loved him and that's where he ended up, at Cronulla, initially. *1989* First Division: St Helens 50 Featherstone Rovers 11 at Knowsley Road. One of the highlights was a superb try from New Zealander George Mann on his home debut, who surged in for a brilliant 30 yarder at the Edington End. *2002* Loose forward Paul Sculthorpe became the first player to retain the prestigious Man of Steel award. He was really in his pomp then. It was little wonder that he later went on to become the sporting face of the Gillette company. A major coup for rugby league at the time. *2010* A memorable evening: the leaving of Knowsley Road Gala Night, hosted by television presenter Gordon Burns in a marquee on the famous turf, during which the club's Greatest 17 were unveiled. So many memories. So, who are the Greatest 17? Paul Wellens, Tom van Vollenhoven, Duggie Greenall, Paul Newlove, Alf Ellaby, Leslie Fairclough, Alex Murphy, Alan Prescott, Keiron Cunningham, Cliff Watson, Chris Joynt, Dick Huddart, Vince Karalius, Sean Long, Paul Sculthorpe, George Nicholls and Kel Coslett. What a fantastic array of talent.

Farewell Festival 2010: the legendary Alex Murphy OBE is inducted into the club's Greatest 17 in the huge marquee on the pitch at Knowsley Road, to rapturous applause. [Bernard Platt]

All smiles for Murph (left) as he receives his Greatest 17 framed commemoration from Eamonn McManus. Eamonn presents Club President and '17' incumbent Kel Coslett with his souvenir of a fantastic occasion. [Bernard Platt]

16 OCTOBER

1944 At the committee meeting at Knowsley Road, it was resolved that Committee member Mr J. Yearsley should be asked to fix a new rope to the flag pole before the next home match. ***1963*** Test match #137 Great Britain 2 Australia 28. This was the first test match to be played under floodlights; first to be played at Wembley and resulted in a record winning margin for Australia in an Ashes test. Alex Murphy and front-rower John Tembey were in the British ranks, but they couldn't stop Australian 'gun' centre Reg Gasnier, who flew in for a brilliant hat-trick of tries. ***1988*** First Division: St Helens 9 Hull FC 20 at Knowsley Road. Not in the script this one. Short-contract Australian stars Michael O'Connor at centre and loose-forward Paul 'Fatty' Vautin made their debuts, but the visitors were by far the better team on the day.

17 OCTOBER

1914 Lancashire Cup Round 1: Swinton 13 St Helens 11 at Swinton. Powerhouse winger Tom Barton scored a brace of tries – the fourth match in a row when he achieved this feat, beginning at Oldham on 19 September. He had great power and pace, for sure. This remarkable document – written by the man himself – charts his impressive sporting career. [Alex Service]

Born St Helens   T. Barton
Winder Juniors (Association) where I learned football
Started for Saints 1899–1900 Seasons
International Cap 1905 + 6 Season against other Nationalities at Wigan (Fullback Position)
Captain for Saints for 9 or 10 years Selected for County Twice & 3 times Reserve once Reserve against Kangaroos
Winner of 5 Gold Medals at Soccer
2 Gold Medals at Rugby 1 of which is Runner up for

Northern Union Cup against Huddersfield 1914 + 15
One when we beat Wigan for a Charity Cup 1912 Season by 13 pts to 8 pts
Was Officialy selected to to tour New Zealand & Australia in the year 1910
Won the Proffesional footballers sprint open to all Soccer & Rugby players at Liverpool
I retired in the Season 1922 + 3 received a benefit against Rochdale Hts in 1921 + 2
Won many prizes on the track & took a relay team X to Preston & won it of X St Helens players

1982 Tour Match: St Helens 0 Australia 32 at Knowsley Road. A 'test strength' Australian outfit were too good for a weakened Saints' team with a future Lancashire Cup Final the following Saturday in mind. Not a good idea, really; a public relations disaster and the Lancashire Cup match was lost as well, 16–0 to Warrington. Paul Forber played his first competitive match in the second row.

18 OCTOBER

1912 Welsh international rugby union forward James Webb signed for the Saints for a signing-on £80. He had played union for Abertillery and was aged 27. He was captain of club and county, had 20 caps for Wales and played for his county on 30 occasions. *St Helens Newspaper*: 'With a reputation like this, Webb should indeed be a useful man to the St Helens team and the pack should be wonderfully strengthened by his inclusion." Unfortunately, James played just five matches for the Saints. Things didn't work out quite as well as he hoped. *1971* Northern Rugby League: St Helens 50 Oldham 2 at Knowsley Road. The true spirit of rugby league. A half-time collection was held for the family of former player Jackie Pimblett, who had died, tragically, after playing for Pilkington Recs when a scrum collapsed. The amount raised was £170-77p. The Saints' players played for nothing: their match fees were later added to the total as a donation from the club. *1992* Lancashire Cup Final: St Helens 4 Wigan 5 at Knowsley Road. The last one. Fittingly, they were our first opponents when the competition began. A gruelling, pummelling 'derby' clash, with little to choose between the teams. A disappointing outcome for Saints' fans in the packed crowd of over 20,000. A great occasion, though. You just had to be there.

19 OCTOBER

1929 Northern Rugby League: St Helens 18 Salford 12 at Knowsley Road. Alf Ellaby and his centre partner Alf Frodsham both scored 'doubles' in a closely-fought encounter against the Red Devils *1970* Northern Rugby League: St Helens 42 Bradford Northern 0. Loose-forward and captain Kel Coslett booted over an incredible 12 goals from 12 attempts, including three penalties of over 50 yards. Follow that!

Jackie Pimblett (back row second from left) in the St Helens schoolboys team in 1958. Two other future Saints include Frank Barrow (next to him on the left) and Jeff Heaton, far right on the back row. [Alex Service]

2002 Grand Final: St Helens 19 Bradford Bulls 18 at Old Trafford. In one of the most dramatic and exciting matches ever seen at the Theatre of Dreams, Sean Long's last-minute drop-goal won the game for the Saints. They were the best side in the league, after all.

Day after the night before. Its celebration time at Knowsley Road as the Saints parade the Super League trophy after the defeat of Bradford Bulls in 2002. The happy chappies are: Tommy Martyn, Paul Newlove, Skipper Chris Joynt and Barry Ward. [Bernard Platt]

20 OCTOBER

1951 Tour match: St Helens 10 New Zealand 33 at Knowsley Road. A crushing victory for the men with the silver ferns. Saints' points were scored by the Welsh triumvirate of George Parsons and Ray Cale with tries and centre Vivian Harrison with two goals. **1956** Lancashire Cup Final: St Helens 3 Oldham 10 at Central Park. Oldham were a really powerful outfit at this time and deservedly won the trophy in front of almost 40,000 fans. Winger Frank Carlton registered Saints' only points with a try. 35 years later, things were different, however. **1991** Lancashire Cup Final: St Helens 24 Rochdale Hornets 14 at Wilderspool. The groundwork had been done after dismissing Wigan in the semis. Second-rower George Mann scored two typically barnstorming tries, with Phil Veivers also notching a brace. **1993** Keiron Cunningham, a young lad from Thatto Heath, playing for Wigan St Judes, signed full professional forms for the Saints. A cliché, maybe, but the rest is history.

21 OCTOBER

1876 Friendly match: St Helens versus Birkenhead Flamingoes, at Boundary Road. This match, against such engagingly-named opponents from over the water, ended in a draw. **1899** Northern Rugby League: St Helens 17 Stockport 3 at Knowsley Road. Former St Helens Recs full-back James Crossley made the first of his four appearance for the Saints, as a left winger. His centre, Jim Barnes, scored two tries. **1984** Division One: St Helens 32 Oldham 5 at Knowsley Road. Mal Meninga led the way for the homesters, with a brace of tries.

Left: His defence was thunderous too. Mal Meninga threatens to dump an Oldham attacker at Knowsley Road; right: workhorse Tony Burke takes the ball up in the same match. Neil Holding and Shaun Allen (rear) are also in the frame. [Brian Peers]

2017 A sad time for all Saints' fans and the rugby league community. Karel Thomas van Vollenhoven passed away in Gauteng, South Africa, aged 82. He will be sadly missed by so many people. A special commemorative book was opened at Saints' stadium, which received a multitude of memories from fans and team-mates for his family to treasure. Indeed, like a number of Saints' fans with a turntable, we put on the original copy of the Vollenhoven Calypso single and shed a quiet tear or two. As vocalist Reggie Byron sang the words: "the idol of them all" in his gorgeous Caribbean lilt, we nodded our heads in agreement. In his pomp, he certainly was. Great times indeed.

22 OCTOBER

1978 First Division: St Helens 8 Warrington 10 at Knowsley Road. A dynamic player in his younger days, Chris Arkwright made his senior debut at left centre and a star was born, as they say. *1981* John Player Trophy Round 1 Replay: Barrow 17 St Helens 0 at Craven Park. A poor evening for the Saints. The teams drew 16–16 at Knowsley Road four days before.

23 OCTOBER

1948 Northern Rugby League: Keighley 12 St Helens 10 at Lawkholme Lane. Second-rower George Parr scored a try on debut. He made 125 appearances for the club from 1948 to 1955 and, ironically, died on the same date in 2003, aged 78. *1963* Powerful second-rower John Warlow was signed from Llanelli RUFC. He was 'billeted' at Minnie Cotton's house in St Luke's Road and later formed a fabulous back row partnership with other union converts, Ray French and John Mantle, at Wembley in 1966.

1982 Lancashire Cup Final: Warrington 16 St Helens 0 at Central Park. Only 6,462 witnessed this one-sided affair. Saints rested a number of key players for the previous match against the visiting Australians at Knowsley Road, and had lost heavily, but it made no difference against the rampant Wire. The Saints did get some revenge, beating the Wire 16–11 the following week at Knowsley Road.

24 OCTOBER

1942 Yorkshire Cup Round 1, first leg: St Helens 21 Wigan 8 at Knowsley Road. Yes, that's right – the *Yorkshire* Cup. There was a dearth of Lancashire teams still operating during the War, hence the anomaly. Right winger Bob Grundy scored a brace, as did his centre, Jimmy Stott. Saints lost the second leg 32–11 in extra time after the aggregate scores were level. The team won only two league matches during a desperate season.

1953 Lancashire Cup Final: St Helens 16 Wigan 8 at Station Road. A record crowd for this Final of 42,793 saw Saints triumph with tries from full-back Glyn Moses and stand-off Jimmy Honey. Stand-off sensation Peter Metcalfe kicked five goals. Sadly, by 2018, affable Welshman Glyn Moses was the only surviving member of that famous team.

1964 Lancashire Cup Final: St Helens 12 Swinton 4 at Central Park. What's not to like about the Cup Kings of Lancashire? Saints won their fifth consecutive Lancashire Cup in their seventh successive final appearance. *1967* Tour match: St Helens 8 Australia 4 at Knowsley Road. A fine victory against the visitors, who cut up a bit rough during the match, with a dazed and bloodied Tom van Vollenhoven one of the unfortunate recipients. 17,300 saw Saints win with two Kel Coslett goals and two drop-goals from scrum-half Tommy Bishop.

25 OCTOBER

1910 *St Helens Newspaper* announced the signing of the club's first Australian player: "Rupert Upton, the new professional from the Recs Cricket Club has arrived here and intends starting work in the town. Upton is a wing or centre threequarter back, who, in Australia played with Hickey, the famous international for the Glebe Club and since his arrival in England during the last football season, he has assisted Barrow in several of their engagements." *1958* Lancashire Cup Final: St Helens 2 Oldham 12 at Central Park. The third successive win for the Roughyeds in the competition. Saints were hampered with an injury to hooker Tom McKinney after just eight minutes. Crowd: 38,780. Ten years later, it was all so different.

1968 Lancashire Cup Final: St Helens 30 Oldham 2 at Central Park. A game of two halves. Saints slipped into gear to blow the Roughyeds away in the second half after being 2–0 down at the interval. Welsh winger Frank Wilson glided over for two cracking tries.

2002 Tour Match: St. Helens 26 New Zealand 38 at Knowsley Road. The last match of its kind. Saints, the week after their Grand Final success over Bradford Bulls, were somewhat exhausted and fielded a somewhat weakened side. Yet it was a tremendously enjoyable 12-try spectacular for the 5,612 fans at Knowsley Road, not least for the 'hidden' goalkicking skills of front-rower Barry Ward. Saints, with Kiwi legend Sean Hoppe captain for the evening, were in contention right until the 73 minute, when second-rower Tony Puletua scored his second try. He would become a Saint himself, in 2009.

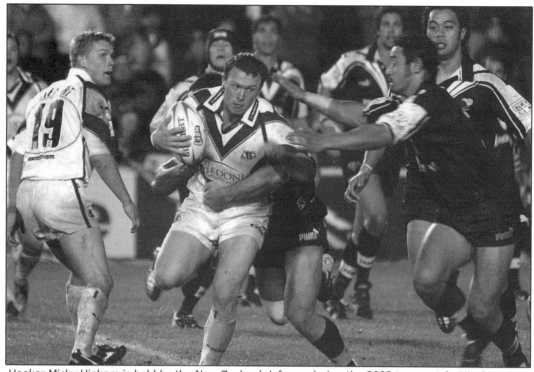

Hooker Micky Higham is held by the New Zealand defence during the 2002 tour match. Nigel Vagana (right) is about to finish the job. [Bernard Platt]

26 OCTOBER

1929 Northern Rugby League: St Helens 10 Castleford 20 at Knowsley Road. International centre Arthur Atkinson of Castleford kicked an incredible 'wind-assisted' penalty goal from 75 yards towards the goal at the Pavilion End. At one stage in the 1930s, the St Helens club built a windbreak at the Eccleston End, which was classed, for a time, as the world's largest billboard and was sponsored by Lewis's department Stores in Liverpool.

Left: Castleford's long-distance kicker Arthur Atkinson (middle) on tour with Saints' players Albert Fildes (left) and Alf Ellaby en route to Australia on the SS Jervis Bay in 1932 [Alex Service]

1929 County Championship: Cumberland 7 Lancashire 15 at Whitehaven. Legendary right-winger Alf Ellaby scored the only hat-trick by a Saints' player for the Red Rose county. A fine achievement on the day. **1957** Northern Rugby League: St Helens 36 Leeds 7 at Knowsley Road. Tom van Vollenhoven, the legendary 'Flying Springbok', made a memorable debut with a late try in front of 23,000 spectators. You just had to be there, they say.

184

1963 Lancashire Cup Final: St Helens 15 Leigh 4 at Station Road, Swinton. A break from their 'usual' opponents, Swinton, Saints had a backline that read as follows: Len Killeen (one try), Tom van Vollenhoven (one try), Keith Northey and Peter Harvey. The 'Vol in the centre' experiment was soon disbanded, however. *1965* From the Boardroom: "A request by the Coach for new training kit for the First Team was agreed by the Board. It was also agreed that in future any new strip ordered be made with a red vee on white and that permission be obtained from the RFL for a change of colours to be registered." White with a red vee it has been ever since.

27 OCTOBER

1962 Lancashire Cup Final: St Helens 7 Swinton 4 at Central Park. The two old foes locked horns once more, with Saints coming out on top, with a try from Tom van Vollenhoven and two Kel Coslett goals. Saints had a barely-out-of-teens half-back combination of Billy Benyon and scrum-half Jeff Heaton on view and they lived up to expectations. *1972* New offices and a souvenir shop were opened at the Knowsley Road ground, well-received improvements that kept the club up with the more progressive members of the league. The shop became a well-appointed Superstore in the new stadium, but from small acorns. *1985* Tour match: St Helens 8 New Zealand 46 at Knowsley Road. The Premiership winners were expected to give the tourists one of their biggest examinations and the match was shown live 'Down Under'. Unfortunately, it was rather a one-sided affair, as the score suggests. Great Britain second-rower Roy Haggerty scored Saints' only try, with Australian centre Ross Conlon pitching in with two goals. *2016* Jimmy Goodier, Saints' hooker during the Second World War years, celebrated his 91st birthday, at his home in Thatto Heath that he had built himself.

28 OCTOBER

1966 Northern Rugby League: St Helens 16 Leeds 3 at Knowsley Road. There was a ground collection at the match in aid of the Aberfan Fund, which raised £360. This was a truly heart-breaking scenario for the Principality, which remains in our thoughts to this day. *1976* Keiron Cunningham, (left) one of a family of 11 siblings, was born in Thatto Heath, St Helens. It should be mentioned that by this time, his elder brother Eddie had already won a Challenge Cup winner's medal when Saints beat Widnes 20–5 some six months before. A fine sporting family, for sure. Keiron is pictured playing for England Schoolboys at Knowsley Road in 1992 [Alex Service]. *1984* Lancashire Cup Final: Wigan 18 St Helens 26 at Central Park. A stupendous match. Saints dominated the first 40, with two tries from Australian superstar Mal Meninga. Wigan came back menacingly, with Saints' only points after the interval courtesy of the trusty boot of Sean Day. The cup came back to Knowsley Road for the first time in 16 years.

29 OCTOBER

1960 Lancashire Cup Final: St Helens 15 Swinton 9 at Central Park. The start of Saints' early 1960s domination of the trophy. 31,755 saw tries by Tom van Vollenhoven, his centre Ken Large, together with stand-off Austin Rhodes, who also kicked three goals for good measure.

1961 Lancashire Cup Final: centre Ken Large gives Tom van Vollenhoven the perfect reverse pass at a packed Central Park. [Alex Service]

2011 Bridging the gap. The main section of the bridge linking the town centre with the new Stadium at Langtree Park was lifted into place during a complex operation. The superb structure was later named the Stephen Prescott Bridge and won several design awards.

2017 World Cup Group Match: France 18 Lebanon 29 at Canberra Stadium. Stand-off Theo Fages captained the French team. He became the first Saints' player to achieve this honour.

Left: Easy does it! The new bridge to Langtree Park takes shape early in 2011 [Ron Lee]; right: Le Capitaine! Theo Fages in a pre-World Cup photoshoot [RLPhotos.com]

30 OCTOBER

1907 Tour match: St Helens 5 New Zealand 24 at Knowsley Road. The first tourists were dubbed the All Golds as a result of their professional status. In the visiting team was Australian star 'Dally' Messenger, a superb footballer, who was a huge attraction on the tour itself. **1933** Original Saint and 'Chemical King' David Gamble (left) passed away, in his mid–70s. One of 13 forwards in the club's first-ever match, against Liverpool Royal Infirmary early in 1874, he was one of four sons of Irish-born Sir David Gamble, the First Baronet of Windlehurst. The family manufactured soda for the soap industry and bleaching powder. Following his death, he left over £90,000 in his will. [Image: St Helens Townships Family History Society]

31 OCTOBER

1933 Back-rower Bill Shiels was born in St Helens. Bill was mostly a member of the 'A' team, making six appearances for the seniors before moving to Liverpool City. **1959** Lancashire Cup Final: Warrington 5 St Helens 4 at Central Park. Warrington's Australian winger Brian Bevan scored a controversial try which essentially was the match-winner. Following a kick from centre Ally Naughton, he jumped up to celebrate his touchdown that many people thought was non-existent. No video refs in those days, unfortunately, but his positive body language won the day. **2011** Len Killeen, the left-wing maestro and a member of both the St Helens and Balmain Halls of Fame, passed away in Port Elizabeth, South Africa, aged 72. Len was laid-back and a brilliant footballer with a superb array of skills. He had pace, swerve and the ability to totally bamboozle opposing defenders with a tremendous array of tricks. He had a long place kick and, contrary to some opinions, Saints knew all about his potential with the boot when they signed him from the Uitenhage Swifts club. He became the talisman in the four cups season of 1965–66. What would they have done without him?

November

Winter closing in!

The demise of the Great Britain team at the end of 2007 caused widespread disappointment. Here's the marvellous Paul Sculthorpe dictating play during the 2001 Ashes series against the Aussies and the chance to pit his skills against the likes of Brad Fittler (13), a player he so much admired.
[Bernard Platt]

November is the most important month in Saints' history, when the inaugural meeting took place at the Fleece Hotel in Church Street with the object of forming a rugby club. Apparently, founder William Douglas Herman wanted to establish a team at the Pilkington Crown Glassworks, where he was head chemist, but it came to nought and a town team was established. In 2018, St Helens RFC celebrated its 145th birthday, with hopefully, many more to come. We've come a long way, baby. And yes – November. The month is now taken up with international rugby league, a crucially important time to enhance the game's widespread appeal. This has included test match series by both Kiwis and Kangaroos, together with Tri and Four Nations competitions. The World Cup has also been a crucial part of this particular time slot, with Langtree Park hosting the Australia versus Fiji clash in 2013.

1 NOVEMBER

1966 BBC2 Floodlit Trophy Round 2: Barrow 16 St Helens 16 at Craven Park. Frank Barrow was at full-back; his brother, Tony joined him in the centre. Both were from Thatto Heath and Saints through and through. Frank would bowl over defenders with the ball in hand and smash into would-be attackers who dared to break the line. He was a hugely popular character during his time at Knowsley Road as a player and later assistant coach. *1987* Tour match: St Helens 52 Auckland 26 at Knowsley Road. Denis Litherland came off the bench to play the last of his 142 games for the club. It was a much-needed morale victory for the Saints, who were having a mixed run of results. *2000* World Cup Group 1: England 76 Russia 4 at Knowsley Road. The attendance was a disappointing 5,736. Paul Wellens at full-back and Sean Long, on the bench, were the Saints' representatives. Man-of-the-match for the Russians was front-rower and captain Ian Rubin, from Sydney City Roosters.

Frank Barrow (left) during the 2013 St Helens Players' Association lunch; another popular Saint – winger Adam Swift models the new 'home' jersey for 2018 at Ruskin Sports Village. [Alex Service]

2 NOVEMBER

1934 Jack Bradbury was signed from Bradford Northern, although he was born in St Helens. He went on to play 231 games for the Saints as player and player-coach, sometimes as a centre, scrum-half or loose-forward. He was as tough as they come. *2013* World Cup Group match: Australia 34 Fiji 2 at Langtree Park. On a cold, windswept night, Australia's tries were scored by Papali, Boyd, Jennings, Josh Morris, Cherry-Evans and Luke Lewis, who was injured when he slid into the fence at the Western Terrace end. Johnathan Thurston kicked five goals, including one beauty from the North Stand touchline into the teeth of the gale. How did he do that? Pure genius. *2017* Saints' new home and away playing jerseys were revealed for the first time for the 2018 Super League campaign. The home jersey was based on the 'inlaid vee' from the late 1980s, which was a popular design.

189

3 NOVEMBER

1914 The *St Helens Newspaper* carried the following item of news which was very much a sign of the times: "[Jim] Flanagan joined the Pals battalion of the South Lancashire Regiment and has been vaccinated, which prevented him turning out on Saturday." *1945* Northern Rugby League: Swinton 5 St Helens 5 at Station Road. Back-rower Jack Fearnley played his last match for the club, his 140th, before eventually moving to Belle Vue Rangers. He later became business development manager at the showground and zoo complex at Belle Vue. *1970* From the Boardroom: Following a letter sent to the club by Tom van Vollenhoven, Saints expressed an interest in bustling South African centre Tobias du Toit, although his signing was not forthcoming and he eventually joined Warrington. *1991* First Division: Wakefield Trinity 20 St Helens 12 at Belle Vue. A surprising defeat for the Saints, who scored tries from left-winger Les Quirk and Phil Veivers, playing loose forward. Full-back Dave Tanner kicked two goals.

4 NOVEMBER

1891 Billy Cross made his county debut for Lancashire against Cambridge University. Arguably the first Saints' 'great' Billy was a silky-smooth operator at fly-half and captain of the Saints for a number of years. *1961* Test Match #127: Great Britain 35 New Zealand 19 at Station Road. Scrum-half Alex Murphy and hooker Bob Dagnall scored tries in the biggest win to date over the Kiwis, and the series was won 2–1. Mighty Dick Huddart was also in the second row. *2006* Gillette Tri-Nations Game four Test Match #318: Australia 12 Great Britain 23 at Aussie Stadium, Sydney. A triumph for the British and the Saints. Representing their country with distinction were Paul Wellens, Leon Pryce, Sean Long, James Roby, Lee Gilmour and Jon Wilkin. Jamie Lyon also played left centre for Australia. A superb Paul Wellens score really unsettled the home side just before the interval, with Lee Gilmour also going over in the 61st minute. Sean Long kicked three from five and a drop-goal for good measure, despite some 'unwanted attention' from Willie Mason. A classic victory to savour, while it lasted.

5 NOVEMBER

1963 From the Boardroom: "The Chairman [Harry Cook] reported that [John] Warlow had arrived in St Helens to stay and had been fixed up in lodgings with Mrs. Cotton." Perhaps the date is significant. Cue future fireworks, one might say? Minnie Cotton, bless her, thought the world of Welshman John and, of course, she sprang to his defence with an umbrella after ructions in the 1966 Challenge Cup Semi-Final against Dewsbury. *1978* Test Match #203: Great Britain 18 Australia 14 at Odsal. The first Sunday Ashes test match to be played in England. Over 26,000 fans saw the Brits level the series 1–1. Ironically, they were dubbed 'Dad's Army', especially in the forwards. Second-rower George Nicholls was the only Saints representative, who was in his early 30s, but he was still at the very top of his game. *2009* Former Sydney Roosters' centre-cum-back-rower Sia Soliola arrived in St Helens on an initial three-year contract. His first season was virtually wiped out after damaging knee ligaments against Warrington on 19 March 2010, although he returned for Saints' play-off campaign. Despite the initial setback, Sia became a huge favourite with the fans, winning a Grand Final ring against Wigan Warriors in 2014 before joining Canberra Raiders.

2017 World Cup: Fiji 72 Wales 6 at Townsville Stadium, Queensland, Australia. Saints' forward Morgan Knowles played for Wales on his 21st birthday and scored their only try of the match [left: RL Photos.com]. A bitter-sweet experience, no doubt?

6 NOVEMBER

1918 Austin Cooper Carr was the first President of St Helens RFC. He passed away in a Liverpool nursing home, aged 59. An iron works proprietor and horse breeder, he played for the club in the second season of its existence. A former alumni of St John's College, Cambridge, Austin's father was the Vicar of St Helens. **1983** John Player Trophy Round 1: Kent Invicta 7 St Helens 40 at Maidstone United FC. A long way to travel for the fans – and there were a number who did – but they witnessed a convincing victory. Saints went on to the Semi-Final only to be beaten 18–4 by Widnes at Wilderspool. **2009** Paul Clough and Paul Wellens took part in a photoshoot for the latest club catalogue of leisure wear from sportswear company Puma, with the Knowsley Road ground as a backdrop.

Left: Austin Cooper Carr in military garb [St Helens Townships Family History Society]; right: an unlikely catwalk for rugby league players! Cloughy and Wello strut their stuff. [Bernard Platt]

191

7 NOVEMBER

1959 Northern Rugby League St Helens 40 Liverpool City 17 at Knowsley Road. South African Percy Landsberg made his debut at right centre to fellow countryman Tom van Vollenhoven, who scored three tries. During his time at St Helens he proved to be a popular player with the fans and team-mates alike. He passed away aged 82, in March 2018 and always treasured his Saints' jersey above all his sporting memorabilia. *1978* BBC2 Floodlit Trophy Round 2: St Helens 47 Castleford 5 at Knowsley Road. Both centres, who were also great stand-offs, Peter Glynn and Bill Francis, registered a hat-trick of tries. Saints reached the Final, when they lost to Widnes, 13–7, also at Knowsley Road.

8 NOVEMBER

1884 Friendly match: St Helens 1 try 8 minors Crawford Village 1 try 2 minors, at Boundary Road. An early 'derby' clash against the lads from down Rainford way. *1952* Test Match #81 (50th Ashes test match): Great Britain 21 Australia 5 at Station Road. Right centre Duggie Greenall scored twice in front of over 32,421. Duggie's second try, converted by Ernest Ward, was on the final whistle and series-winning celebrations could begin. *1958* Northern Rugby League: St Helens 42 Rochdale Hornets 12 at Knowsley Road. South African Jan Prinsloo made a two-try debut. He had watched his first game of rugby league three days before when Salford took on Leeds at Old Trafford, the home of Manchester United FC.

Jan Prinsloo (left) combined power and pace on the flanks; Jackie Waring, a footballing centre right out of the top drawer, wears his England jersey with pride. [Alex Service]

9 NOVEMBER

1884 Saints winger Christopher Chavasse OBE MC TD was born Oxford. He was the Curate at St Helens Parish Church when he made six appearances for the Saints, scoring three tries. Christopher was an Olympic athlete, became a military Chaplain and was later appointed the Bishop of Rochester. Quite a guy. *1940* War time international: England 8 Wales 5 at Watersheddings. Centre Jackie Waring and stand-off Frank Tracey were the Saints' representatives. The match was stopped in the first half after an air raid warning. The players were taken off and the match resumed later after the all-clear given. *1970* Tour match: St Helens 37 Australia 10 at Knowsley Road. Wow, what a game. Australia came over to Lancashire on the back of a World Cup Final victory at Headingley the previous Saturday and were blown away by Saints' attacking rugby, typified by a brilliant hat-trick from stand-off Alan Whittle. "What a pity the cameras missed this one" said Brian Batty in the *Daily Mail*. How right he was! *2013* The great full-back Steve Prescott MBE lost his battle against illness, at the age of 39. An inspiration to so many people with some unbelievable fund-raising challenges, Saints and Hull FC later inaugurated the Steve Prescott Cup in his honour. The Man of Steel Trophy was re-named after him too – quite appropriate.

10 NOVEMBER

1932 Saints' Harry Ince died after a long illness, aged 57. His nephew, Stan was a member of the St Helens Board of Directors in the 1970s. Harry is buried in St Helens cemetery and on his gravestone is the following inscription: 'When the Great Scorer comes to write against your name, he writes not that you won or lost, but how you played the game." Marvellous stuff. *1951* Test Match #78: Great Britain 20 New Zealand 19 at Station Road. A landmark moment. Front-rower Alan Prescott made his debut in test match rugby. This was also the first televised test match. Alan Dixon was the commentator, aided by Harry Sunderland. Eddie Waring was the half-time summariser. *2007* Test Match #324: Great Britain 28 New Zealand 22 at the JJB Stadium, Wigan. The last time, at the time of writing, that a Great Britain team took the field. Paul Wellens, Ade Gardner and Jon Wilkin were in the starting line-up, with James Roby and James Graham on the bench. Indeed, 'Jammer' Graham scored a real 'powerhouse' try, brushing aside six attempted Kiwi tacklers in the process, but it wasn't the last try for Great Britain. That was scored by Danny Maguire of Leeds Rhinos.

11 NOVEMBER

1969 From the Boardroom: "It was reported that there had again been complaints regarding the lack of hot water in the Referees Room, it was agreed to look into the possibility of having an additional tank installed to provide hot water direct by means of an immersion heater." A golden rule: always look after the ref. When dressing facilities later moved to the Main Stand, there was an eye-test chart in the officials' changing room. They were warmer by then and had a sense of humour. *1972* World Cup Final (Test Match #186): Great Britain 10 Australia 10 at Stade de Gerland, Lyon. John Walsh, at left centre, was the only Saints representative. Leeds's John Atkinson was outside him. After 20 minutes extra time, there was no further scoring. Great Britain were awarded the World Cup on a superior points-scoring average in the final table. *1984* First Division: St Helens 59 Barrow 2 at Knowsley Road. Barry Ledger, normally a winger, was at stand-off and scored three tries. His scrum-half was Neil Holding.

12 NOVEMBER

1887 Friendly match: Kendal Hornets 1 goal 5 tries 4 minors St Helens 0 at Kendal. The match report in the *Athletic News* highlighted the difference between the teams: "the passing of [Buff] Berry and Cross to the threequarter backs very much puzzled the St Helens players, who hardly knew where they had the ball." Ball handling wizard Billy Cross would become a Saint in later years. **1910** Northern Rugby League: St Helens 13 Merthyr Tydfil 3 at Knowsley Road. Right centre Jimmy Greenwood suffered 'shock and internal haemorrhage' and was in a potentially 'grave' condition after a crunching tackle from his opposite number and spent time in St Helens Hospital, who were, according to the local press: "besieged with enquiries about his well-being!" Fortunately, he made a full recovery. **1989** First Division: St Helens 62 Barrow 18 at Knowsley Road. A cracking four-pointer from stand-off Tommy Frodsham was one of many highlights. He scored a try in his next two games, against Hull and Oldham. Scrum-half Neil Holding scorched in for three tries – the last one of five hat-tricks for the club during his career. **2015** A plaque was unveiled at the top of a specially-constructed stone plinth on the site of the playing pitch at the former Knowsley Road ground to commemorate the 120th anniversary of the first-ever match under Northern Union (later, of course, rugby league) rules. The project was a partnership between Knowsley Road developers Taylor Wimpey, the RFL, St Helens RFC and the local council. Saints' Chairman Eamonn McManus performed the opening ceremony. RFL chief executive Nigel Wood was also in attendance.

A moment of closure? The commemorative plinth and plaque are opened by Saints' Chairman Eamonn McManus and Mayor, Councillor Stephen Glover (fourth and fifth from the left respectively). Former St Helens forward and star of stage and screen, Adam Fogerty, is on the far right.
[Alex Service]

13 NOVEMBER

1905 Rugbyite, in the *St Helens Newspaper*, revealed the club President's good fortune at the races and his good nature: "The St Helens club are indeed lucky enough to have a President like Captain Michael Hughes, for apart from the interest which he takes in the doings of the team, his generosity is unlimited. This splendid sportsmanship was revealed in a striking manner when he announced that he was giving to the club the stakes which a horse of his had won that day at the Manchester Races, a 'small matter' of about £70 which is a vast sum to the St Helens club. The fact that Capt Hughes does not win out of his turn on the turf makes his gift all the more generous." The well-connected [later Colonel] Hughes, of Sherdley Hall was a major owner and breeder of racehorses and there was a special six furlong gallop created for them in the grounds of his home at Sherdley Park. One of his horses, Aesop, was second in the 1893 Grand National. [Image courtesy of Sutton Harriers AC]

1909 Exhibition match: St Helens 21 Hull FC 33 at Great Heath ground, Coventry. The local rugby union team had been suspended for three months by the RFU for flirting with professionalism. This was an opportunity too good to miss. The Northern Union sent down two teams to play an exhibition game, which aroused much interest locally and a Coventry team later joined the Northern Union. **1926** Test Match #33 England 21 New Zealand 11 at the Boulevard, Hull. Stand-off Leslie Fairclough became the first Saints player to take part in a test match and scored a try on debut. He was joined by Albert Fildes (St Helens Recreation and later a Saint) in the second row, who also scored a try.

1973 Tour match: St Helens 11 Australia 7 at Knowsley Road. A brilliant victory for the Saints, although Welsh front-rower Mel James suffered a broken leg which effectively kept him out of contention until he returned as a substitute against Wakefield Trinity in the Challenge Cup on 22 February 1975.

Left: Welsh front-rower Mel James, who fought back from injury to become a stalwart of the St Helens club. He is photographed taking on the Leeds defence at Wembley in 1978. Graham Liptrot is behind him.
[Alex Service]

14 NOVEMBER

1931 Early Northern Union stalwart William Briers died aged 56 after an appendectomy. He is buried at Christ Church, Eccleston. *1928* Representative match: Wales 15 England 39 at Sloper Road, Cardiff. George Lewis was at right centre for Wales; Saints' Englishmen were: right winger Ellaby, who scored a blistering hat-trick, Alf Frodsham, who scored a try from the other flank and schemer Leslie Fairclough at scrum-half. *2009* Gillette Four Nations Final: England 16 Australia 46 at Elland Road, Leeds. England were in contention, 16–22, until Australia produced four killer tries in the last 13 minutes. Gut-wrenching stuff for the packed crowd. Saints' representatives were: Kyle Eastmond, James Graham, James Roby and Jon Wilkin.

James Roby off-loads to Kevin Sinfield (Leeds Rhinos) during the 2009 Four Nations Final at a packed Elland Road. Another Saints' representative, Kyle Eastmond, is in the background. [Bernard Platt]

15 NOVEMBER

1889 According to the local press: "Mr Leopold Weisker, of the Wellington Hotel, St Helens applied to Messrs. R. Pilkington and JC Gamble, at the Police Court on Tuesday morning, for an occasional licence for St Helens football field, Dentons Green on the occasion of the illuminated football match on Thursday evening. Mr Weisker stated that the match was being played with the aid of Wells lights and he asked for a licence from six to nine o'clock. Superintendent Barker objected to the granting of the application on the grounds that it might conduce to disturbance at night. The bench stated that the application would be refused." The Wellington Hotel, in Naylor Street South was the club headquarters at the time. *1919* Centre supreme Jimmy Stott was born in Parr, St Helens. A Scorpio feels things very deeply and he was a man of principle in the way in which rugby should be played, a true Corinthian in that respect.

The newly-constructed Edington Stand is photographed at the Eccleston End of Knowsley Road. As it says on the advertising board, steelwork was by local company Todd Brothers. [Alex Service]

1950 Work on the new enclosure at the Eccleston End, later named the Edington Stand, began, with steel fabrication from local company Todd Brothers. The enclosure was renowned as the 'away' end for visiting spectators at Knowsley Road. **1972** Tour match: St Helens 9 Australia 24 at Knowsley Road. The Kangaroos had to be at their best to beat this Saints' team, whose points came from a Frank Wilson try and three goals from Kel Coslett.

16 NOVEMBER

1895 Northern Union: St Helens 0 Wigan 0 at Knowsley Road. The first 'derby' clash in the new professional competition, was as you might expect, a game of relatively few chances.
1929 Tour match: St Helens 18 Australia 18 at Knowsley Road. A breathless exhibition of open rugby from both sides. Both Saints' wingers scored two tries: Kiwi flyer Roy Hardgrave on the right and Ben Halfpenny – normally a second-rower – on the left.
1935 Northern Rugby League: St Helens 31 Bramley 3 at Knowsley Road. Five goals for front-rower Bill Fletcher, who later moved to Holme Farm, virtually next door to Saints' ground, behind the Eccleston End.
1963 First Division: St Helens 11 Featherstone Rovers 11 at Knowsley Road. Former St Patricks (Widnes) junior Duggie Laughton made his debut. A fine loose-forward, with excellent hands and organisational ability, it was a shame that his tenure at Saints was relatively short, with 78 appearances and 14 tries, from 1963 to 1965.

17 NOVEMBER

1964 From the Boardroom: "Mr F and J Yearsley reported on the trip to Newport to watch Newport [RUFC] player John Mantle, it was agreed that the player should be watched as often as possible by various directors...." The importance of 'getting things right' was paramount in assessing new signings and getting the signature of 'Big John' was a big plus for the club.
1985 Rangy centre Mark Elia signed from the Te Atatu club in New Zealand. An effective ball runner and finisher, Mark was also an exceptional cricketer, who played in the Yorkshire leagues for a spell.

18 NOVEMBER

1893 Friendly: St Helens 25 Tuebrook 3 at Knowsley Road. A disappointing crowd of just a few hundred watched this match. Saints scored seven tries: Doherty (2), Traynor, Cross, McLees, Jones and Gladwin, with captain Billy Cross also chipping in with two goals. A tantalising piece of memorabilia remains from this match, [below: Alex Service] with the Saints' team printed on card, the forerunner of today's club programme. *1984* John Player Trophy Round 1: St Helens 60 Keighley 8 at Knowsley Road. Left winger Sean Day kicked 10 goals, a feat he achieved three times in the 1984–85 campaign. His achievements with the boot, albeit in a short time scale, frequently go 'under the radar'. True fans know different.

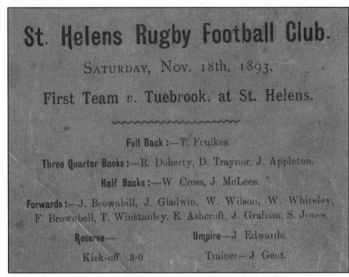

19 NOVEMBER

1873 Where it all began. St Helens RFC was formed at a public meeting on a Wednesday evening in the Fleece Hotel. Some other rugby league clubs also formed in 1873 include Salford, Wakefield Trinity, Halifax and Millom ARLFC. *1938* Leonard Michael Anthony Killeen was born in South Africa. Scorpios can control any situation they can find themselves in and, needless to say, Len was in command of most scenarios on the field. He scored 115 tries in 187 appearances from 1962 to 1967, including nine hat-tricks. Some player. *2011* Four Nations Final: England 8 Australia 30 at Elland Road, Leeds. The last hurrah as a Saints' player for front-rower James Graham before his move to Canterbury Bankstown Bulldogs in Australia. Such a pity that despite his phenomenal reputation at international level, he had not been in a team that has beaten Australia, up to and including the 2018 World Cup Final.

20 NOVEMBER

1926 Lancashire Cup Final: St Helens 10 St Helens Recreation 2 at Wilderspool. A landmark moment: Saints' first-ever major trophy triumph. This 'derby' clash in the pouring rain and cloying mud was essentially settled in the first half, with tries from winger Alf Ellaby and stand-off Leslie Fairclough, who danced around Recs' second-rower Albert Fildes to score under the posts. Centre George Lewis kicked two goals.

1961 Representative match: Rugby League XIII 22 New Zealand 20 at White City Stadium, Manchester. Tom van Vollenhoven was on the right wing; Warrington's Brian Bevan (two tries) on the other. For the Kiwis, Ken McCracken was in the centre, father of Jarrod, who played for the Saints in 1992–93.

Paul Loughlin (left) a superb all-round centre in both domestic and representative rugby league; right: Paul Groves was a superb hooker who had a penchant for scoring vital tries. [Brian Peers]

21 NOVEMBER

1914 Northern Rugby League: St. Helens 26 Dewsbury 16 at Knowsley Road. This game marked the debut of Afro-Caribbean scrum-half James Peters, signed from Barrow. The former Bristol, Plymouth and England Rugby Union international lost three fingers in a serious accident at work in the Royal Naval dockyard at Devonport in 1909, which must have limited his effectiveness somewhat on the rugby field. He played just two matches for the Saints, before, presumably, retiring from rugby. *1989* First Division: Hull 24 St Helens 34 at the Boulevard. A try and five goals for Great Britain centre Paul Loughlin, but the star of the show was hooker Paul 'Kit Kat' Groves with a stunning hat-trick of touchdowns. *1993* Stones Bitter Championship: Oldham 2 St Helens 12 at Watersheddings. Young full-back Steve Prescott kicked his first goal for the seniors. Try scorers? Front-rower Andy Dannatt and substitute Jon Griffiths. Scrum-half Gus O'Donnell also popped over two drop-goals.

22 NOVEMBER

1947 Northern Rugby League: Liverpool Stanley 10 St Helens 7. Stand-off Frank Brown made his debut for the seniors. He is reputedly the only man to have played for Saints (four matches), St Helens RUFC and St Helens Town AFC. He was quite the all-round sportsman. *1958* Representative match: Northern RLXIII 8 France 26 at Knowsley Road. The club pairing of left centre Duggie Greenall and Tom van Vollenhoven was replicated in this international clash. Alas, even with Warrington's Brian Bevan on the other flank, there were no tries to cheer from the homesters. The only points came from four goals from Vic Yorke of York. Georges Fages of Albi was scrum-half for the French.

1983 Lord Pilkington died aged 78. A member of the famous glass-making family, he was Club President and loved watching both amateur and professional rugby league, with his wife, Lady Mavis.

23 NOVEMBER

1903 Committee Meeting at Talbot Hotel: "Resolved that: 2,000 Handbills to be printed and 2 sandwich men engaged for Wakefield Trinity match." Publicity was of paramount importance, even in the 'olden days'. **1921** Tour match: St Helens 8 Australia 16 at Knowsley Road. Tries from Tommy Gormley and Harold Bradbury, plus a goal from Teddy McLoughlin gave Saints some respectability against a talented Kangaroos outfit. **1968** Flying winger Anthony Sullivan was born in Hull. His father was the great Clive Sullivan and Anthony certainly created his own niche in Saints' history with his try-scoring exploits: 213 tries from 305 appearances in the red vee. Says it all. **1986** First Division: St Helens 50 Hull FC 10 at Knowsley Road. John Fieldhouse, signed from Widnes as part of the Harry Pinner transfer made his debut from the bench. He played 57 times for the club overall.

Two great Saints' wingers. Local born Alf Ellaby (left) was a professional footballer with Rotherham County before taking the rugby league world by storm; right: Anthony Sullivan flies in for another touchdown at Knowsley Road. Saints' kit for the RFL Centenary Season in 1995, blue and white stripes, with blue shorts, looked absolutely fantastic.
[Alex Service]

24 NOVEMBER

1902 Alfred Henry Ellaby, the son of Oliver, a St Helens licensee first saw light of day in St Helens. Alf realised his value as a try-scoring phenomenon to the St Helens club and was paid accordingly. You could say, without exaggeration, that he was a real 'superstar' in his pomp. Saggitarians have a 'bright, sharp intellect and enjoy mental challenges.' Alf loved to out-think his opposite number on the field, for sure. But his pace was a big advantage too.

1956 Tour match: St Helens 44 Australia 2 at Knowsley Road. A record defeat for the Kangaroos, including a try from every Saints forward. Take a bow: Alan Prescott, Frank McCabe, Abe Terry, Nat Silcock, Josh Gaskell and Vince Karalius! *1964* From the Boardroom: "It was reported that [Australian centre David] Wood had been found employment in the menswear department of the St Helens Cooperative Society." Suits you, Sir!

25 NOVEMBER

1975 County Championship: Lancashire 36 Other Nationalities 7 at Knowsley Road. Geoff Pimblett, on debut, played right centre, although he was normally the last line of defence. His team-mates Dave Eckersley and George Nicholls were also on the bench. *2017* World Cup semi-final: England 20 Tonga 18 at Mount Smart Stadium, Auckland. A difficult assignment for England, with the 'neutral' stadium full of Tongan fans, all of whom seemed to be waving a flag. James Roby and Alex Walmsley were on the interchange bench.

26 NOVEMBER

1932 Northern Rugby League: St Helens 21 Leeds 5 at Knowsley Road. A straightforward victory for the League Champions, who scored five tries from Bob Jones, Roy Hardgrave, Tom Winnard, Alf Ellaby and Ben Halfpenny. Winnard added a goal and Jack Arkwright went one better, with a double. *1945* From the Boardroom: "Camp Commandant (Mersey) North West District, Liverpool, wrote intimating that he intended to surrender the Treasurer's Room and small brick building known as Ladies Supporters Hut from requisition as from about the 30th November 1945." Parts of the Knowsley Road ground were indeed requisitioned by the military in the Second World War, including sections of the Pavilion and the St Helens club had no say in the matter. *1938* Northern Rugby League: Broughton Rangers 10 St Helens 7 at the Cliff. This ground later became the training base for Manchester United FC. Frank Ellaby, who originated from Salford, and no relation to winger Alf, made his debut in the second row. *2003* The Saints' Heritage Society's website was launched in the Cabaret Lounge at Knowsley Road. Legendary former player Geoff Pimblett did the honours, as the site went fully on line.

Geoff Pimblett – who else – launches the Saints Heritage Society's new website. Dave Dooley (left), one of the prime 'movers and shakers' behind the project admires Geoff's IT skills. [Alex Service]

One they won. Welsh full-back Kel Coslett (left) prepares to kick for touch during the 1963 Lancashire Cup Final against Leigh. Seven years later, the Leythers had their revenge. Below: Bob Jones, a fine all-rounder and local teacher, who was a valuable utility player for Saints between the wars.

[Alex Service]

27 NOVEMBER

1926 Northern Rugby League St Helens 54 York 3 at Knowsley Road. This landslide victory included a stunning hat-trick of tries from Les Fairclough, who normally created them. Surprisingly, it was his only three-try performance at club level. *1988* John Player Trophy Round 2: St Helens 16 Hull 13 at Knowsley Road. Saints, the holders, eventually progressed to the semi-finals, where they lost 20–18 to Widnes.

28 NOVEMBER

1942 War Emergency League: Wakefield Trinity 36 St Helens 3 at Belle Vue. St Helens-born Ted Kerwick made this single appearance for the Saints at stand-off. His scrum-half was Eli Dixon. Both had played for local rivals St Helens Recreation before the outbreak of the War. *1970* Lancashire Cup Final: St Helens 4 Leigh 7 at Station Road, Swinton. Captain and loose forward Kel Coslett kicked two goals as Saints fell to local rivals Leigh, whose captain-coach Alex Murphy came back to haunt his former club.

Don Gullick, the Welsh 'Rambo' in the centre, was always a real handful as shown against a desperate Warrington defence. [Alex Service]

29 NOVEMBER

1902 First Division: Broughton Rangers 23 St Helens 0 at Wheaters Field. Forward James Rennie played his last match for the club. He later died, tragically, as a result of a colliery accident underground. *1952* Lancashire Cup Final: St Helens 5 Leigh 22 at Station Road. The first final in the Jim Sullivan era resulted in a convincing victory for Leigh, although the Saints ended the campaign as League Champions. Powerhouse centre Don Gullick scored the only try, with George Langfield kicking a goal.

30 NOVEMBER

1963 Test Match #139 Great Britain 16 Australia 5 at Headingley, Leeds. Front-rower Cliff Watson, hardly a shrinking violet in test match football, was sent off after 51 minutes to add to the woes of the home team; the great running forward Dick Huddart also played in his last Ashes Test. *1968* Test Match #164: Gt. Britain 34 France 10 at Knowsley Road. This was a good performance from the Brits, who were captained by scrum-half Tommy Bishop, on his home turf. John Warlow was the other Saints' representative, who was in the front row, with Dennis Hartley and Kevin Ashcroft. The attendance of 6,080 was somewhat disappointing. *1971* BBC2 Floodlit Trophy Semi-Final: Leeds 0 St Helens 17 at Headingley. Two tries from John Walsh and four Coslett goals capped a brilliant victory over the powerful Yorkshiremen and revenge for the previous season's Final reversal at the same venue. Saints went on to win the Final this time, against Rochdale Hornets, at Knowsley Road, but the real groundwork had been done in West Yorkshire.

December

It'll soon be Boxing Day!

Festive fun – and how. George Mann takes the ball up to the Wigan defence in
the 1992 Boxing Day classic against Wigan at Knowsley Road. Saints' jerseys
had a different sponsor (Coors) for this particular match. [Alex Service]

Before the advent of the Summer Super League, the end of December was one of the most
eagerly-awaited times of the year for rugby league fans. Boxing Day was, more often than
not, Saints versus Wigan; packed crowds, a brilliant atmosphere and fantastic rugby.
Remember 1992? One of our favourites: St Helens 41 Wigan 6. Now we are just left with our
memories and misty eyes. The festive season is, effectively, now a rugby league free zone.
So sad. It seems so unlikely now, but there were games on Christmas Day, as well as Boxing
Day, for many years. The first was in 1895, at Knowsley Road, St Helens 6 Widnes 0. Between
the wars, it was the date of the first St Helens 'derby' clash against the Recs. Christmas Day
or not, it appears that there was little general bonhomie between the supporters; the return
was on New Year's Day. After the Second World War, Liverpool Stanley filled in for the Recs
and, in the 1950s, Leigh were regular opponents. In fact, the last Christmas Day game was
against the Leythers in 1959, at Knowsley Road, when the Saints won 14–10. Remember,
too, the BBC2 Floodlit Trophy Finals, which, from 1965 to 1979 were shoe-horned into the
crowded fixture list. Saints appeared in seven, winning the trophy twice, in 1971 and 1975.

1 DECEMBER

1928 Northern Rugby League: St Helens 21 Oldham 3 at Knowsley Road. Long-serving scrum-half Walter Groves played his first game at loose-forward, a move that extended his career with his home town club. He played there in the club's first-ever Championship Final success against Huddersfield in 1932. *1948* Australian winger Lenny Kenny signed from Leeds for a £500 fee. His nickname was 'pivot on a penny Lenny Kenny' and, as such, it is possible to see why he was such an elusive customer on the flanks. A great lover of horse racing too. *1956* Northern Rugby League: St Helens 51 Huddersfield 4 at Knowsley Road. Left-winger Frank Carlton led the scorers with four tries. Second rower Roy Robinson also notched a memorable hat-trick of three pointers.

2 DECEMBER

1937 Tour match: Saints-Recs XIII 7 Australia 15 at Knowsley Road. 7 players from Saints; 6 from Recs. A measure of the relative strength and status of the two sides by the mid–1930s in that they no longer warranted individual matches with the Kangaroos. This did not go down well with the hard-core fans from either side, however. The match was played on a Thursday afternoon – half-day closing – yet the crowd was still disappointing, to say the least. The match programme, below, tells us that the home team played in Recs' change strip of black and white hooped jerseys. [Alex Service]

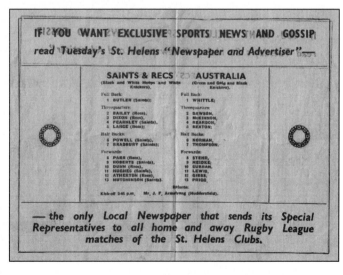

1961 Northern Rugby League: Hull KR 12 St Helens 5 at Craven Park, Hull. Second-rower Jim Measures played his last game as a Saint before his transfer to Widnes. He won a Challenge Cup Final with the Chemics in 1964 and played for Great Britain. *1967* Lancashire Cup Final replay: St Helens 13 Warrington 10 at Station Road. Great to see skipper Tom van Vollenhoven, in his last season as a player, lift the famous old trophy on high. Les Jones, John Warlow and young Eric Chisnall were the try-scorers, with substitute John Houghton kicking two goals. The crowd was a disappointing 7,577.

This one's for you. Skipper Tom van Vollenhoven shows the Lancashire Cup to the fans after the replayed Final at Swinton against Warrington in 1967. John Mantle, John Warlow, Kel Coslett and Eric Chisnall are the other jubilant Saints in the picture [Alex Service]

1979 St Helens Past Players' Association was formed after a meeting of interested parties at Knowsley Road. Ray French was the first chairman; secretary was the recently-retired Geoff Pimblett, far left on image below, and Peter Harvey was treasurer. Initial membership was 45. The organisation has grown and continues to thrive ever since. [Alex Service]

2017 World Cup Final: Australia 6 England 0 at Suncorp Stadium, Brisbane. James Roby, Alex Walmsley and Jonny Lomax played in a terrific display of sheer grit and determination against the reigning World Champions. A game of paper-thin margins, for sure. So near, yet so far. We really felt for them. In the image below, Jonny Lomax puts his body on the line for the England cause. [RLPhotos.com]

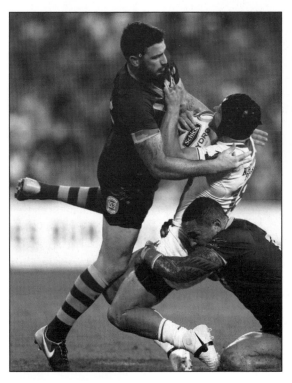

3 DECEMBER

1963 From the Boardroom: "The Chairman reported that he had interviewed Huddart who said that he had made up his mind to migrate to Australia at the end of this season." And he did – in a £10,000 move to the St George Club in Sydney. Dick suffered from asthma and thought the climate would suit him better.

1995 Centenary Season: St Helens 58 Workington 10 at Knowsley Road. Big money capture Paul Newlove made an immediate impression with a try on debut. So light on his feet for a big man, selection for the Greatest 17 beckoned in future years.

4 DECEMBER

1926 International match: Wales 34 New Zealand 8 at Taff Vale Park, Pontypridd. A good thumping for the Kiwis, in front of 18,000 fans. Saints' captain George Lewis made his Welsh debut. He was the 96th player to make his first appearance for his native country. *1973* BBC2 Floodlit Trophy Semi-Final: Bramley 13 St Helens 12. A real upset. Bob Goulding senior made his debut. John Mantle and hooker Tony Karalius were with him in the front row.

5 DECEMBER

1970 European Championship: St Gaudens 11 St Helens 30 at Toulouse. An excellent victory for the Saints, who clinched the trophy with a win in the second leg at Knowsley Road at the end of the season. Billy Benyon and Les Jones both scored two tries; John Walsh kicked six goals. *2004* Youth International: England Academy Under–17s 28 Australian Institute of Sport 22 at South Leeds Stadium. Saints had three young stars on view: Ian Hardman, James Graham and Andy Bracek. In what was a fine victory, the *Rugby Leaguer and League Express* Man-of-the-Match award went to front-rower James Graham. A brilliant career in the XIII-a-side code, on two continents, was just beginning.

Toulouse here we come, suited and booted! Left to right: Harry Cook (chairman), Cliff Watson, Frankie Barrow, Eric Chisnall, Tony Karalius, Bill Sheffield, Eric Prescott, Les Jones, Graham Rees, Jeff Heaton, Alan Whittle, John Mantle and Bill Sayer about to board the coach for Liverpool airport.
[Alex Service]

6 DECEMBER

1952 Northern Rugby League: Workington 5 St Helens 22 at Derwent Park. Centre Duggie Greenall scored four tries and kicked two goals. Duggie was a fine try-scorer himself as well as a provider. *1964* Test Match #142 France 18 Great Britain 8 at Stade Gilbert Brutus, Perpignan. The visitors featured an all-St Helens front row of Warlow (on debut), Dagnall and Tembey, with captain Alex Murphy at scrum-half. The game was staged where the Saints have played the majority of their matches against Catalans Dragons in the Super League competition. *1992* Regal Trophy Round 2: Featherstone Rovers 8 St Helens 25. A difficult assignment for the Saints, including a try from Kiwi centre Jarrod McCracken. It was a strong backline too: Quirk, Connolly, McCracken and Sullivan. Great players all.

7 DECEMBER

1971 Greatest 17 incumbent Chris Joynt was born in Wigan. Chris impressed with his first club, Oldham and proved to be one of the finest-ever signings. Saggitarians are the real go-getters of the world, enthusiastic and idealistic. He proved to be a belting captain of St Helens RFC and we must not forget that he played 22 times for Great Britain too. *1955* Representative match: Northern RLXIII 24 New Zealand 11 at Odsal. Young Vince Karalius had his first taste of representative rugby. All the threequarter line, including right centre Duggie Greenall, scored a try. *2016* Saints' and Great Britain loose-forward Harry Pinner launched his autobiography *A Born Leader* at Central Library St Helens, with a large group of former team-mates and friends. The famous old Lancashire Cup was another attraction on the day.

Harry Pinner (left) at his book launch, with Peter Lush (chair, London League Publications Ltd) and guest speaker George Nicholls. The Lancashire Cup is a gleaming reminder of rugby league's great times. [Alex Service]

8 DECEMBER

1926 Tour Match: St Helens 22 New Zealand 12 at Knowsley Road. Alf Ellaby flew in for a brace of tries, with his centre, George Lewis, kicking five goals. *1962* Northern Rugby League: St Helens 13 Leeds 6 at Knowsley Road. Hooker Joe Egan, son of the Wigan legend of the same name, made an impressive debut. Keith Northey was Saints' try scorer; Kel Coslett, also in his debut season, kicked five goals.

9 DECEMBER

1894 Alderman Thomas Charles Wilcock, owner of the Phoenix Brewery in Sutton and Saints' Chairman, died of typhoid fever, aged 52. His funeral was at Lowe House Church but, according to the Liverpool Mercury: "As Mr Wilcock succumbed to an attack of typhoid fever, the coffin was not taken into church, but was allowed to remain in the churchyard until the close of the service." Such sad circumstances for his family to bear. *1961* Northern Rugby League: Wakefield Trinity 12 St Helens 10 at Belle Vue. Jackie Pimblett, playing on the left wing, scored a try on his full debut. Jackie later lost his life as a result of a scrummage collapse, while playing for Pilkington Recreation in 1972. *1984* First Division: St Helens 48 Leeds 16 at Knowsley Road. A stunning victory for the home team, characterised by a sensational hat-trick from stand-off Chris Arkwright. *2006* St Helens RFC were the deserving winners in the BBC Team of the Year at the *Sports Personality of the Year* Awards. Eyebrows were certainly raised and it was so good to see such achievements and the sport of rugby league recognised on a national platform.

10 DECEMBER

1963 From the Boardroom: "A letter of protest [from a local primary school] about the playing of Sunday football because of the effect it had on children attending Sunday school was read to the Board." *2002* Stuart 'Steve' Llewellyn died aged 78. A lovely man, who was widely respected both from his deeds as a dashing winger – he dived over for virtually every try he scored – and as a Deputy Headteacher at Grange Park High School, in Thatto Heath.

All smiles! They must all be Saints' fans. Steve Llewellyn with his class at Grange Park High School in the early 1950s. [Alex Service]

11 DECEMBER

1970 Augustine 'Gus' O'Donnell was born in Billinge. Gus developed kidney problems, which subsequently ended his career, but we will remember him for being in the side that thwarted Wigan's 'Grand Slam' bid in the 1993 Premiership Final at Old Trafford. *1977* BARLA Lancashire Cup Final: Pilkington Recs 12 Latchford Albion 0 at Knowsley Road. The famous old ground also became the focus for many of Pilkington Recs' greatest triumphs in the amateur code. Indeed, Recs had not conceded a try in any rounds of the competition, either.

12 DECEMBER

1896 Lancashire Senior Competition: Broughton Rangers 3 St Helens 0 at Wheater's Field. A disappointing loss for the visitors, against the team that would finish as league leaders. *1978* BBC2 Floodlit trophy Final: St Helens 7 Widnes 13 at Knowsley Road. The Saints were starting to show the need for an infusion of new blood by this time. Skipper Geoff Pimblett kicked two goals and front-rower Dave Chisnall scored the only try.

13 DECEMBER

1966 From the Boardroom: "It was reported that [Bill] Sayer had been signed at a fee of £1,750. The action taken was approved by the Board." This was another fine piece of business by the Saints! This was definitely Wigan's loss and although Bill was at the veteran stage, he could have played for his former club at Wembley against St Helens in the Challenge Cup Final when they lacked personnel in the hooking department. *2008* Vince Karalius died in the Isle of Man, aged 76. He had been suffering from prostate cancer for some time. Tributes to the great man came in from far and wide. When St Helens and Widnes meet they play for the Vince Karalius Cup. A fitting honour indeed.

The first game at the superb Langtree Park Stadium was in the Karalius Cup between St Helens and Widnes Vikings on 2012. Nothing could have been more appropriate. [Bernard Platt]

14 DECEMBER

1895 Northern Rugby Union: Oldham 0 St Helens 0 at Watersheddings. Saints played centre Billy Jacques and were subsequently fined when it was realised he was still registered by Hull. This glitch cost the club two league points. *1965* BBC2 Floodlit Trophy Final: St Helens 0 Castleford 4 at Knowsley Road. This was the first final of this much-maligned competition. Saints' fans were scratching their heads as to why their team didn't score in this one. Normally reliable goalkicker Len Killeen had an off-day with the boot, which didn't happen very often in the 'four cups' season. *1971* BBC2 Floodlit Trophy Final: St Helens 8 Rochdale 2 at Knowsley Road. Our first success in the competition, albeit on home turf. In the Hornets' team were several former Saints: Glover (5), Myler (6), Gartland (7) and Sheffield (12).

15 DECEMBER

1954 Solomon Huyton died aged 87 and is buried in St Helens Cemetery. One of the Saints' most forceful forwards in the early days, he played in the club's first-ever match against an international touring team, when the Maoris came to Dentons Green on 14 March 1889. It was their 67th match since arriving in Britain the previous October. *1961* Effervescent scrum-half Neil Holding was born in St Helens. Saggitarians, apparently, are always constantly reinventing themselves which is quite appropriate, as Neil had everyone in stitches with his comedy routines and impersonations. Like Alex Murphy, he was tremendously quick off the mark and capable of the unexpected. A real crowd-pleaser. *1970* BBC2 Floodlit Trophy Final: Leeds 9 St Helens 5 at Headingley. A closely-fought encounter, but Saints had to slot in a gruelling replayed Semi-Final against Wigan at Knowsley Road, two days before, winning 16–15, which was clearly a factor in this defeat.

Left: Neil Holding, a superb number 7 and master of the 'chip and chase' scores against Featherstone in 1989. [Alex Service]

16 DECEMBER

1975 BBC2 Floodlit Trophy Final: St Helens 22 Dewsbury 2 at Knowsley Road. Some brilliant rugby for the television viewers to savour. David Hull played at centre; Frank Wilson at stand-off, with two blistering tries from powerhouse winger Roy Mathias. *1967* Northern Rugby League: St Helens 10 Oldham 2 at Knowsley Road. Rhodesian Garth Robertson made his debut at stand-off.

17 DECEMBER

1968 BBC2 Floodlit Trophy Final: Wigan 7 St Helens 4 at Central Park. Loose-forward Kel Coslett kicked two goals. Fellow Welshman Cen Williams, normally a centre, was at full-back. Just over a week later, the Boxing Day match against the two sides at Knowsley Road was abandoned at half-time. *1993* First Division: St Helens 23 Hull KR 22 at Knowsley Road. The pre-Christmas attendance of 3,239 was a disappointment in a match that could have gone either way. Young full-back Steve Prescott booted over five goals and generally showed us why he would be a future favourite with the fans, with his pace and elusive running.

A young Steve Prescott (above) lines up a conversion at Knowsley Road in the 1994–95 season [Alex Service]; right: in action during his special fund-raising match at the same venue on 22 April 2007, when his devastating illness had been diagnosed. The jerseys were signed by his team-mates and later auctioned for the cause. [Bernard Platt]

18 DECEMBER

1926 Northern Rugby League: Leigh 6 St Helens 3 at Mather Lane, Leigh. Saints' try was scored by the new wing sensation, 24-year-old Alf Ellaby. Saints' fans simply couldn't believe that the club had unearthed anyone so good. *1943* War Emergency League: St Helens 0 Wakefield Trinity 10 at Knowsley Road. Wigan's stellar full-back Martin Ryan guested for the Saints at scrum-half. At stand-off was another famous Wiganer, Tommy Bradshaw. Saints centre Jimmy Stott also guested for the Riversiders during the conflict. *1948* Northern Rugby League: St Helens 61 Whitehaven 0 at Knowsley Road. Right winger Lenny Kenny, the Australian flyer signed from Leeds, roared in for a hat-trick of tries.

19 DECEMBER

1937 Former chairman Tom Phillips died aged 70. Born in Widnes, Tom came to St Helens to take over the Headship of Windle Church of England School in 1904 and later took charge of the new Rivington Road Senior School. Former pupils such as Leslie Fairclough and Charlie Crooks were just two of his sporting successes for the Saints. During the First World War he received national acclaim for his work with the Food and Fuel Control agencies, which were acclaimed as the most efficient in the British Isles. His great communication skills were utilised in obtaining the assistance of Pilkington Brothers in providing the funds to build the Pavilion in 1920. His greatest achievement, however, was the setting up of schoolboy rugby competitions in the town, which began to flourish in succeeding years.

1961 Coach Alan Prescott's contract was terminated by the Board after a disappointing series of results threatened the club's future status in the new First Division. His position had been under threat for some months, with Jim Brough and later Cliff Evans of Swinton being linked to the job. In the interim, former wing legend Stan McCormick took charge of affairs and this was later made permanent. Alan Prescott later joined Leigh in a similar capacity

All smiles in the dressing room as new signing Percy Landsberg (centre, in Rhodesian blazer) is introduced to fellow Southern Africans Jan Prinsloo (left) and Tom van Vollenhoven (right). Secretary Basil Lowe is to the right of Landsberg; coach Alan Prescott (to his left) is all smiles. [Alex Service]

20 DECEMBER

1930 Northern Rugby League: Rochdale Hornets 2 St Helens 9 at Athletic Grounds. Saints' wingers were the match winners, with two tries for Alf Ellaby and one for New Zealander Roy Hardgrave. A deadly duo indeed. **1947** Test Match #68: Great Britain 25 New Zealand 9 at Odsal. A home record 42,680 fans packed in to the famous ground for it's first-ever test match to see the Brits beat a very competent Kiwi outfit and secure the rubber 2–1. Len Aston was Saints' representative in the second row.

21 DECEMBER

1903 Committee Meeting at Talbot Hotel: "Mr JF May of Harris Street was elected a member of this committee vice Mr Bridge". Jim May later became chairman of the club in the late 1920s, during the club's first real era of success and helped to get seven St Helens-based players – three from the Recs; four from the Saints – onto the 1928 Australian Tour. **1957** Northern Rugby League: St Helens 52 Wakefield Trinity 5 at Knowsley Road. New signing Tom van Vollenhoven continued to score virtually at will against the visitors, who were seemingly powerless to stop him crossing the whitewash on six occasions. He equalled Alf Ellaby's individual match record, too. Simply stunning for the 15,000 fans.

1986 First Division: St Helens 28 Oldham 6 at Knowsley Road. Welsh centre Steve Bayliss came off the bench to begin his second spell as a Saint, which lasted a further nine matches. He had previously played for Fulham.

22 DECEMBER

1945 Northern Rugby League: St Helens 5 Workington Town 20 at Knowsley Road. Saints struggled against the league's new boys. Centre Jack Waring scored a try and Welsh stand-off Stan Powell kicked a goal. *1956* Northern Rugby League: St Helens 37 Whitehaven 6 at Knowsley Road. Vince Karalius, perhaps more famed for his 'destructive' qualities, scored his first hat-trick of tries for St Helens.

23 DECEMBER

1939 Second-rower Ray French was born in Cowley Hill Maternity Hospital, St Helens and spent his early life in McFarlane Avenue, quite close to Saints' ground. A Capricorn, so he is a practical problem solver and an excellent organiser – something that this former English teacher excelled at since his retirement from playing rugby. Signed from St Helens RUFC at the start of the 1961–62 campaign as a replacement for Wakefield Trinity-bound Don Vines, he made 204 appearances and won every honour with the Saints before his transfer to Widnes. In later years, he replaced Eddie Waring as BBC Television's 'Voice of Rugby League' and remained a tireless worker for both codes of rugby in the town, rewarded by the MBE in 2010. Richly deserved. *1968* From the Boardroom: "A letter from the league asking for reports on the experiment of the upward movement of the ball when feeding the scrum was read. It was agreed to inform the league that we were not in favour". Quite right too. *2007* Centre supreme Duggie Greenall died aged 80. The end of an era. He joined the club just after the war, when fortunes seemed bleak. He went on to play in the club's inaugural Challenge Cup success in 1956 and their second Championship Final victory in 1959, when he partnered Tom van Vollenhoven. Quite a turnaround in fortunes.

Old team mates and close friends re-united. Tom van Vollenhoven, Duggie Greenall and Glyn Moses share a sofa and copious memories in 2007. [Alex Service]

24 DECEMBER

1938 Northern Rugby League: Leigh 10 St Helens 18 at Mather Lane, Leigh. The great Alf Ellaby scored his final try for the club, in his second spell as a Saint. It was his 280th touchdown and for this game, his centre was the young Welshman Stan Powell. Alf's business interests in Blackpool were taking prominence and, by the end of January 1939, he had announced his retirement, triggering a flood of tributes from friend and foe alike. *1972* Northern Rugby League: Blackpool Borough 14 St Helens 33 at Borough Park, Blackpool. A game witnessed by just 700 hardy fans. Saints did enough to win at a canter, with a brace of tries from Les Jones and Dave Eckersley. Borough eventually won just four of their 30 matches during the campaign and for the visitors, there was the prospect of the 'derby' clash with Wigan on Boxing Day at Knowsley Road to prepare for. As it happened, the old antagonists drew 15–15.

25 DECEMBER

1919 Northern Rugby League: St Helens Recs 21 St Helens 6 at City Road. Recs – the 'Babes' of the rugby league were up and running, with home-grown talent in abundance. It took the Saints several years to redress the balance of power in the town. *1946* Northern Rugby League: St Helens 16 Liverpool Stanley 17 at Knowsley Road. The trialist stand-off, who played under the alias 'Johnson' was later revealed as Lieutenant Len Constance RNVR. "We had to see Constance, just to make sure that this star turn was no dream", wrote one scribe, after his 'outing' match against Wigan 24 hours later at the same venue.

1950 Northern Rugby League: St Helens 12 Leigh 2 at Knowsley Road. The last Saints' game for second-rower Len Aston before his premature retirement through illness, a tremendous loss to the club.

26 DECEMBER

1905 Northern Rugby League: St Helens 5 Wigan 13 at Knowsley Road. Over 6,000 saw this first-ever Boxing Day clash between the old foes. Winger Billy Hillen scored a try; Charlie Creevey kicked a goal. *1920* Northern Rugby League: St Helens 4 Wigan 22 at Knowsley Road. The new pavilion at Knowsley Road, including offices and dressing rooms, was opened by club President Lord Derby. At last the club was inclusive on one site: no more trips to and from the ground for both teams by wagonette to get changed in the Talbot Hotel in Duke Street – a massive step forward.

1949 Northern Rugby League: St Helens 15 Wigan 8 at Knowsley Road. A ground record of 35,695 fans packed themselves in for this memorable 'derby' victory. Skipper Jimmy Stott scored a try and kicked 3 goals, whilst other 3 pointers came the way of flying winger Stan McCormick and hooker Reg Blakemore.

1969 Northern Rugby League: Wigan 11 St Helens 53 at Central Park. Loose forward Kel Coslett kicked 10 goals; flying winger Les Jones scorched in for a brilliant hat-trick of tries. They scored first, early on, too and subsequently imploded. Bring on the 1970s.

1970 Northern Rugby League: St Helens 5 Wigan 12 at Knowsley Road. Front-rower Albert Halsall played his last – 120th – game for the club.

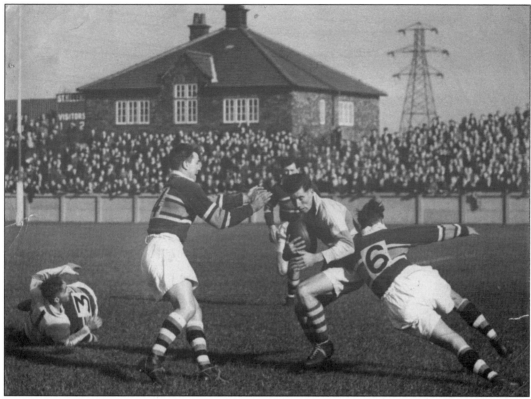

No wagonettes here. Left winger Bill Adair is tackled by the Hunslet defence during Saints' 20–14 league victory at Knowsley Road on 7 October 1950. The Pavilion and concrete terrace wall provide a splendid backdrop. In the post-war attendance boom, there were 16,000 fans at the match.
[Alex Service]

27 DECEMBER

1886 Friendly: Ossett RUFC 1 goal, 4 minors St Helens RFC 5 minors. Difficulties for the Saints, according to the *Athletic News* report the following day: "The visitors arrived at eleven o'clock yesterday, after being in an alarming railway collision at St Helens Junction, which severely shook the players. The ground being very hard through the severe frost, a drawn game was arranged."

1952 Northern Rugby League: Wakefield Trinity 11 St Helens 20 at Belle Vue. This hard-fought win included a try on debut for Peter Metcalfe. He was an excellent footballer, who aspired to county and international honours as a stand-off. After his premature retirement he coached the Pilkington Recs amateur team with great success. *1987* Stones Bitter Championship: Wigan 22 St Helens 32 at Central Park. At one stage it was 22–6 for Wigan, until one of the greatest comebacks ever seen in any 'derby' clash secured the spoils. Tries were scored by Phil Veivers with two, Dave Tanner, Kevin McCormack and Les Quirk. Paul Loughlin kicked six goals. Pure festive joy – if you were a Saints' fan.

Dave Tanner at his best, scoring a vital try during Saints' marvellous 27–26 victory against the visiting Kiwis at Knowsley Road on 1 October 1989. Notice the referee in trainers too. Dave also kicked five goals for good measure and was a key member of the squad who could play at full-back or anywhere in the threequarter line with great effectiveness. [Brian Peers]

28 DECEMBER

1907 Northern Rugby League: St Helens 16 Bramley 3 at Knowsley Road. Saints' half-backs, Matt Creevey and Fred Trenwith scored tries, together with hooker Jack Pope and the evergreen Billy Briers. *1980* Slalom Lager Championship: Barrow 11 St Helens 8 at Craven Park. The Blues were a good side in those days and Saints were in the midst of rebuilding. Both centres, Chris Arkwright and Denis Litherland, scored tries, but not enough in the final analysis. The team finished in 8th position at the end of the campaign, a real comedown for fans who were (over?) used to success.

29 DECEMBER

1970 Front-rower John Stephens was signed from Wigan for a £4,000 fee. He was a fine player, who excelled in the big matches. Remember his fine try in the 1972 Challenge Cup Semi-Final replay against Warrington? John was a chef and later, a restauranteur. He joined his hometown team, Widnes after leaving Saints at the start of the 1974–75 campaign. *1974* Division One: Salford 0 St Helens 14 at the Willows, Salford. A valuable two points for Saints against one of their strongest rivals. John Walsh and George Nicholls scored the tries; skipper Kel Coslett kicked four goals. The team went on to win their one and only First Division title at the end of the season. They lost four matches in 30 – now that's the mark of Champions.

30 DECEMBER

1899 Lancashire Senior Competition: Tyldesley 3 St Helens 14 at Tyldesley. During what was the last Saints' game of the 19th century, right centre David Traynor ran in a spectacular hat-trick of tries and kicked a goal. A further three-pointer came from left-winger Bob Doherty. *1985* Back-rower Paul Jones was signed from Leigh East amateur club. He was tall and powerful, making 52 appearances for the seniors before he was transferred to Oldham, with scrum-half Sean Devine, as part of the £56,500 deal that saw Chris Joynt leave Watersheddings for the Saints.

Pride of the Red Rose. Talented threequarter David Traynor (left), wearing his county jersey and cap; fast forward to the 1970s: rugged front-rowers John Stephens and Mick Murphy keep up the Lancashire tradition. [Alex Service]

31 DECEMBER

1892 St Helens began their New Year tour of the North East with a match against Northumberland Cup holders Rockcliffe. Sunday was given over to 'religious meditation and some sightseeing' with two further matches played: against West Hartlepool (2 January) and South Shields, where almost 6,000 spectators watched the proceedings. Saints were unbeaten throughout. *1954* Former Saints' front-rower Jonty Pilkington made headlines in the northern edition of the *Daily Mirror*. When he was in the army, Irish Guardsman Pilkington asked his Sergeant Major for a weekend pass so that he could play for the Saints in October 1946 and was told: 'get out of my sight'. Jonty took him literally and was absent for eight years. Jonty told the court martial at Pirbright in Surrey that during his absence, he had lived openly at home and his name and image had frequently been seen in the local newspapers. The authorities took a dim view, however, as you might expect. Yet the ever-popular Jonty remained a colourful character, boxing and all-in wrestling were amongst his other interests and, whisper it, a love of classical music and opera.

What an appropriate epilogue! 1966 Championship Final: St Helens 35 Halifax 12. The St Helens supporters in the huge crowd at Swinton are looking forward to a double celebration of Challenge Cup and League Championship, reflected in the supporters' banner. Their optimism was duly rewarded. This superb image is a reflection of community, family, friendships, young and old, enjoying a special rugby league occasion. Times have changed but one thing still rings true: Saints' fans still passionately follow their team resplendent in the famous red vee. Long may it continue!
[St Helens Local History & Archives/*St Helens Reporter*]

A new novel from Geoff Lee

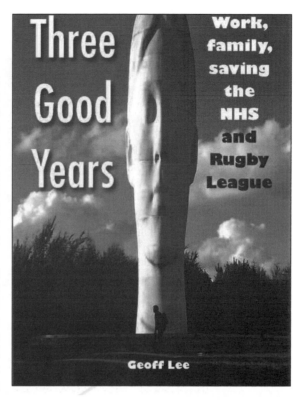

The latest novel by Geoff Lee is set between the years 2006 and 2008 with much of the action taking place in the drawing office of the Wilkinson's Engineering Works in the fictional South Lancashire town of Ashurst. It is the sixth in a series about northern working class life and is inspired by Geoff's love and links with the sport of rugby league and the old saying about work that "They could write a book about this place. It would be a best seller".

The main character continues to be the draughtsman Alan Greenall along with Thelma, who in "One Winter" had drifted north from Cardiff into the town during the summer of 1962. By the time of "Three Good Years", they are married with two children Rebecca and Robert and two soon to be three grandchildren Josh, Joanna and then Daisy.

The Greenalls are both keen rugby league fans watching the Saints at home for every game and frequently enjoying their trips into Yorkshire, particularly to Headingley, Odsal Stadium and Wakefield. They are also keen Crown Green bowlers with Alan a regular member of the Southport Edge Miners' Welfare club.

He still works at Wilkinson's with the firm now run from a company in Amsterdam. In 1962 over 8,000 people worked there but now that number is down to little more than 300.

Among some of the interesting chapter titles are *The Jehovah's Widnes*, *Lord Beeching has been beaten before*, *"I follow Marlborough League"*, *Callaghanism and Neo Liberalism* and *The Church of the Everyday Saints* along with the cliff hanger *"He's in St Helens Hospital"*.

One moving story told is about the details of Thelma's mother who had died in 1944 when Thelma was less than a year old. It is discovered that she had grown up in Tiger Bay and may well have gone to the same school around the same time as Billy Boston, Johnny Freeman and Shirley Bassey had gone there.

Published in September 2018 at £9.95. Available from www.llpshop.co.uk or Amazon or Abe Books for £9.50, including postage to the UK. Can be ordered from any bookshop at £9.95 (ISBN: 9781909885196). Also on sale in the St Helens RLC club shop.

Other St Helens books from London League Publications Ltd:

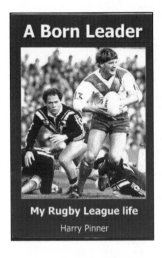 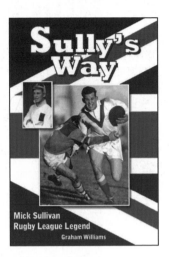 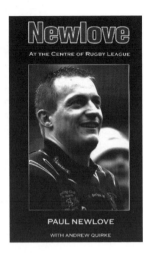

A Born Leader **by Harry Pinner**: Autobiography of St Helens and Great Britain legend. One of the great loose-forwards of post Second World War rugby league. Published in 2016 at £12.95, available from www.llpshop.co.uk or Amazon or Abe Books at £12.50 including postage to the UK. Can be ordered from any bookshop (ISBN: 9781909885127)

Sully's Way **by Graham Williams:** Biography of Mick Sullivan, who made the joint record appearances for Great Britain in test matches. Signed by St Helens for a then world transfer fee. Published in 2015 at £12.95, available from www.llpshop.co.uk or Amazon or Abe Books at £12.50 including postage to the UK. Can be ordered from any bookshop (ISBN: 9781909885097)

Newlove – At the centre of Rugby League **by Paul Newlove with Andrew Quirke:** Autobiography of former Great Britain and St Helens centre, who played a crucial role in the club's success in the early years of Super League. Published in 2004 at £14.95 (hardback), now available from www.llpshop.co.uk or Amazon or Abe Books at £6.95 including postage to the UK. Can be ordered from any bookshop (ISBN: 9781903659199).

All the above books are available as E-Books for Amazon Kindle.

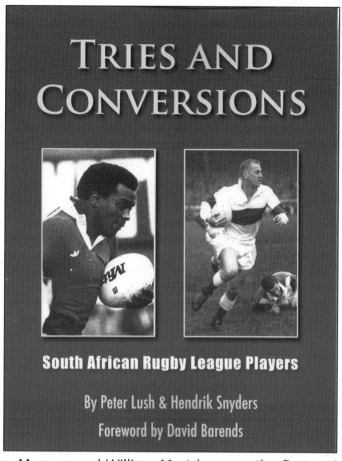

In 1910, James Megson and William Mart became the first native-born South Africans to sign for British rugby league clubs. Since then, South African players have made a significant contribution to rugby league. This book is the first comprehensive study of their contribution to rugby league. It covers players who played in Great Britain and Australia. Some were very successful, such as Attie van Heerden and George van Rooyen in the 1920s, Tom van Vollenhoven, Alan Skene, Jan Prinsloo and Len Killeen in the 1950s and 1960s, and Mark Johnson and Jamie Bloem in the Super League era. But there were also players who never made it after switching codes to play rugby league, and their stories are also told here.

Available for just £13.95 post free in the UK direct from London League Publications Ltd or from Amazon.co.uk or Abe Books. Credit card orders via www.llpshop.co.uk; payment by cheque to PO Box 65784, London NW2 9NS. Available in bookshops at £14.95.
Also available as an E-Book for Kindle from Amazon.

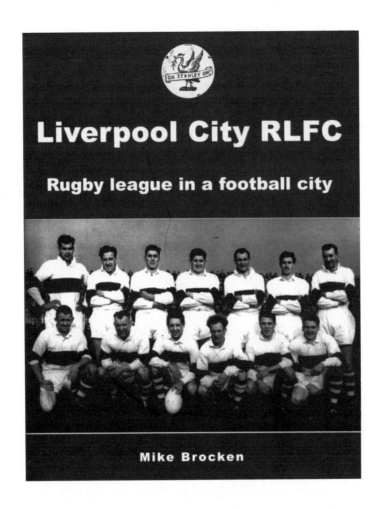

The full story of rugby league in Liverpool from the sport's earliest days to the modern era. Based on extensive research and interviews, a fascinating story of a struggle against the odds.

246 page paperback available direct from London League Publications Ltd for £14.95 post free in the UK. Visit www.llpshop.co.uk to order (credit cards via Pay Pal) or write to London League Publications Ltd, PO Box 65784 London NW2 9NS (cheques payable to London League Publications Ltd). Also available on Amazon and Abe Books. Can also be ordered from any bookshop (ISBN 9781903659403)

Also available as an E-Book for Kindle on Amazon.